Budget Weddings
FOR DUMMIES®

by Meg Schneider

Fitchburg Public Library
5530 Lacy Road
Fitchburg, WI 53711

WILEY

Wiley Publishing, Inc.

Budget Weddings For Dummies®

Published by
Wiley Publishing, Inc.
111 River St.
Hoboken, NJ 07030-5774
www.wiley.com

Copyright © 2009 by Wiley Publishing, Inc., Indianapolis, Indiana

Published simultaneously in Canada

No part of this publication may be reproduced, stored in a retrieval system or transmitted in any form or by any means, electronic, mechanical, photocopying, recording, scanning or otherwise, except as permitted under Sections 107 or 108 of the 1976 United States Copyright Act, without either the prior written permission of the Publisher, or authorization through payment of the appropriate per-copy fee to the Copyright Clearance Center, 222 Rosewood Drive, Danvers, MA 01923, (978) 750-8400, fax (978) 646-8600. Requests to the Publisher for permission should be addressed to the Permissions Department, John Wiley & Sons, Inc., 111 River Street, Hoboken, NJ 07030, (201) 748-6011, fax (201) 748-6008, or online at http://www.wiley.com/go/permissions.

Trademarks: Wiley, the Wiley Publishing logo, For Dummies, the Dummies Man logo, A Reference for the Rest of Us!, The Dummies Way, Dummies Daily, The Fun and Easy Way, Dummies.com, Making Everything Easier, and related trade dress are trademarks or registered trademarks of John Wiley & Sons, Inc. and/or its affiliates in the United States and other countries, and may not be used without written permission. All other trademarks are the property of their respective owners. Wiley Publishing, Inc., is not associated with any product or vendor mentioned in this book.

LIMIT OF LIABILITY/DISCLAIMER OF WARRANTY: THE PUBLISHER AND THE AUTHOR MAKE NO REPRESENTATIONS OR WARRANTIES WITH RESPECT TO THE ACCURACY OR COMPLETENESS OF THE CONTENTS OF THIS WORK AND SPECIFICALLY DISCLAIM ALL WARRANTIES, INCLUDING WITHOUT LIMITATION WARRANTIES OF FITNESS FOR A PARTICULAR PURPOSE. NO WARRANTY MAY BE CREATED OR EXTENDED BY SALES OR PROMOTIONAL MATERIALS. THE ADVICE AND STRATEGIES CONTAINED HEREIN MAY NOT BE SUITABLE FOR EVERY SITUATION. THIS WORK IS SOLD WITH THE UNDERSTANDING THAT THE PUBLISHER IS NOT ENGAGED IN RENDERING LEGAL, ACCOUNTING, OR OTHER PROFESSIONAL SERVICES. IF PROFESSIONAL ASSISTANCE IS REQUIRED, THE SERVICES OF A COMPETENT PROFESSIONAL PERSON SHOULD BE SOUGHT. NEITHER THE PUBLISHER NOR THE AUTHOR SHALL BE LIABLE FOR DAMAGES ARISING HEREFROM. THE FACT THAT AN ORGANIZATION OR WEBSITE IS REFERRED TO IN THIS WORK AS A CITATION AND/OR A POTENTIAL SOURCE OF FURTHER INFORMATION DOES NOT MEAN THAT THE AUTHOR OR THE PUBLISHER ENDORSES THE INFORMATION THE ORGANIZATION OR WEBSITE MAY PROVIDE OR RECOMMENDATIONS IT MAY MAKE. FURTHER, READERS SHOULD BE AWARE THAT INTERNET WEBSITES LISTED IN THIS WORK MAY HAVE CHANGED OR DISAPPEARED BETWEEN WHEN THIS WORK WAS WRITTEN AND WHEN IT IS READ.

For general information on our other products and services, please contact our Customer Care Department within the U.S. at 877-762-2974, outside the U.S. at 317-572-3993, or fax 317-572-4002.

For technical support, please visit www.wiley.com/techsupport.

Wiley also publishes its books in a variety of electronic formats. Some content that appears in print may not be available in electronic books.

Library of Congress Control Number: 2009935227

ISBN: 978-0-470-50209-9

Manufactured in the United States of America

10 9 8 7 6 5 4 3 2

WILEY

About the Author

Meg Schneider is an award-winning writer with more than two decades of experience in journalism and public relations. She has authored or coauthored several books, including *COPD For Dummies* and *Making Millions For Dummies* (both published by Wiley). When she married in 1999, she and her fiancé had just closed a restaurant and had very little money to work with, so they looked for creative ways to keep wedding costs down while still having the kind of ceremony and reception they wanted. The final tally was less than $6,000 for a wedding with 100 guests that included professional musicians, butler-passed hors d'oeuvres, a three-course meal, professional photography, and a professionally baked cake.

Meg's journalism honors include awards from the Iowa Associated Press Managing Editors, Women in Communications, the Maryland-Delaware-D.C. Press Association, Gannett, the New York State Associated Press, and the William Randolph Hearst Foundation.

A native of Iowa, Meg now lives in upstate New York.

Dedication

This book is dedicated to Mark Dixon, whose favorite saying comes from a Geico commercial: "I saved. I thought that meant something to you."

Author's Acknowledgments

No man is an island, and no book comes to market through the efforts of a single person. I gratefully acknowledge the support and contributions of:

Barb Doyen, my agent and ardent cheerleader, and a fierce proponent of saving money where you can.

Tracy Boggier and Sarah Faulkner, my editors. I thank Tracy for her skills in coming up with interesting projects, and Sarah for her ability to take reasonably good text and make it even better.

Copy editor Jessica Smith and technical reviewer Gloria Boyden. Jessica, thanks for keeping my voice active. Gloria, thanks for making sure my advice is sound.

Mark Dixon, who makes me laugh, and who has adapted remarkably well to the loopiness that so often accompanies life with a writer. (Plus, he buys me cheesecake when I finish writing a book.)

Jan and Dick Schneider, my parents, who, among other things, made planning my wedding as nearly stress-free as possible, and who have encouraged me to express my personality (even when that means breaking the rules) in every venture of life.

Publisher's Acknowledgments

We're proud of this book; please send us your comments through our Dummies online registration form located at http://dummies.custhelp.com. For other comments, please contact our Customer Care Department within the U.S. at 877-762-2974, outside the U.S. at 317-572-3993, or fax 317-572-4002.

Some of the people who helped bring this book to market include the following:

Acquisitions, Editorial, and Media Development

Project Editor: Sarah Faulkner

Acquisitions Editor: Tracy Boggier

Copy Editor: Jessica Smith

Assistant Editor: Erin Calligan Mooney

Editorial Program Coordinator: Joe Niesen

Technical Editor: Gloria Boyden

Editorial Manager: Christine Meloy Beck

Editorial Assistants: Jennette ElNaggar, David Lutton

Art Coordinator: Alicia B. South

Cover Photos: iStock

Cartoons: Rich Tennant (www.the5thwave.com)

Composition Services

Project Coordinator: Sheree Montgomery

Layout and Graphics: Claudia Bell, Joyce Haughey, Jennifer Mayberry

Illustrator: Elizabeth Kurtzman

Proofreaders: Cynthia Fields, John Greenough

Indexer: Sherry Massey

Special Help Todd Lothery, Elizabeth Staton

Publishing and Editorial for Consumer Dummies

    Diane Graves Steele, Vice President and Publisher, Consumer Dummies

    Kristin Ferguson-Wagstaffe, Product Development Director, Consumer Dummies

    Ensley Eikenburg, Associate Publisher, Travel

    Kelly Regan, Editorial Director, Travel

Publishing for Technology Dummies

    Andy Cummings, Vice President and Publisher, Dummies Technology/General User

Composition Services

    Debbie Stailey, Director of Composition Services

Contents at a Glance

Table of Contents

Introduction

● ●

*W*hen I began planning my wedding in earnest, I bought a copy of a wedding planning guide for working women. I assumed, from the title, that it was aimed at women who didn't have a lot of time or interest in planning a spectacularly formal and lavish wedding. Imagine my chagrin when I began flipping through it and came across a section on hand-rolled, personalized, individually written (in calligraphy, no less) thank-you-for-attending scrolls for each guest's dinner setting. Appalled, I flipped some more, gaping at advice about fancy bridal party breakfasts, in-law cocktail receptions, and hot-house orchids for a winter wedding.

I immediately called my mother, demanding to know whether I was expected to do any of this blankety-blank nonsense for my wedding and who on earth was supposed to pay for it. My mother, who is a wonderful mother, said (this is a direct quote), "P'fft."

"In the first place, you're on a budget, so you have to set your priorities," she continued. "But, even more important, your wedding should express your personality. Don't do anything you don't feel comfortable with." I don't know when I've loved her more.

A year later, I had the wedding of a lifetime — personal and lots of fun for our guests — and *affordable*. It was in an atrium rather than a church because neither of us was particularly religious. We gave our guests kazoos imprinted with our names and the date and invited them to serenade us during the recessional (which they did, with exceptional vim if not precise harmony). We had butler-passed hors d'oeuvres and pink flamingos on the wedding cake, including a flamingo bride and groom that I fashioned myself out of swizzle sticks, black ribbon, and lace from the local craft store. The final price tag for the wedding was less than $6,000, but my husband and I never felt that we had cut corners for the event — and neither did our 100 guests.

About This Book

Budget Weddings For Dummies is about making your wedding memorable and fun without going into hock up to your eyeballs. Contrary to what the wedding industry would like you to believe, you can have the fabulous day you've always dreamed of for far less than the down payment on a house. Your wedding should be a reflection of what matters to you, not what matters to the wedding industry.

So you won't find tips here on how to snag that designer wedding gown for only $5,000; instead, you find ways to look beautiful for a tenth of that price or less. This book examines every facet of planning a wedding and applies practical, real-world advice for getting the most out of every wedding dollar you spend. After all, let's face it: Money matters. And there's no point in racking up a bunch of wedding bills that will give you and your new spouse indigestion for months after you exchange your vows.

What's great about this book is that you don't have to read it from cover to cover. It's organized in such a way that you can read what you need when you need it without feeling like you're jumping in blind. All the chapters stand alone, so jump around as you wish.

Conventions Used in This Book

For the sake of consistency and readability, I use the following conventions throughout the text:

- Terms I introduce for the first time are in *italics,* with a plain-English definition or explanation nearby.
- Keywords in bulleted lists and the action part of numbered steps are in **bold.**
- Web addresses are in monofont.

When this book was printed, some Web addresses may have been split into two lines of text. If that happened, rest assured that I haven't inserted any extra characters (such as hyphens) to indicate the break. So, when using one of these Web addresses, just type in exactly what you see in this book as though the line break doesn't exist.

What You're Not to Read

Occasionally I include information that doesn't directly relate to saving money on your wedding, such as the history behind certain wedding traditions and the meanings of various flowers. These fun (but nonessential) tidbits are generally set off from the main text in shaded boxes; you can skip them if you like.

And, of course, you can ignore any information in this book that doesn't apply to your situation. If you're already planning a church wedding, for example, you clearly don't need to read the sections in Chapter 4 about other ceremony locations. (However, the information about combining ceremony and reception sites may be useful to you.) Likewise, if you've already decided to wear your mother's (or other relative's or friend's) wedding gown, you can save yourself the time and trouble of reading the gown information in Chapter 6.

Foolish Assumptions

When researching and writing this book, I made some assumptions about you, the reader. For instance, I assume that you

- Are getting married, are related to someone who's getting married (and probably are footing at least some of the bill), or are helping a friend plan an affordable wedding.
- Don't have unlimited funds to spend on your wedding, and you don't want to go into debt to pay for it.
- Don't want to elope.
- Don't want to give your guests the impression that you're skimping or cutting corners on your wedding.
- Are looking for creative ideas to keep costs down.
- Want suggestions on where to look for bargains.
- Have a computer (or access to one) and are familiar with online shopping and other online functions.
- Are more interested in simplicity and convenience than in complexity and unnecessary work.

One thing I *don't* assume is that I know what your wedding priorities are — aside from keeping expenses under control. That's for you and your betrothed to determine (and I show you how to do it in Chapter 1). This book is designed to show you how to have the wedding *you* want at a price *you* can afford.

How This Book Is Organized

For Dummies books are known for breaking a topic down into broad subtopics so you can easily find the information you need without having to slog through a lot of information you don't. This book breaks up the concept of budget weddings into five main pieces, with chapters that explore specific topics in detail.

Part I: Coming Up with a Game Plan

This part provides you with the basics, such as coming up with a vision for your wedding, establishing a budget, and getting your timeline in order. I also offer a sample budget to help you get started.

Part II: Planning the Ceremony

In this part, I get into the nuts and bolts of your wedding ceremony — the who, what, and where for exchanging your vows. Chapter 4 focuses on ceremony locations, from the traditional church wedding to really offbeat sites (and everything in between). Chapter 5 focuses on ways to keep your wedding-party costs down. Chapter 6 is devoted to the marrying couple's attire, including options for lowering wardrobe expenses. Chapter 7 covers the ceremony details, from selecting a celebrant and hiring musicians to decorating the ceremony site. Chapters 8 and 9 explore ideas for keeping floral and photography and videography costs under control. Chapter 10 looks at invitations and other printed materials.

Part III: Celebrating with Your Guests

The reception typically carries the biggest price tag of anyone's wedding because so much goes into it: food and drinks, entertainment, favors, and decorations. This part shows you how to host a terrific party on a budget as well as how to make the most of other wedding events. Chapter 11 takes you through selecting a reception site, and Chapter 12 addresses your food and beverage needs. Chapter 13 looks at entertainment and décor options. Chapter 14 covers the rehearsal dinner, bachelor and bachelorette parties, and other pre- and post-wedding get-togethers. And, finally, Chapter 15 wraps up the part by providing advice for getting good deals for your honeymoon.

Part IV: The Part of Tens

I love the Part of Tens, because it's such a convenient way to get a lot of information into an easy-to-read format. Here you find ten ways to get the biggest bang for your wedding buck, ten inexpensive (but still classy) wedding favors, and ten wedding traditions you can ditch if you're pinching pennies.

Part V: Appendixes

This part serves as your own personal workbook for keeping track of everything related to your wedding. With the pages in this part, you can fill out a planning calendar, keep a record of prices from various vendors, keep track of what's been done and what still needs to be done, and write down your budget. Whew! You better get busy!

Icons Used in This Book

Throughout the text, you'll see icons that alert you to certain types of information. These can help you find exactly what you're looking for. Here's a glossary of those icons and what they mean:

This icon indicates a better, cheaper, or more convenient way of doing something.

This icon highlights important information you should keep in mind, especially when you're making plans, researching, or signing up vendors for various elements of your wedding.

In all likelihood, nothing will actually explode if you ignore the bits of text next to this icon. But you could end up spending more than you need to (or making another kind of mistake) if you don't heed my warnings.

Where to Go from Here

The beauty of *For Dummies* books is that you can go straight to the info you want and ignore everything else. If you haven't figured out your wedding budget yet, turn to Chapter 2. If you haven't even decided what you really want for your wedding, start with Chapter 1.

Otherwise, check out the table of contents or index to find the topic you're most interested in at the moment. For example, if you're trying to save money on your wedding attire, Chapter 6 is for you. If you're interested in low-cost photography and videography options, turn to Chapter 9.

One last thing before you dive in: We were a budget wedding couple, and many of our friends and family members commented on how elegant and fun our wedding was. So don't let anybody — and especially not the $40 billion wedding industry — tell you that the measure of a "perfect wedding" is how much money you spend.

The true measure of your perfect day is how you express your love for and commitment to each other, and how you make your guests feel welcome and valued as participants in your celebration.

Part I
Coming Up with a
Game Plan

"Are you quite sure Barbara's receptive to an inexpensive wedding?"

In this part...

Planning your wedding can be a lot of fun, but it can be extremely stressful, too. Before you get caught up in the hype of so-called "must-haves" for your perfect day, you need to figure out what your own dreams and limitations are. In this part, I show you how to focus by concentrating on what really matters to you and your spouse-to-be. I also show you how to create your wedding budget, taking into consideration the things that are high priorities for you.

A lot of wedding experts tell you that you need a year to 18 months to properly plan a wedding. But you can do it in a much shorter time frame. I show you the tasks that need to be done and the best order in which to do them (regardless of whether you have two years or two months to pull it all together). Finally, I take you through the often baffling task of lining up vendors and other assistance to make your wedding as seamless and snag free as possible.

Chapter 1

Bringing Your Wedding Dream to Life

As soon as you announce your engagement, you're inundated with advice and exhortations to make your wedding all that it can be: romantic, elaborate, *perfect*. This generally well-meaning advice can, and usually does, come from every quarter — parents, friends, the media, and (not least of all) vendors. As a result, planning your wedding can easily become an all-consuming venture that exhausts all your resources — mental, emotional, physical, and financial.

In this chapter, you can discover how to separate your own dreams and desires from the pressures you get from outsiders. You also can get tips for setting goals and priorities with your fiancé(e), for deciding how much you want to spend on your wedding, and for staying focused on what really matters to you as a couple.

Embracing the Real Magic of Weddings

People in the wedding industry call it "white blindness" — the tendency of so many brides and grooms to succumb to the glitz and fantasy of "the perfect wedding" regardless of the price tag. Of course, many wedding vendors encourage this response; after all, they can't count on your repeat business (despite the ever-higher divorce rate), so they try to make as much money as they can from each customer. And they do it by selling emotion as well as their product or service.

Unfortunately, many couples readily buy into the idea that their love for each other is rightfully measured by the expense and extravagance of their wedding day. This belief doesn't hold sway because the couples aren't smart or otherwise savvy consumers. It occurs because of a marketing ploy in which the wedding industry keeps hounding you with emotionally charged messages like "You'll look like a princess!" or "You only get married once!"

If you want an excuse to throw a fancy party and wear a princess-bride get-up, wait until October and host a Halloween party. For your wedding, remember that you won't find magic in orchids or tiered cakes. The real magic lies in the fact that you and your betrothed want to build a life together as partners, and you want to publicly proclaim your love for and commitment to each other.

Make a pact with your spouse-to-be: Whenever one of you seems to be suffering from white blindness, the other is authorized to say, "What matters is that we're getting married," until the symptoms abate.

Establishing Goals and Identifying Your Priorities

Planning a wedding is a big project, but few couples have anything but the vaguest idea of what they want to accomplish with their ceremony and reception. Even fewer can identify what they want to accomplish in their first year of marriage. As a result, many couples spend money on things that aren't really important to them and, therefore, end up exceeding their budget to get the things that are on their priority lists.

Like any major undertaking, a well-planned wedding requires a mission — a reason for being (beyond the obvious one of entering into a legal and spiritual union, of course). Read on to find out how setting goals and determining your priorities for your big day can help you stick to your budget.

Setting goals together

You may find the idea of setting goals for your wedding rather strange. After all, isn't the goal of any wedding to get married?

Well, yes and no. Certainly, the primary purpose of any wedding is to join two loving hearts in wedlock. But most couples also want to have a celebration that their guests enjoy and that allows them to express their own tastes and personalities. These desires may be goals for your wedding as well. To minimize stress and misunderstandings during your wedding planning, and to make sure you set a budget you can stick to, you and your spouse-to-be need to discuss the goals you have for your big day.

Your wedding goals won't necessarily be practical or realistic. Your fiancé's main goal, for example, may be for everything to be perfect for you. So, when the inevitable snags and snafus arise during the planning, he may worry about *your* reaction. However, if you talk about your goals beforehand, you can reassure him that you don't expect a perfect day, and he'll feel less stress. At that same time, you can set a new goal together — say, to enjoy yourselves even if not every detail is perfect.

Here are some ideas for starting your own goals discussion:

- **List what you've liked and disliked about weddings you've attended.** Making this type of list helps you visualize your wedding from your guests' points of view. Plus, it's an easy way to identify any pet peeves you and your betrothed have about weddings ("The Chicken Dance" and smashing cake in each other's faces, for example).

- **Talk about wedding traditions and whether you want to follow them.** You may choose to ignore the traditions of throwing the bouquet and the garter, for example — and, of course, doing so saves money on those items. Or you may forgo the traditional wedding garb or agree not to have any attendants. See the nearby sidebar, "Putting wedding traditions in perspective," to understand the real reasons behind some popular wedding customs. You may decide you don't really want to devote money to some of these things.

- **Think about how you want to remember your wedding.** Focus on how you want to feel when you look back on your big day. Do you want an intimate gathering so you can remember every guest and nearly every moment? Do you want to feel that you included everyone you possibly could? Do you want to recall how your creativity kept your celebration under budget? Do you want to feel that you had fun doing the planning and that you were relaxed enough to enjoy your wedding?

- **Consider how you want your guests to remember your wedding.** Naturally, you want them to have a good time; otherwise, why would you be throwing a party? So go a little deeper into what you want your guests to experience. Maybe you want to make sure everyone is well fed, personally welcomed, or pampered a little. Maybe you want to ensure that they don't feel obligated to take home a favor, to stay to the very end of the reception, or to participate in a "dollar dance."

✔ **Discuss what you want to accomplish in the year after the wedding.** This discussion is a good way to break out of the fairy tale mind-set that so often surrounds wedding planning; it forces you to recognize that, after the wedding is over, you still have to build a life together. So talk about what each of you wants to do during your first year of marriage. Do you want to buy a house? Replace one of your aging cars? Start a business? Start a savings account for any of these things? Listing your financial goals for your first married year helps you keep the reins on your wedding spending.

Begin this discussion when the two of you are alone and can focus your attention on your wedding goals — perhaps during a walk or over a quiet dinner. Encourage each other to be honest and to listen to what the other one says.

Figuring out your priorities

Talking about your goals makes it easier to decide what really matters to each of you, and identifying your priorities makes it easier to create your wedding budget and stick to it.

To figure out your priorities and whether you need to compromise (see the next section for tips on compromising), each of you should sit down and list five specific things (like fresh flowers, your favorite DJ, or professional video — not vague items like "everyone having a good time") that you really want for your wedding and five things you don't care much about. Compare your lists; cross off anything that's on both your "don't care" lists and highlight any matching priorities on your "really want" list. Finally, discuss the remaining items, noting how important they are to each of you and ways you can make sure each of you gets your top priorities.

Another option is to go through the wedding checklist in Appendix C and assign a number to each item — using a scale from 1 to 5, with 1 being least important and 5 being most important. You and your betrothed can do this together or separately. Either way, when you identify different degrees of importance, that's your cue to start talking about compromises.

Putting wedding traditions in perspective

Most people take wedding traditions for granted. Some are sweet and romantic, some have odd or spooky origins, and still others are just traditional because it was the fashion hundreds of years ago. The ones I list here have costs associated with them, so if you're trying to decide which traditions you want to follow and which you can do without, this primer may help.

✔ **The best man:** In the days when men raided neighboring villages for their brides, a prospective groom often took with him a buddy who was skilled in hunting and warfare to help him fight off any angry kin of the bride's. (By the way, the bride originally stood to the left of the groom so he could use his right hand to defend himself — and her — if her family showed up and demanded her return. In many early churches, weapons even were hidden beneath the altar in preparation for such a scenario.) See Chapter 5 for details on minimizing the costs associated with the wedding party.

✔ **The diamond engagement ring:** Engagement rings may be vestiges of times when women were considered property; even today, a ring on the third finger of a woman's left hand indicates she's "spoken for." Until the 1940s, diamonds were seldom, if ever, used in engagement rings.

✔ **The ring pillow:** Since ancient times, crowns were carried on lush pillows at the coronations of new kings and queens. Eventually, this custom was adapted to weddings to present the most precious element of the ceremony: the rings that symbolize a new unity and unending love.

✔ **The veil:** In ancient Rome, brides wore full-length veils that later served as their burial shrouds. Veils also were common in societies that arranged marriages; the bride's identity was hidden until the end of the marriage ceremony so the groom couldn't back out if he didn't find her attractive.

✔ **The wedding cake:** Wedding cake started out as rice or wheat cakes that guests broke over the bride's head (or tossed at the couple) to ensure fertility. By the Middle Ages, guests simply tossed rice at the couple and brought their own scones or biscuits to the wedding; leftovers were distributed to the poor after the ceremony. In the British Isles, the guests piled their biscuits together and the couple exchanged a kiss over the top; the bigger the pile, the more good fortune the couple was supposed to have. The elaborate tiered wedding cakes we know today didn't come into being until the mid-1600s.

✔ **The white wedding dress:** Before Queen Victoria's time, people simply wore their best clothes when they were married; color didn't matter. Queen Victoria popularized the white wedding gown in the mid-1800s, and Empress Eugenie (wife of Napoleon III) set the standard for the elaborate styling and details of wedding dresses.

Ban the phrase, "Whatever you want," from your priorities talk, because that just puts pressure on the other one (usually the bride-to-be) to take responsibility for every aspect of planning, without really knowing what her partner prefers. Instead, discuss what really does — and doesn't — matter to each of you. The areas you should discuss include

- **The ceremony location:** Do you want to get married in a church, or do you have another location in mind? Do you want an indoor or outdoor ceremony? Religious or civil? Formal or informal? See Chapter 4 for information on choosing a ceremony site you can afford.

- **The wedding party:** How many attendants do you want (if any at all)? Will you pay for their clothing and accessories, hotel rooms, and other expenses? See Chapter 5 for ways to keep your wedding-party costs under control.

- **Your attire:** Do you want a fancy, traditional wedding gown and black tuxedo? Do you want to buy, rent, or make your own gown, or do you want to borrow your mother's? Chapter 6 covers clothing options for the bride and groom as well as ways to minimize these expenses.

- **The ceremony itself:** Do you have a minister, priest, or other clergy member in mind, or do you want a friend or relative to officiate? Do you want live or recorded music? Do you want a soloist? How will you decorate the ceremony site? See Chapter 7 for more on working out the details of your ceremony.

- **Flowers:** Do you want fresh or artificial flowers? Do you want fancy bouquets and floral centerpieces for the reception? Chapter 8 provides information on how the kind of flowers you select and the quantity you buy can affect your budget. It also offers some less expensive alternatives to flowers.

- **Photography and video:** What kind of photos and video do you want? Do you want to hire a professional, and, if so, how long do you want her to shoot? Or are you okay allowing your cousin to handle the photography or videotaping? Check out Chapter 9 for ways to keep these expenses under control.

- **Invitations and other printed materials:** Formal weddings dictate formal invitations, which typically are more expensive than less formal options. Discuss whether you want other materials like save-the-date cards, response cards, announcements, ceremony programs, printed napkins for the reception, place cards, and thank-you notes. For money-saving tips on your printed materials, refer to Chapter 10.

- **The reception:** What kind of party do you want to throw? Do you want a sit-down meal or a buffet, a cocktail reception, a picnic, or a brunch? How many guests can you afford to fete?

Will you serve alcohol, and, if so, will you offer a full bar or wine and beer only? Will it be a cash bar or an open bar? Do you want to provide traditional wedding cake or a different dessert? Will you party to a DJ or a band?

The reception often is the main expense of a wedding, so flip to Chapters 11, 12, and 13 to find ways to cut costs and make smart decisions.

✔ **Related events:** Do you want to throw an engagement party or a luncheon for your bridesmaids? How about a hometown reception for people who can't make it to the wedding? Will you invite guests to a gift-opening party the day after the wedding? Chapter 14 discusses a variety of pre- and post-wedding events and how they can affect your budget.

✔ **The honeymoon:** Do you want to take your honeymoon immediately after your wedding, or do you want to wait a while? What kind of trip do you envision? See Chapter 15 for information on planning and paying for your honeymoon.

Talk about the vision you have for your wedding day and related events. You and your affianced may have different mental pictures of what your wedding and reception will look and feel like. Maybe you've always imagined an elegant evening wedding with a string quartet and butler service, and your fiancé(e) pictures a backyard ceremony followed by a pool party. Bounce ideas off each other, and don't be afraid to combine elements from different kinds of weddings to create a celebration that expresses both your personalities.

If you have a difficult time choosing among competing priorities, try running them through the Prioritizer tool at the CNN/Money Web site (`cgi.money.cnn.com/tools/prioritize/prioritize_101.jsp`). You enter the financial items that you're trying to decide among, and the tool asks you to select the most important ones among various pairings. When you finish your selections, the tool ranks your priorities for you. (This tool is great if you're having trouble balancing your wedding wishes with your other financial goals, too.)

When you get your priorities in order, write them down and post them in a place where you'll see them often. You may even want to make a copy to carry with you in your wallet so you can refer to it when you're doing your wedding shopping.

Working out compromises

Unless you and your fiancé(e) have nearly identical tastes and priorities, you'll probably identify one or more areas of your wedding where you need to compromise. You also may need to compromise if one (or more) of your priorities turns out to be a budget buster.

 The key to an effective compromise is fairness. Each of you should be willing to give up something that's only of moderate importance to get something that you really want. Say you really want your favorite local band for the reception, and your future spouse really wants the matching platinum wedding rings with the diamond chips. You may be willing to use artificial flowers instead of fresh so you have more money for the wedding rings, and your partner may be willing to limit the dinner menu so you can afford the band.

Estimating Your Budget

Much of the stress that accompanies wedding planning can be traced straight to money issues — how much to spend, what to spend it on, and where it's coming from. (Family feuds over guest lists come in a close second.) Chapter 2 covers wedding budgeting in detail. But before you and your intended get too far along in your planning, agree on a ballpark figure by asking each other how much your wedding day is worth to you in dollars.

You may be surprised at your answers. Here's why: When one of you says or even thinks, "I want to spend $20,000 on our wedding," you're almost bound to start thinking about what $20,000 represents in your life. If you make $30,000 a year at your job, for example, $20,000 represents eight months of your salary. Do you really want to work eight months to pay for a single day? Or, similarly, you may realize that you can buy a really nice car for that much money — or put a down payment on a house.

 Putting a dollar estimate on your plans prevents you from succumbing to tunnel vision, because you'll see your wedding budget in relation to your other financial goals and obligations. Your financial big picture acts as a natural brake on your wedding spending.

So how do you come up with a dollar estimate? Try one or more of these methods:

✔ Limit your budget to between 10 percent and 20 percent of your annual combined income.

✔ Find out what wedding goods and services cost in your area and use those numbers to build your estimated budget. This is useful if you really have no idea what's realistic. Keep in mind that you still have to focus on your priorities, not just expand your budget to accommodate prices in your area.

✔ My preferred method is less scientific than the preceding options but more personal. I recommend that you say dollar figures for the overall budget out loud in descending order until you get to one that doesn't make you feel like you've been kicked in the stomach.

I'm serious. Your emotions are more tied up in money issues than you realize, and it's difficult to sort through your feelings, especially when they're mixed together with your emotions about getting married. This technique is a quick way to determine your breaking point for your wedding budget. The highest dollar figure you can say out loud without flinching is the upper limit of your wedding budget comfort zone.

As you get deeper into your planning, you'll fill in the details of your budget, such as who's paying for what and so on. At the beginning, though, you and your future spouse should agree on a maximum so both of you know what your limits are.

Staying Focused and in Control

When it comes to your wedding budget, impulse is your enemy, and pressure is its co-conspirator. Wedding vendors — and sometimes family and friends — may do their best to get you to spend more, and it's easy to get swept away by the glitz and emotion.

So how do you arm yourself against impulse and pressure? Think WEDDING:

✔ **Wait:** Give yourself at least 24 hours to consider a purchase before you sign a contract or fork over the cash.

✔ **Evaluate:** Get quotes from at least three vendors, and be sure the quotes have as much detail as possible so you can compare prices, services, and value.

✔ **Define:** Identify how each purchase or expense helps you create the wedding of your dreams. If a purchase doesn't quite fit your vision, it's expendable.

✔ **Discuss:** Talk with your spouse-to-be, a friend, or a relative about the pros and cons of various options. A third party's viewpoint can help you clarify your own thoughts and feelings.

✔ **Insure:** Have a backup plan in case of glitches or unexpected expenses. For example, have a good suit for the groom in case the rented tux doesn't fit, or start a slush fund to cover items that go over budget.

✔ **Negotiate:** Ask for what you want, and know what you're willing to give on and what you want to stand firm for.

✔ **Get away:** Take a break from wedding planning and do something else you enjoy, even if it's just an hour in the garden or watching a favorite TV show. Take a break at least once a week — and more often if you can — just to remind yourself that a whole world exists that has nothing to do with weddings.

Here are some other ways to help yourself stay focused on your priorities and within your budget:

✔ **Keep your budget, list of priorities, and financial goals in easy view.** The more you see what you and your future spouse have agreed upon, the less likely you are to forget those things in the excitement of a bridal show or vendor meeting. Use the forms in the appendixes at the end of this book, and post them prominently on the fridge, your computer monitor, the bathroom mirror, or any other place where you'll see them regularly.

✔ **Take your wedding budget with you when you shop.** Refer to it as often as necessary to remind yourself of what you agreed to spend. It's even useful to get vendors to ease up on their hard-sell approach; just show them your budget for their service or product and say, "I'm sorry, but this is really our absolute limit." If your wedding is at a low-demand time, the vendor may shade his prices to fit your budget.

✔ **Pass the buck.** Tell vendors, family members, and friends that you have to discuss things with your future spouse before making decisions. This tactic buys you time, which is the best antidote for impulses and pressure. (Besides, it should be true; after all, it's your future spouse's wedding, too.)

✔ **Leave your checkbook and credit cards at home or in the car when you meet with vendors.** Doing so forces you to take a break from the excitement, even if only for a few minutes, so you're less likely to make a decision you'll regret later.

Your wedding day is a big day, but it *is* only one day. More important is the foundation you and your fiancé(e) build for your life together. Discussing goals and priorities, working out compromises, and sticking to the plan you've created are skills that will serve you well throughout your married life, helping to ensure that your own "happily ever after" really does come to pass.

Chapter 2

Working with a Wedding Budget

Consider this sad, but true story: In 2009, a groom-to-be in Austria robbed four banks to get the money he needed to pay for his fiancée's lavish fantasy wedding. (Her must-have list included a Chanel wedding gown, a new car to drive to the ceremony, a 500-person guest list, and a Caribbean honeymoon.) The man stole nearly $500,000 before he was caught. He told the court, "The money from the first robbery went in a day, so I just kept going."

Most couples, of course, don't resort to crime to pay for their weddings. But plenty go overboard with their wedding spending, racking up thousands of dollars in debt and starting their married lives that much further behind in the financial security game.

This overspending isn't entirely the couples' fault. Not only does the word "wedding" add a price premium of between 10 percent and 30 percent to virtually any item or service, but the wedding industry itself persistently promotes ideals of lavish spending to achieve a "perfect, special day." It takes stamina and determination to stand firm against the hype and pressure you're bound to encounter as you put the pieces of your wedding together. And you must know upfront what you and your intended really want and what you can do without.

In this chapter, I show you how to figure out how much you have available to spend on your wedding and how to decide where that money should go. I also give you tips on helping your family and others who may be involved in the planning process understand the financial limits you've set. Even more important, I provide pointers on how to say no — without hurting anyone's feelings — when a relative, friend, or vendor presses for an extravagance that you don't want to pay for. Finally, I show you how to match the size of your wedding to your budget and provide a sample budget for you to review. You can plug your own numbers into a budget form in Appendix D.

Figuring Out the Cash Flow

The traditions of the groom's family paying for the rehearsal dinner and honeymoon and the bride's family paying for just about everything else are solidly behind us. These days, a third of marrying couples pay all the wedding bills themselves; another third get some financial help from their parents and other relatives but bear the brunt of the costs on their own. In this section, I help you determine where your wedding funds are coming from.

Establishing who's paying for what

Before you begin planning your wedding in earnest, you need to know where the money will come from. It's all too easy to assume, for example, that your parents will pay for your reception, only to get a shock when it's time to put down the deposit on the venue. So gently broach the subject as early as you can after the engagement.

Maybe your parents *do* want to pay for your reception — or maybe they aren't in a position to help with expenses. No matter how it works out, you need to know upfront whether either set of parents plans to contribute to the wedding, how much they intend to give, and whether they want to pay for specific things or let you use the cash as you see fit. You can't create your wedding budget without this information.

Sometimes people who give you money to pay for some or all of your wedding expenses think that the gesture gives them the authority to make decisions about your wedding. Of course, you should be flexible, but don't let the generous offer force you into something you don't feel comfortable with.

The best way to counter this is to be clear from the beginning about what you want and how that person's money will be spent. For example, if your parents offer to give you $1,000, you may tell them that you'll use that money to pay for the photographer or put it toward the reception. If, for some reason, your parents would rather pay for the invitations and the flowers, they can say so upfront, and you can adjust your own budget accordingly.

Calculating what you can afford

No matter who's paying the bills or contributing funds, you and your intended need to have an honest discussion about what you want and what you can realistically afford. And, if you aren't combining your bank accounts right away (or at all), you need to decide whether to split every cost 50-50 or whether to divvy up the items or services each of you is paying for.

Most important, however, you need to figure out where the wedding funds that you'll be offering up are going to come from. Do you have savings that can be used for wedding expenses? If not, or if your savings account won't cover your costs, how will you finance the rest of your wedding budget? In the following sections, read about three common ways to come up with the money you need — and the potential dangers with each method.

Agreeing on a savings and spending plan

Depending on how much time you have before your wedding day, you may be able to create a monthly savings plan that will cover your wedding budget. Go over your finances together and discuss areas where you can cut back temporarily to meet your wedding budget goals. Maybe you can agree to limit or cut back on a few things, such as eating out, clothes shopping, the daily morning mochas, or cable, in order to divert the money to your wedding budget.

Consider opening a joint checking or savings account specifically for wedding expenses so that each of you can keep track of how much wedding money you have and how much you've spent.

Even if you do have a significant amount of money in your savings account, you and your fiancé(e) should discuss how much of it you want to use for your wedding. Check out Chapter 1 for tips on setting goals and priorities for your big day.

Here are two potential hazards you may run into if you plan to save for your wedding:

> ✔ **Life happens, and it wipes out your savings account.** To paraphrase the old saying, unexpected snags can smash the best-laid plans to hash. Car repairs, medical bills, unplanned travel expenses — any of these or a dozen other inconvenient

problems can decimate your savings, leaving you without the funds you planned on for your wedding.

✔ **One or both of you fail to live up to your wedding savings agreement.** In this case, you end up with not only less money than you budgeted for, but you also have a great strain on your relationship. Money is one of the top three stressors in any marriage, and you certainly don't want to spend your engagement with that stress. Make sure you're both committed to your savings plan and be realistic about what you're willing and able to save. (And make sure you keep track of what each of you contributes, just in case the wedding is postponed or canceled.)

Come up with a Plan B to cover either of the preceding scenarios. Your Plan B may be using credit cards, taking out a personal loan, or even putting the wedding off for a few months to give you more time to save. Or you can go over your list of priorities (see Chapter 1) and do some further weeding to trim expected costs.

Using credit cards

Many couples charge their wedding expenses on credit cards. Under certain circumstances, this may be a good option. For instance, it may make sense if you

✔ Have a credit card with a low interest rate (lower than you'd pay for a personal loan, for example)

✔ Get useful rewards when you use your credit card — cash back, frequent flyer miles, or points you can exchange for hotel stays or other goods you'll actually use

✔ Will be able to pay off the wedding bills within your first year of marriage

Credit cards are chock-full of pitfalls, however, including the following:

✔ **Your interest rate may rise.** Don't think you're safe if you pay all your bills on time and never exceed your credit limit; credit card companies have the right to raise your interest rate at any time.

✔ **You may spend more than you planned.** Researchers have proved that your brain reacts differently depending on whether you pay with cash or plastic. Using cash activates the brain's pain center, which acts as a brake on spending. But your brain doesn't register that same "pain" when you use a credit card, so the spending brake doesn't engage automatically.

✔ **You may fool yourself into thinking you can pay off your credit card debt with cash gifts from your wedding guests.** The truth is that most couples receive far less in cash gifts than they spend on their weddings. Indeed, most couples receive far less cash than they expect even if they don't plan to use it to pay off wedding bills.

✔ **The "best-laid plans" adage that I mention earlier can wreak havoc after your wedding, too.** Unexpected expenses can delay your pay-off plans, which will cost you more in finance charges.

Borrowing money

If you don't have savings available to cover your wedding plan and don't want to rack up charges on your credit cards, you can explore borrowing money — either from relatives or from your bank or credit union.

Lots of couples feel shy about asking their families for wedding money, and this can be especially true if you're older and have been out on your own for several years. Making it more of a business transaction can help ease your discomfort: Ask for a loan rather than an outright gift.

Explain to your families what you intend to use the money for. Better yet, give them a copy of your proposed budget. It'll likely make both of you feel better to know that you have a plan based on your own priorities.

When you make your request, propose a repayment plan with a modest interest rate. This approach gives your relatives a chance to offer the money as a gift, to decline the offer of interest, or to make part of the money a loan and part a gift.

If your relatives can't help out, look into getting a personal loan from your bank or credit union. In most cases, you can take up to five years to pay it back, and you may get a break on the interest rate if you agree to have payments automatically deducted from your checking or savings account.

Some lenders market "wedding loans" to help couples finance the day of their dreams. The problem is that interest rates on these loans — like anything else that has the word "wedding" in front of it — are often astronomical. You're better off using a credit card or personal loan.

Never, never, never borrow against your home or from your 401(k) to finance your wedding. If you default on any kind of loan that uses your home as collateral, you could lose your house. And when you borrow from your 401(k), you can lose far more than the amount of the loan because you have less principal working for you — which can seriously affect your retirement plans no matter how young you are.

If you're thinking of taking on a great deal of debt for your wedding — no matter where you're borrowing from — it's time to sit down with your beloved and revisit your goals and priorities. Yes, your wedding is an important occasion, but it's not worth digging yourself into a financial hole. In the long run, both of you will be happier if you have a wedding you can truly afford.

Calling for a Reality Check

Consider yourself forewarned: This section may depress you and make you feel that your dream wedding is out of reach. After all, weddings aren't cheap — at least, they aren't if you don't follow the advice in this book.

However, knowing what other couples pay for their weddings is useful when you're crafting your own budget, because it forces you to think about what's most important to you. You may look at some of the dollar figures here and think, "There's no way I'm paying $400 for invitations!" Or you may say to yourself, "If I need to budget $850 for flowers, I'll have to look for other places to cut costs."

Read on to see what the average engaged couple spends on their wedding and how to use those numbers to start creating your own budget. And, because budgeting on paper is different from complying with it in your daily life, check out the tips to stick to your financial plan.

Understanding average wedding costs

How can a wedding cost as much as a new car or the down payment on a house? Where on earth do couples spend all that money? According to The Wedding Report (www.theweddingreport.com), an industry research site, the top three expenses are the reception, the honeymoon, and the engagement ring. Together, these account for 70 percent of a $25,000 wedding.

Actual wedding costs depend mainly on size, scale, and location. A formal wedding with 250 guests obviously costs more than a backyard fete with 60 guests. And a wedding in New York City costs more than the same function in Iowa City. So before you get too discouraged, do some research to find out the average costs in your area.

Doing some legwork early in the wedding planning process can save you money later. Attend a bridal show or two and make a note of the prices vendors advertise. Or call around to several wedding vendors in your area and ask what the average package costs and what it includes. Vendors should be able to give you a range of prices. A print shop manager, for example, may say that his wedding customers spend an average of $250, but that he's had some who have spent as little as $75. With this information, you'd know that your stationery budget should be somewhere between $75 and $250, depending on the quantity and kind of materials you have printed.

Knowing the average costs for vendors in your area gives you a basis for constructing your budget. It also helps you identify whether a given vendor's prices are out of line.

Budgeting for tips and gratuities

Believe it or not, many of the vendors you pay for your wedding expect tips on top of their fees, and, in any case, etiquette demands that you give tips to certain people.

Tips and gratuities can easily run into the hundreds of dollars, which makes them a real budget-buster if you don't plan for them in advance.

Some tips are required and others are optional. For instance, tips are required for the following people (when gratuities aren't already included in the contract):

- **Altar boys/girls:** $10 to $15 each
- **Bartenders:** 10 percent of the liquor bill
- **Chauffeurs:** 10 percent to 15 percent of the bill
- **Coat check/restroom attendants:** 50 cents to $1 per guest
- **DJ:** $50 to $100
- **Hair stylist/makeup artist:** 10 percent to 15 percent of the bill
- **Valet parking attendants:** 50 cents to $1 per car
- **Waitstaff:** 15 percent of the catering bill

Check your contract with the reception site to see if gratuities for bartenders and waitstaff are included with the fees. If they are, you don't have to tip these folks extra. However, if one of the staff delivers exceptional service at your reception, you may want to show your appreciation with an extra tip.

Generally, you don't need to tip business owners; for them, a sincere thank-you note is appropriate. However, if the person actually providing the service is an employee, or if the service greatly exceeds your expectations, you may want to offer a tip. Tips are optional for the following professionals:

- **Baker/cake designer:** $10 to $20
- **Catering/reception manager:** $50 to $100
- **Musicians:** $5 to $10 per hour for each musician
- **Florist:** $10 to $20 per staff member
- **Officiant:** $75 to $200 (which may be in the form of a contribution to the church)
- **Photographer/videographer:** $50
- **On-site wedding coordinator:** $50
- **Wedding planner:** 10 percent of her total bill

Pay tips in cash. Place them in envelopes and arrange for them to be distributed right before the vendor or staff person leaves. This way, you can better judge how much of a tip she's earned. The best man usually takes charge of distributing tips and final vendor payments; if you don't have a best man, designate a trusted person to take care of this for you.

Insuring against budget-busters

The tighter your budget, the more important it is to build in a cushion for unanticipated expenses. A slush fund of between 10 percent and 15 percent of your total budget gives you breathing room when one of your line items costs a bit more than you expect. Plus, by setting this money aside upfront, you don't have to frantically redo your budget to find the extra funds.

Keep your slush fund separate from your regular wedding fund so you only tap into it when you need it. This way you're more likely to reach your wedding day at or below your budget — a great way to start your married life!

Agreeing on limits

Nearly half of all couples go over their set wedding budgets. In some cases, cost overruns may be unavoidable. If fuel prices spike, for example, your wedding vendors may raise their rates to compensate for their extra expenses. This is a good reason to include a slush fund in your budget (see the preceding section for details).

In many other cases, however, extra expenses arise because couples give in to impulses or requests from family members and close friends. Or they simply don't keep a close eye on what they're spending.

Here are some tricks to help you stick to your budget:

✔ **Make sure you both understand and agree to the budget you've worked out.** Think of it as good practice for merging your finances after the wedding.

✔ **Post your budget in a place where you'll see it often, such as on the refrigerator.** If you and your fiancé(e) don't live together, make sure each of you has a copy of the budget you've agreed on.

✔ **Discuss any adjustments before you include them in your budget (or pay vendors more than the budgeted amount).** For example, if you find a cake topper you *love,* but it costs $50 more than you budgeted for, talk to your intended before you commit to spending the extra money.

✔ **Look for other areas you could trim to compensate for an additional expense.** Say you forgot to include your great-aunt and her husband in your guest list, and your mother insists that you invite them. If your reception cost is $40 per guest, you'll need to shave $80 from somewhere else in the budget — perhaps by deciding on a less expensive bouquet or choosing less expensive centerpieces.

✔ **Write down any changes or adjustments you've agreed to.** That way, you won't experience misunderstandings later.

Getting Others on Board with Your Budget

It's one thing for the two of you to establish your budget. Getting others to respect it is a different challenge altogether. As soon as you announce your engagement, you'll get (often unwanted) advice and questions about your wedding. And when you meet with vendors, they may be far too busy painting roseate pictures of wedding-day bliss to pay attention to your financial limits.

Dealing with pushy friends and family

Anytime someone begins a sentence with, "Are you going to . . .?" or "You should have . . ." be on guard for suggestions that are likely to wreak havoc with your budget.

Of course, when these suggestions come from people far removed from your inner circle, you can easily shrug them off. Just listen politely, say, "That's an interesting idea," and then go ahead and do what you already planned to do. But when the advice or ideas come from family members and close friends, you may feel pressured to give in — perhaps because you aren't sure how to politely tell them that their suggestions don't fit your financial reality. Plus, saying no to these family members and friends goes against the almost universal desire to please and be considered a "good person." Many people feel so guilty at the thought of saying no that they say yes far more often than they should.

You may be able to preempt some of these awkward discussions by sharing your written budget with those who have a financial stake in your wedding — any family member or friend who's contributing money. In fact, these stakeholders may be more comfortable if they have a clear idea of the limits you've set; most people won't offer suggestions that are out of your range if they know what your range is.

Here are some ways to say no without feeling guilty or like a "bad" person:

- ✔ **"I wish I could, but our budget is really tight."** This response avoids the appearance of singling out a request for denial and explains the reason you're saying no. If the person making the request urges that it wouldn't cost that much extra, you can counter with the research you've done. Or you can even let the requester see your budget.

- ✔ **"I haven't seen Aunt Tilly since I was seven. I think I'll just send her an announcement."** When others urge you to add virtual strangers to your guest list, this response alerts them to your actual relationship. The suggestion of a more appropriate gesture — sending an announcement — also makes clear that you aren't ignoring the family tie.

- ✔ **"We've decided that we only want to invite family and close friends."** This statement is useful if a family member or friend wants to invite business associates or clients — a surefire way to bloat your guest list and shatter your carefully crafted budget. It also reaffirms that this is *your* wedding, and you have the final say.

✔ **"We've made so many tough decisions on the guest list already, and we really can't squeeze anyone else in. Maybe we can all get together for dinner after we get back from our honeymoon."** Use this response when someone you've invited asks to bring an extra guest (commonly a boyfriend- or girlfriend-of-the-moment). It offers a peek at the thought you've put into your guest list as well as a hospitable alternative.

✔ **"That's a good idea, but I don't have the time or money to do it."** If your mother or your best friend wants you to create elaborate favors or centerpieces, pleading lack of time is the perfect answer. The requester is sure to understand that you have lots to do. Plus, it may prompt her to offer to do it herself, which also could ease the strain on your budget (as long as that person pays for the supplies, of course).

It's your celebration, your wallet, and your sanity. Say yes when you can, but don't be afraid to say no when it's in your best interests.

Handling overzealous vendors

Don't count out wedding vendors when it comes to unwanted advice. They almost always try to *up-sell* clients — that is, convince them to spend more than they were planning to. They usually play on your emotions: "Aren't you worth the super-deluxe package? You'll look just like Princess Diana!" or "I've known so many brides who regretted not having the four-tier cake they really wanted."

It's often easier to say no to vendors than it is to those nearest and dearest to you, but if you've ever been in the same room as an overzealous wedding vendor, you know how difficult it can be to decline their services or suggestions. So be sure to take your budget with you when you meet with the vendors. Having your budget in hand can do wonders for your common sense; it's the only known antidote to emotion-based overspending.

Matching Your Guest List to Your Budget

The question of whether you should set your guest list or your wedding budget first is sort of like deciding whether the chicken or the egg came first.

If you set your budget first, you can figure out the per-guest cost, which gives you your guest list limit. Say, for example, your reception budget is $2,500, and the cost per person at the site you want is $25 for food and $15 for the bar (wine, beer, and soda). That limits your guest list to about 60 people ($60 \times \$40 = \$2,400$).

On the other hand, you can figure that you'll have 100 guests, which means you need to keep reception costs at $25 or less per person. That per-guest cost likely rules out most traditional reception halls, so you may have to start brainstorming nontraditional ideas for your reception.

Neither method is better than the other; it depends on your circumstances and priorities. If you and your betrothed have large families, maybe you'd rather have a cookout reception so you can invite all your relatives. If you expect your guest list to be smaller, though, you can let your budget dictate the number of people you invite.

Ballpark figures also help you eliminate venues that are out of your price range or are too small or too big for the number of guests you expect. Whether you start with your budget or your expected guest list, you should come up with at least a ballpark figure for your guest list before you start visiting possible ceremony and reception sites. No matter what kind of ceremony and reception you have, the site should fit both the ambience you want to create and the number of people you expect to host.

A vast church sanctuary is the wrong place for an intimate ceremony, for example, and even a mid-sized ceremony may feel small in a church that can seat several hundred people. On the other hand, stuffing 100 people into a space intended for 50 makes everyone uncomfortable (including your community's fire marshal).

Knowing the rough size of your guest list helps you eliminate sites that don't fit your vision, allowing you to spend your time and energy looking at appropriate sites for your ceremony and reception.

With most ceremony and reception sites, you can get by with a handful more guests than you originally expected. But if that handful grows too much, it may push you out of those affordable sites and force you to come up with a new plan for your celebration. And reworking your plan definitely creates a lot more work and may cause stress overload.

Before you get too far into your planning, share your budget and your ballpark guest list figure with your parents and your future in-laws; they're the people who are most likely to insist on additional guests. If they know upfront what you can afford and what you have in mind, they're more likely to curb their own requests.

If either set of parents still insists, tactfully remind them of your limits and suggest that you'd be happy to invite their extra guests if they're willing to cover the additional expenses (assuming, of course, that your site can accommodate extra guests). If you need guidance in the best ways to say no, see the earlier section "Dealing with pushy friends and family."

Looking at a Sample Budget

The sample budget in this section uses the form from Appendix D, which has been modified to reflect the priorities of a bride and groom. (In the interests of conserving space, this sample doesn't include the items the couple decided against.)

The budget is for an evening wedding with 100 guests. The couple has chosen to have the ceremony and reception at the same location. The bride will wear an ivory bridesmaid dress rather than a traditional wedding gown, and the groom will wear a suit. The contract for the reception includes gratuities for bartenders and servers, table linens, and decorations for the ceremony area. Friends of the bride's family are to provide the ceremony music, and a friend of the groom has agreed to DJ the reception for a modest fee. This couple also has decided to delay their honeymoon until after their first year of marriage. As you can see, this couple used less than $100 of their cushion — a result of good planning and shopping around for the best deals.

Sample Wedding Budget

	Estimated	Actual
Total Budget	$6,790	$6,822
Cushion	$750	$32

Apparel	Estimated	Actual
Bride's shoes	$30	$30
Engagement ring	$300	$275
Groom's suit	$200	$250
Hosiery	$10	$10
Wedding dress	$100	$100
Wedding rings	$200	$220
Other _Alterations_	$50	$30
Total apparel	**$890**	**$915**

Decorations	Estimated	Actual
Candles	$50	$25
Table centerpieces (nonfloral)	$100	$75
Total decorations	**$150**	**$100**

Gifts	Estimated	Actual
Attendants	$100	$120
Bride and groom	$150	$150
Readers	$25	$25
Singers	$100	$100
Total gifts	**$375**	**$395**

Flowers	Estimated	Actual
Bridal bouquet	$30	$20
Bridesmaid bouquets	$25	$25
Boutonnieres	$40	$35
Corsages	$50	$30
Flower girl flowers	$15	$15
Head table flowers	$60	$75
Maid/matron of honor bouquet	$30	$30
Total flowers	**$250**	**$230**

Miscellaneous expenses	Estimated	Actual
Beauty treatments	$150	$125
Cake knife	$10	$10
Card basket	$5	$10
Guest book and pen	$10	$15
Hotel rooms	$150	$250
Marriage license fee	$30	$30
Rehearsal dinner	$150	$200
Toasting flutes	$5	$10
Total miscellaneous	**$510**	**$650**

Music	Estimated	Actual
Ceremony singers	$100	$100
Reception DJ	$150	$150
Total music	**$250**	**$250**

Photography/Videography	Estimated	Actual
Candids	$200	$200
Negatives	$500	$500
Total photography/videography	**$700**	**$700**

Printing/Stationery	Estimated	Actual
Invitations	$150	$95
Postage	$30	$30
Programs	$15	$12
Thank-you notes	$25	$25
Total printing/stationery	**$220**	**$162**

Reception	Estimated	Actual
Alcohol	$1,100	$1,100
Cake-cutting fee	$125	$100
Catering*	$1,500	$1,495
Favors	$75	$75
Taxes	$250	$245
Wedding cake or other dessert	$225	$230
Total reception	**$3,275**	**$3,245**

* Many reception sites, as in this case, waive the hall rental fee if you use the in-house catering department.

Tips/gratuities	Estimated	Actual
DJ ($50 to $100)	$50	$50
Hair stylist/makeup artist (10% to 15% of bill)	$20	$25
Officiant ($75 to $150)	$100	$100
Total tips/gratuities	**$170**	**$175**

Chapter 3

Deciding When to Get Married and Organizing Your Timeline

In This Chapter

▶ Planning the best time for your special day

▶ Working on your guest list

▶ Being the first to book your ceremony and reception sites

▶ Staying on schedule with some important milestones

*P*lanning a wedding is kind of like looking at a class syllabus at the beginning of a new school semester: There's so much to do that your brain freezes, stunned by the enormity of the task. But, just like when you were in school, all these tasks don't have to be done at once. Some, like getting your marriage license, even *have* to wait until you get much closer to your wedding date. Organizing your timeline thaws out your brain and allows you to break this massive project into manageable pieces.

Creating a timeline also can save you money. Everything about your wedding — from the date you exchange vows and the time you dance your first dance, to the number of people you invite and the lavishness of your decorations — has a price tag attached. So how does following a timeline save you money? It stops you from procrastinating, which can cause you to have to settle on high-priced alternatives.

The average span between getting engaged and getting married is 16 months, and the conventional wedding planning timeline is a year. But lots of people pull together lovely weddings in a quarter of the conventional time, even if they're on a budget. No matter how much time you have to plan your wedding, the key to staying organized and within your budget is to set your priorities (see

Chapter 1) and do first things first. The timeline in Appendix A shows you which tasks need to be completed first and which can wait; if you have less than a year to plan your wedding, simply compress the tasks in the appendix to fit your timeline.

In this chapter, I show you how setting and following your timeline can ensure that you get what you want at a price you can handle.

Choosing a Date and Time to Suit Your Wallet

Perhaps it has never occurred to you to have your wedding on any day other than a Saturday evening in June. But, then again, maybe you didn't realize that you can save quite a bit of money by choosing a Tuesday afternoon in April or a Friday evening in October.

The sooner you decide on a wedding date, the sooner you can begin researching locations that fit with your vision for your wedding. Maybe you've always dreamed of a spring wedding that's all daisies and sunshine. Or maybe (especially if you suffer from hay fever) you've always thought a winter wedding would be nice, with crackling wood fires and warming drinks. Whatever your vision is, you're more likely to score the venue you want (at a price you can afford) if you start your search early.

 Begin with your ideal date, day, and time, and then research the basic costs for it — location rental and catering. If the costs strain your budget too far, look into how changing the day of the week and the time of day would affect the price.

In the following sections, I show you how to choose a date and time that are less expensive than that traditional Saturday evening in June.

Understanding how dates and times affect prices

Your wedding date and the time of your reception can affect prices for everything from the catering to the photography bill by 30 percent or more. June and September are the most popular wedding months in the U.S., which means more couples are competing for ceremony and reception space and the usual wedding services. In basic supply-and-demand fashion, vendors naturally charge their highest prices when their services are most in demand; the couples who are willing and able to pay those prices get the contracts.

Evening weddings are the most popular and usually the most expensive. An evening wedding typically is more formal, which means more expensive attire, accessories, flowers, decorations, and food. And, of course, Saturdays are the most popular days for weddings. So a Saturday evening in June or September is likely to be the most expensive option for your wedding.

You can stick to your budget if you get married on a Saturday evening in June; I did. If the date or time of the wedding is one of your top priorities, you simply need to look for other ways to save in order to balance out the more expensive wedding date. See the sample budget in Chapter 2 to figure out where you can save.

Selecting cheaper months

June and September are the most popular wedding months in large part because, in most areas of the country, the weather is neither too cold nor too hot. You gamble more on the weather earlier in the spring or later in the fall, especially if you want an outdoor location.

January, March, April, and November can be far less expensive months for marrying. Venue prices may be lower, and vendor prices are likely to be significantly lower simply because the demand isn't as great.

Notice that this list of cheaper months doesn't include February, May, July, August, October, or December. February and December aren't value priced because of St. Valentine's Day and Christmas. Lots of couples get married on or around the lover's holiday, which means more competition for venues and vendors. In December (and on New Year's Eve), your competition may not be other marrying couples but holiday parties that use many of the same venues and vendors that weddings do. July and August dates tend to fill up fast with couples who didn't book their June or September dates early enough. And May and October are popular wedding months in the Midwest.

Meetings and conventions can ruin your plans, too. Call your local chamber of commerce or convention bureau to find out when these kinds of gatherings are scheduled so you can plan around them. Also check dates for local college or high school reunions and homecoming weekends. If you live in or are getting married in a Spring Break hot spot like the Florida Keys or Mexico, you may want to avoid planning a February, March, or April wedding.

Some wedding experts recommend Memorial Day and Labor Day as good weekends to get married, because venues and vendors often are cheaper and guests have more time to travel. However, travel is more difficult and more costly on these holidays, which may prevent some guests from attending. Plus, holiday crowds may overrun hotels, beauty salons and spas, and other locations like parks and beaches. Be sure to weigh the pros and cons before you settle on a holiday wedding date.

Selecting cheaper days of the week

Ceremony and reception site rental rates are typically least expensive on weekdays and Sundays. Hotel rates usually are lower Sunday through Thursday, too — something to consider if you'll be paying for your own wedding suite or for a room for a VIP guest from out of town (such as a relative or friend who's serving as officiant).

Airfares are typically cheaper on weekdays, too, so you could save money on your honeymoon travel costs if you get married on, say, a Tuesday and leave for your honeymoon on Wednesday. See Chapter 15 for more on saving money on your honeymoon.

Other vendor rates also may be lower on these days, especially photographers, florists, DJs, and bakers or cake designers. Fridays and Saturdays are busy days for these folks, so they can charge more. But the weekdays, especially Tuesdays and Wednesdays, and Sunday are usually slower business days, so you may be able to negotiate a lower rate even if the vendor doesn't automatically offer a discount. (Refer to Chapters 8, 9, 11, and 13 for more on getting the best prices from specific vendors.)

The main reason most couples get married on a Saturday is because they figure it's easier for guests to attend. But if you get married on a Thursday, your out-of-town guests can get cheaper airfares, and your local guests should be able to arrange to take the day off from work if you give them the usual six to eight weeks' notice.

Selecting cheaper times of the day

Food and drink gobble up the lion's share of most wedding budgets. However, you can cut these costs dramatically simply by changing the time of your wedding. For example, you can explore the following options:

- **A 9 a.m. ceremony followed by an elegant brunch:** Breakfast food is much cheaper than lunch or dinner fare, and you can fill out the menu with fresh fruit, made-to-order omelet stations, and delicious breads and pastries. Because of the lower food cost, you can even invite more guests or provide a wider variety of food and still stick to your budget.

- **A 2 p.m. wedding with a cake reception:** Serve cake and a variety of beverages (punch, coffee, tea, and soda, for example) and supplement it with a sweet-and-salty snack buffet. You also can include a chocolate fountain with fresh fruit, graham crackers, pretzels, and potato chips for dipping.

✔ **A 4 p.m. wedding followed by a cocktail party:** Arrange for butler-passed hors d'oeuvres and stations with cheese, crackers, fruit, and veggies.

If you get the timing right, you can give your guests a wonderful (and appropriately filling) experience at a fraction of the price you'd pay for a traditional sit-down meal — or even a buffet dinner. Of course, timing is key: You don't want to serve only hors d'oeuvres when your guests expect a full meal. If you've set your heart on a 6 p.m. ceremony, you have to give your guests dinner afterwards. Chapter 12 provides everything you need to know about figuring out a food budget.

Avoiding expensive wedding dates

No matter what month in which you choose to get married, you may be competing with holidays, religious observances, and even sporting events — all of which can punch big holes in your budget. You may pay a hefty surcharge for opening a venue or using a vendor that's normally closed on a secular or religious holiday, for example. In addition, travel arrangements may be more challenging and costly, and accommodations for out-of-town guests may be scarce and pricey.

Here are some dates you may want to avoid:

✔ **Federal holidays:** In addition to the expense of the following dates, the people you most want to share in your celebration may have other plans for popular travel holidays like Memorial Day, July 4th, and Labor Day:

- New Year's Day (January 1)
- Martin Luther King, Jr. Day (third Monday in January)
- President's Day (third Monday in February)
- Memorial Day (last Monday in May)
- Independence Day (July 4)
- Labor Day (first Monday in September)
- Columbus Day (the Monday closest to October 12)
- Veteran's Day (November 11)
- Thanksgiving Day (fourth Thursday in November)
- Christmas Day (December 25)

✔ **Religious observances:** The days and/or dates of these holidays change from year to year, so be sure to check the calendar for the year you intend to get married:

- Ash Wednesday
- Christmas Day
- Christmas Eve
- Easter Sunday
- Good Friday
- Hanukkah
- Kwanzaa
- Muharram
- Orthodox Easter
- Palm Sunday
- Passover
- Ramadan
- Rosh Hashanah
- Tisha B'Av
- Yom Kippur

✔ **Major sporting events:** If you're getting married in or near a city that's hosting a big sporting event (or that has a team playing in the event), reception halls, hotel rooms, and caterers may be hard to come by. Here are some of the biggest sporting events to be aware of:

- Super Bowl (late January/early February)
- NCAA Men's Basketball Tournament (March/April)
- NHL Stanley Cup Playoffs (May/June)
- NBA Championship (June)
- World Series (October/early November)
- College football bowls (November through January)

✔ **Other observances:** St. Valentine's Day, Mother's Day, and Father's Day aren't official holidays, but consider the potential problems before scheduling your wedding on one of these days. Flowers — especially red roses — are at their most expensive around Valentine's Day, and florists are busy for both Valentine's Day and Mother's Day. Plus, your guests may have other plans for these dates and may be less likely to attend.

Starting (And Finalizing) Your Guest List

The number of people you expect to have at your wedding is closely tied to both your budget (see Chapter 2) and the kind of locations you need for the ceremony and reception. To come up with a starting figure, make a list of guests that you, your spouse-to-be, and both sets of parents want to invite, and then add another 10 to 20 slots for later additions. Use this number as your rough estimate to determine what size venues you need for the ceremony and reception. (Check out Chapter 2 for more on setting your guest limits and matching your venues with the number of guests you anticipate inviting.)

Unless you plan to have a small, intimate wedding, you'll undoubtedly invite people who won't attend. Most wedding experts put the no-show list at between 10 percent and 20 percent of your guest list. So you can plan to invite up to 120 people if you expect 100 people to actually attend. However, make sure your budget and your location can accommodate everyone you invite in case they all decide to show up.

You don't need to finalize your guest list until it's time to send out the invitations, usually six to eight weeks before the wedding. You need an estimate for the caterer, and you have to provide a final head count the week before the wedding.

Reserving the Venue(s) Early to Cushion Your Budget

Popular wedding venues are booked a year or more in advance, so if you have your heart set on a particular site, book it as soon as possible and secure your reservation with a deposit. Shopping early also helps you lock in prices and may even net you discounts or extra services as an incentive for reserving the space. Also, the earlier you make your reservation, the more leeway you may have in the amount and terms of the deposit. Of course, you need to get all these terms in writing so misunderstandings and unpleasant surprises don't spring up later on.

If you don't have a year to plan, don't panic: Just make finding and reserving a venue the first item on your to-do list. You may have to be more flexible with dates and times to get the venue you want, but you could save money by choosing a less common wedding schedule (see the section "Understanding how dates and times affect prices" earlier in this chapter).

Locking in prices

Wedding prices don't typically fluctuate dramatically, but inflation and other economic pressures can make waiting to reserve your venue a costly proposition. Today's $15-a-person dinner may cost $17 per plate a few months from now. However, if you start early enough, you may be able to lock in today's prices — even if your wedding is a year or more away.

If a venue's prices aren't guaranteed, ask to see a list of estimated prices for your wedding date. Most venues prepare estimated price lists a year in advance; even though they're only estimates, they do give you a fairly solid idea of what your actual costs will be.

 Get a written estimate for each venue you visit, and ask whether a deposit locks in the prices you've been quoted. If the venue has no price guarantee, ask whether it places a cap on any price increase; some venues offer a "not to exceed" limit on any increases between the time you book the site and the day of your wedding.

Exploring early-bird extras

Reception sites don't make any money when they aren't full of people partying, so site managers like their event calendars to be as full as possible as early as possible. This haste to book on the venue's part can give you an edge in negotiating everything from deposits to extra services. For example, the manager may agree to waive the rental fee for table linens or centerpieces. Or she may offer a discount on the bar rate if you guarantee a minimum number of guests for the meal.

 You can further strengthen your negotiating position by setting your wedding on a weekday, a Sunday afternoon, or a Saturday morning, when the site is less likely to be booked. Be sure to check out newly opened venues, too; they're usually eager for business because they aren't as well-known as established venues.

 Generally, the closer you get to your wedding date, the less likely you are to score extras from the venue — unless, of course, your wedding is on a typically slow day for the site.

Wheeling and dealing: Negotiating your deposits

No matter what venue you choose, you'll have to secure your reservation with a deposit. However, keep in mind that the site managers may allow some slack in the amount and terms of initial deposits if you book early. So, for example, you may be able to put down half the normal deposit now and pay the remainder in 30 or 60 days — a great advantage if your cash flow is tight.

When you're ready to reserve a site, get answers to these questions:

- ✔ **How much is the deposit, and when does it have to be paid?** Depending on the venue's policies, you may be able to put a modest deposit down now if you agree to pay the rest of the normal deposit by a specified date. This kind of arrangement buys you time to investigate other venues and save up to pay the remaining deposit if you decide to stick with this venue. Just make sure you understand the refund policy on any deposit you make (see the next bullet).

- ✔ **What's the refund policy on deposits?** Some sites refund your money if you cancel your reservation more than 90 days before your wedding; others pro-rate refunds depending on when you cancel; and still others don't offer deposit refunds at all. Make sure you know the site's policy before you make any payments. For example, if you aren't ready to make a final decision on your venue, you don't want to pay a nonrefundable deposit.

- ✔ **Will the deposit be credited toward the final bill?** Believe it or not, some sites treat deposits as additional income; the rationale is that your deposit pays for taking the site off the market, not for your event. You may be able to negotiate this policy, especially if you're booking a normally slow day or time of year. If the site manager refuses to apply your deposit to your final bill, look for another venue.

- ✔ **What payment methods do you accept?** Nearly all reception sites accept major credit cards; churches and other ceremony sites may accept only cash or checks. How you pay is an important point to keep in mind as you work with your budget, because you need to know which items you need cash for and which you can charge to your (low-interest, reward-offering) credit card.

Set it in stone: Getting your contract in writing

When you reserve a venue for either your ceremony or your reception, the items you've talked about with the site manager mean nothing unless they're included in the reservation contract. Make sure your contract includes the following information:

- ✔ A description of your event, including times, setup information, the number of people expected, and the location

- ✔ Gratuity and tax charges (as a percentage of the total bill)

- ✔ Deposit due dates and refund terms

- ✔ Due dates for information you need to supply, including the menu selections and the final head count

- ✔ A list of contingency fees, such as additional charges if your final head count falls below a certain number

- ✔ Any other terms or special instructions you've discussed with the site manager

Read the contract carefully and make sure you understand it before you sign it or hand over a deposit. The time to resolve questions or misunderstandings with the contract is before you clinch the deal; afterwards, you may just be stuck with whatever you get, and your budget may suffer for it.

Filling In Other Details on Your Planning Timeline

When you and your future spouse have agreed on your goals and priorities for your wedding (see Chapter 1), you can start filling in other important details in your plans — choosing your attendants, finding vendors, selecting your wedding attire, and making sure your union is legal.

The planning calendar in Appendix A provides guidelines on when you should start and finish various tasks for the typical 12-month planning timeline; all you have to do is plug in the appropriate dates for your wedding.

If you have less than a year to plan your wedding, just adjust your timeline to make sure first things come first. If you're getting married in 4 months, for example, first do the tasks in the "12 to 9 Months in Advance" section and so on.

When you figure out your planning dates, mark them on a calendar or post the list of dates where you and your betrothed can refer to them easily.

A written timeline helps you stick to your budget in several ways. If you're paying cash as you go, knowing when specific items have to be paid for helps you follow your savings plan. If you're using a credit card, your timeline can help you estimate monthly charges, payments, and balances. Perhaps most important, keeping track of when your wedding-planning tasks need to be completed prevents last-minute panic buying — and the overspending that often accompanies haste.

Building your wedding party

You probably already know who you want to stand up with you at your wedding. If not, you and your intended should discuss your attendants soon. Either way, after you and your soon-to-be spouse have decided on the wedding party, all that remains is to make the invitation official — and make sure your preferred attendants are available on your wedding day.

As you choose your attendants, keep in mind the costs associated with your wedding party (see Chapter 5). Immediately after your engagement, you may want every friend you can remember to stand up with you. However, your budget may tell you that you're better off limiting your bridal party to a maid of honor and best man — or to not having a bridal party at all.

Enlisting the help of family and friends

The saying, "It's not what you know — it's who you know," may be cynical when you're talking about finding a job, but it's an absolute godsend when you're planning a wedding, especially when funds are limited. Family members and friends represent a wealth of knowledge and skills that you can put to work for you in your quest to save money. For example, you may be able to elicit ideas that wouldn't have occurred to you — everything from possible vendors and inexpensive shopping tips to alternatives that are fun and budget-friendly.

Family and friends may be able to do some of the wedding work, too — another way to cut down on expenses. Most people are happy to help with general planning and relatively minor tasks like addressing invitations or helping to put favors together. If you're fortunate, however, you may have relatives or friends who have the necessary talents, interests, and time to save you a ton of money on major tasks.

Canvass family and friends early in your planning so you have a better idea of which vendors you can forego and which you need to line up (see the following section). Getting early commitments also helps you tweak your budget; for example, if your sister will make your bouquets and centerpieces, you don't have to set money aside for a florist.

Here are a few things people in your circle may be able to do:

- ✔ Arrange bouquets and floral decorations
- ✔ Bake your wedding cake or other dessert
- ✔ Cater your reception
- ✔ Create customized invitations
- ✔ Make the alterations to your wedding attire
- ✔ Provide entertainment
- ✔ Take photos or video

Tell friends and family members you'd like to have their services in lieu of a traditional wedding gift. It's a simple way to let them know how much you value their participation. If they want to give you a traditional gift anyway, that's okay, but you've made it clear that you don't expect one.

When you enlist a relative or friend to do something for your wedding, write a quick thank-you note saying how much you appreciate the help and look forward to the result. It's more than a nice gesture; it serves as a polite reminder of the commitment they made to you and the success of your wedding day. (You need to write a second thank-you note, accompanied by a gift if appropriate, after the wedding, too.)

Lining up vendors before all the good ones are booked

You can eliminate a lot of wedding-planning stress by choosing your major vendors early in the process. By deciding on these vendors early, you'll know what they'll cost and have plenty of time to make any necessary adjustments to your budget. You just might be able to score a discount by booking early as well. (Refer to the earlier section "Exploring early-bird extras" for more on scoring some extra deals.)

If you get married during a popular wedding month, lining up vendors early is even more important. The closer you get to your wedding day, the more you risk your preferred vendors being booked. Your second or third choices may be substantially more expensive, so clearly it pays to avoid procrastination.

Here are the vendors you need to line up as early as possible

- Caterer (see Chapter 12)
- DJ or band (see Chapter 13)
- Photographer and videographer (see Chapter 9)

You can wait to select a baker and a florist as long as your wedding doesn't compete with busy times like graduation, St. Valentine's Day, or Mother's Day. (The planning calendar in Appendix A provides guidelines on when to book these vendors.)

Deciding whether to hire a planner

Most budget-minded couples don't hire independent wedding planners, but if you and your spouse-to-be are pressed for time or overwhelmed by the thought of finding and interviewing individual vendors, you may decide the expense of a planner is worth the aggravation you'll avoid. In general, the earlier you decide whether to hire a planner, the more value you get for your money.

Before you determine that you need a planner, though, find out whether your ceremony and reception venues have on-site wedding coordinators, whose services likely won't cost you anything. The following sections discuss what you can expect from on-site coordinators and independent wedding planners.

Taking advantage of an on-site coordinator

The *on-site coordinator's* sole job is to ensure that everything goes smoothly for your ceremony or reception, and her services usually are included in the rental fee. She also can put you in touch with reputable vendors, saving you some legwork.

At most venues, an on-site coordinator will

- Meet with you (free of charge) to discuss ideas for your ceremony or reception
- Explain what the venue provides
- Help you plan a menu that fits your budget
- Arrange food tastings (you may pay a fee for this)

✔ Create a floor plan for your reception, or provide floor plan options you can choose from

✔ Provide a written cost estimate based on the size and scale of your wedding

✔ Explain deposit policies and payment schedules

✔ Oversee the setup for the ceremony or reception

Hotels and reception halls often have high turnover rates when it comes to their staff, so keep in mind that the on-site coordinator you meet with early in your wedding planning may move on by the time your wedding date arrives. In most cases, the transition to a new employee doesn't present any problems; usually the venue management takes care to make sure all staff members are well-trained and professional. However, at your initial meeting, you may want to ask the coordinator how your arrangements will be handled if she leaves her job.

If you're worried about sounding rude when asking about this, say, "What if you move on to a better job between now and my wedding date?" The assumption that the coordinator would only go on to bigger and better things takes any sting out of the question.

Choosing an independent wedding planner

Independent *wedding planners* — who also call themselves bridal consultants or wedding coordinators — provide a full range of services, from simple consultations to the arrangement of every detail of your wedding and reception.

The service you get from a planner depends on what kind of planner you hire. Consider which of these three types of planners may be the best fit for you:

✔ **A planner who offers one-time-only initial consultations:** This type of planner helps you establish your budget and timeline and gives you tips for working with vendors. He also may offer referrals to vendors in the area. These consultants typically charge on an hourly or per-meeting basis, so it's pretty easy to keep costs under control.

✔ **A planner who offers partial planning:** These planners usually come into the picture a couple weeks before the wedding and make sure all the details are finalized. Some only come in for the rehearsal and the wedding itself to make sure the festivities run smoothly. Partial planning services typically are billed either by the hour or on a flat-fee basis that includes a set number of hours.

✔ **A full-service planner who offers beginning-to-end service:** This type of planner will get to know you, your tastes, and your needs, and he'll help you craft a budget and timeline. He'll make recommendations for food and drink, help you choose flowers and decorations that suit your budget and style, and organize the theme, colors, and other details you choose. He has connections with a broad range of vendors and can help you find ones that fit your budget.

Full-service planners are the most expensive of the three options. They usually charge between 10 percent and 20 percent of your total wedding budget. Some won't even commit to weddings with budgets of less than $25,000.

Theoretically, a wedding planner's job is to get you the best deal with other vendors so you can have the wedding of your dreams while staying on budget. Unfortunately, it doesn't always work that way in practice. The "recommended" vendors a wedding planner deals with often pay fees to the planner to get on his list. Even if the planner offers a referral as a "free" service to you, chances are the vendor pays the planner a commission — which, naturally, is passed on to you in the vendor's bill.

To avoid the shady side of the wedding planning business, look for a planner who either is a member of the Association of Bridal Consultants or who follows the association's code of ethics. The code requires planners to disclose any referral fees before clients sign a contract; most association members don't take referral fees from vendors. Use the search function on the ABC Web site (www. bridalassn.com) to find member planners in your area.

Ordering wedding attire so you have plenty of time to spare

If you and your betrothed are planning to wear traditional wedding attire, including a gown and tuxedo or suit, start your search early. For the perfect gown, start looking six to eight months before your wedding. This timeframe ensures that you have enough time to shop, order, and have alterations made without rushing. After all, you're sure to pay a premium for rush orders, and alterations can take weeks, depending on how extensive they are. (If you have less than a year to plan your wedding, see Chapter 6 for other, less time-consuming attire options.)

If you intend to find your gown at a discount bridal shop, a consignment store, or online through sites like eBay, you can delay starting your search a little longer. However, be sure that you leave enough time for shipping and alterations if necessary.

It hardly seems fair, but finding the groom's attire is less compli-cated and generally requires less time. For a 12-month planning timeline, you can start looking for a tuxedo (either to rent or pur-chase) or suit about 3 months before your wedding; that leaves plenty of time for measurements and alterations. If your timeline is shorter, I recommend starting your search no later than a month in advance, if possible. I say this because rental places and tailors may be booked.

Make it legal: Taking care of your marriage license

Depending on where you live, getting your marriage license may be one of the last things on your list. In many states, licenses are only valid for 30 to 60 days, so you don't want to get yours until you're much closer to your wedding date.

However, for planning and budgeting purposes, call the county clerk or marriage bureau to find out how much the fee is, how long the license is valid, and whether you have to fulfill any other requirements, such as blood tests, waiting periods, residency, or proof of divorce (in the case of a previous marriage).

Here's another reason to call your county marriage bureau early on in the process: In many states, marriage licenses are issued in the county in which the *wedding* takes place, regardless of whether the couple lives in that county. Other states allow their county governments to issue licenses that are valid anywhere in the state.

Part II
Planning the Ceremony

The 5th Wave   By Rich Tennant

"Why didn't you tell me you wanted to get married by the water. We'll move the ceremony into the bathroom."

In this part...

The ceremony is the heart of any wedding celebration. Everything about it — your venue, your wedding party, your wardrobe, the music and readings you select, and even the wording of your vows — speaks symbolically or literally of your attitudes, hopes, and expectations for your marriage. And most of it affects your wallet.

In this part, you can read about each aspect of planning your budget-friendly ceremony: selecting a site, deciding on your wedding party, choosing attire that suits your taste and budget, and figuring out the details of music and décor. Also in this part are chapters on flowers, photography, and printing — all of which are major expenses for most marrying couples — and information on how to keep costs down without sacrificing your priorities.

Chapter 4

Deciding Where to Get Married

*D*eciding where to exchange their vows challenges lots of couples. For some, the question is a matter of religious beliefs. Interfaith ceremonies, for example, often require extra coordination and meetings with the couples' respective clergy members. And when one half of the couple has strong ties to a particular church and the other doesn't, that can raise planning issues as well. When neither of you belongs to a church, the mere range of ceremony site options can induce a sort of wedding-planning paralysis.

In many ways, the site you and your spouse-to-be choose sets the tone for your entire wedding day, reflecting your attitudes and beliefs about marriage as well as your tastes, personalities, and sense of style.

The site also affects your pocketbook; after all, no matter where you get married, you'll fork over at least a little cash. The trick is finding a site that offers the atmosphere you want at a price you're willing (and able) to pay. In this chapter, I cover the most common and some not-so-common wedding venues, explaining the usual costs associated with each and the extra expenses you may have to budget for.

You can save money by having your ceremony and reception at the same location. I cover reception site selection in Chapter 11 on the assumption that you want to hold your ceremony in one place and your reception in another (as most couples do). But the benefits of having the ceremony and reception at the same location include the following:

- ✔ You don't have to worry about transportation between sites.
- ✔ You can cut back on your decorations budget.
- ✔ You may save money on rental fees.

Beginning the Search for the Perfect Location

For many couples, the ceremony location is a given; they've always wanted to be married in their place of worship. However, if you and your betrothed haven't already chosen a ceremony site, your first task is to decide where you want to exchange your vows. No matter which kind of venue you want, you need to investigate availability, costs, and any restrictions that may affect your ceremony.

Unfortunately, it's easy to lose track of which venues offer what amenities. I've created a list of questions that can help you stay organized — and avoid unpleasant financial shocks. Ask these questions of each venue you consider:

- ✔ What hours are available for a wedding?
- ✔ Is the site available for a rehearsal? When, and for how long?
- ✔ What does the rental fee include?
- ✔ What is *not* included in the rental fee?
- ✔ Do you offer any packages or discounts?
- ✔ Do you require a deposit? How much, and when is it due?
- ✔ When is the balance due?
- ✔ What's your refund policy on deposits?
- ✔ Do you have an on-site coordinator to help plan and execute the ceremony?
- ✔ Do you have any restrictions on bringing in outside vendors?
- ✔ How much parking is available?
- ✔ Do you have restrooms, trash receptacles, and electrical service for the ceremony?

    ✔ Will you provide a written estimate and contract?

    ✔ Is there a cancellation clause in the contract?

Always, always, *always* get the rental terms in writing, and make a note of any verbal agreements you reach with the site manager or representative. If a venue won't provide a written estimate, look elsewhere for your ceremony site.

Choosing an Indoor Location

Even though lots of couples choose to exchange vows in parks, gardens, and other outdoor settings, indoor ceremony sites remain the most popular choice — mainly because most couples get married in churches, temples, or other places of worship.

Staying indoors has practical advantages, too. For one, you don't have to worry about rain or wind ruining your ceremony. You also run less risk of having to swat away a mosquito or bee in the middle of your vows. And you can keep your guests comfortable with heat or air conditioning.

Of course, you aren't limited to a church ceremony if you decide on an indoor venue. Many hotels, reception halls, museums, and historic sites also are equipped to host charming nuptials. In this section, I tell you about places of worship and reception halls. (See the later section "Holding to your budget at historic places and civic sites" for more about museums and similar indoor sites.)

Going to the chapel

Most couples have their ceremonies in churches or other places of worship, and then they move to banquet halls for their receptions. But great church weddings don't just happen (for convenience, I use the term "church" here, but the advice applies to any place of worship). Like every other aspect of your wedding planning, you need to select a church that's a good fit for you — in terms of both the ceremony and the cost.

If you and your betrothed have decided to get married in your home church, obviously you don't need to go shopping for a ceremony site. However, you do need to budget for the expenses of using the church — and any extra costs. Check out the list in the later section "Gathering some basic information" for guidance on what you need to know. Then use the answers you gather to make any necessary adjustments to the rest of your wedding budget.

If you aren't a member of a church, or if you and your betrothed are members of different churches, finding a religious site for your ceremony can be a challenge. Here are some of the rules you may come across:

- ✔ Some churches don't permit interfaith ceremonies.

- ✔ Some require that either the bride or groom be a member.

- ✔ Some insist that both the bride and the groom be members.

- ✔ Some allow weddings for members' children but don't require the marrying couple to join.

The bottom line is this: If you have no affiliation with a particular church, synagogue, or mosque, chances are you won't be able to have your wedding there unless you're willing to join the congregation. The main exception is the Unitarian Universalist Church, which welcomes a wide range of spiritual and religious beliefs. This church often opens its facilities to nonmembers who wish to be married there.

You also may want to check out chapels at local colleges or universities; they usually have less strict membership requirements and often are quite inexpensive to rent, especially if you or your intended (or any of your parents) attended the school.

Gathering some basic information

Before you book a church, you need some basic information. Ask about the following items before putting any money down:

- ✔ **Size:** Determine whether the church is the right size for your guest list. Fifty guests can look like a puny crowd in a vast cathedral, for example, and 100 guests will be cramped in a space built to hold 75.

- ✔ **Availability:** Ask whether the church is available at the time you want on the date you want and whether any other functions are scheduled for that day. If so, find out how this will affect your ceremony. Check availability for your rehearsal, too.

- ✔ **Religious requirements:** Find out whether the church requires that both of you become members or that only one of you converts to the church's denomination. Ask whether you must go through premarital counseling as well. If so, only you and your fiancé(e) can determine whether you're willing to meet those requirements.

- ✔ **Ceremony restrictions:** Some churches limit your ability to personalize your service, in many cases by prohibiting secular music and readings or by offering only a standard ceremony.

Some require you to use their organist, which may limit your music selection. Others have restrictions on photography and videography.

Some churches also have rules regarding attire. They may forbid bare arms and legs, for example. If the church you choose has such rules, you may have to invest in a bridal jacket or wrap to wear during your ceremony. (Check out Chapter 6 for more on "temple-ready" wedding gowns.)

✔ **Included services:** Some churches offer pew decorations, aisle runners, and even the use of altar decorations. However, you may be slapped with an additional fee, so be sure to ask whether these things are included in the rental fee.

✔ **Extra services:** Some churches charge a cleaning fee, which may be refunded if you take charge of cleaning up after the ceremony. Other services like parking and coat check may cost extra, too.

When you've gathered the info you need, you and your spouse-to-be may need to discuss the pros and cons of each church you've researched. Depending on your priorities, you may decide that the answers to some of the preceding questions are deal-breakers; others may fall under the category of "the cost of doing business" with the church you prefer. As always, only you and your intended can decide what matters and what doesn't.

Understanding typical costs

According to the Bridal Association of America, the average rental cost for a church runs between $400 and $450. Churches in large cities typically charge more, and some churches charge around $1,000 for a wedding. Depending on the site, that price may include the officiant's fee and a refundable cleaning deposit. The cost will likely include rental of the church for three to five hours for the ceremony itself (to allow for setup time) and a rehearsal, which usually is held the evening before the wedding.

Some churches offer wedding packages that include the services of the officiant and organist as well as decorations. Prices vary widely — depending on the church and region — from around $600 on the low end to $2,000 or more on the high end.

Even with a package deal, you still may run into extra fees. Decorations may not include altar flowers or an aisle runner, for example. If you want to use a unity candle or *chuppa* (a wedding canopy) in your ceremony, you'll pay extra. And you may incur an extra charge if you want the church bells to ring at the conclusion of your ceremony.

You may get a substantial discount if you, your intended, or your parents are church members. Many churches charge only a nominal rental fee — mainly to cover clean-up — for members. Of course, an additional donation to the church is always welcome (and sometimes expected).

Places of worship book up fast, so start your search early to ensure that you get the date and time you want. You may have to pay a deposit — usually around $200 — so be sure to ask about refund policies.

Saying "I do" in a reception hall

Holding your ceremony in a reception hall provides budget-conscious couples several advantages, including the following:

- ✔ You typically pay one rental fee for both the ceremony and reception.
- ✔ You don't have to worry about transporting the wedding party or guests between ceremony and reception venues.
- ✔ You can hire the officiant you want (and thus personalize your ceremony as much as you like).
- ✔ You don't have to pay for decorations for multiple sites.

Unfortunately, reception halls have their disadvantages, too.

- ✔ You may not be able to choose your caterer or bring in your own alcohol.
- ✔ You may find *room turning* — changing the setup from ceremony to reception — to be awkward for you and your guests.
- ✔ Deposits often are nonrefundable or only partially refundable.
- ✔ You may pay the same amount in mandatory gratuities and other miscellaneous charges that you would for a church rental fee.

Turn to Chapter 11 for more on vetting and selecting reception sites.

Exchanging Vows Outdoors

Outdoor ceremonies are lovely and can be extremely cost-effective — or they can cause frustration and empty your wallet. On the one hand, you can keep decoration expenses to a minimum, because nature provides your designer backdrop. On the other hand, nature can be a heartless practical joker, leaving you and your guests uncomfortable and disappointed. And it costs money — sometimes a lot of it — to guard against the unpredictable tricks of nature.

Outdoor ceremonies (and receptions, for that matter) require special amenities that you take for granted in an indoor site. In fact, the issues and challenges for any outdoor location are similar to those for a home wedding. (See the later section "Backyard Nuptials: Getting Married at Home.")

Among other things, you may have to provide the following items for your outdoor fete:

- ✔ Level walkways and seating areas
- ✔ Pest control
- ✔ Power supply
- ✔ Restroom facilities
- ✔ Site clean-up
- ✔ Tents
- ✔ Trash cans

A large tent (or multiple smaller ones) is an absolute must if you don't have an adjacent indoor facility you can use if your wedding day turns out to be miserable weatherwise. And keep in mind that the tent is likely to be your biggest expense.

The following sections discuss some outdoor options that won't break the bank as well as special preparations you need to consider for an outdoor ceremony.

Reviewing some inexpensive outdoor options

The cost of renting some outdoor sites can rival the fanciest reception hall in town. But there are plenty of affordable options, too. Because rates, restrictions, and policies differ greatly from site to site, you need to do some research to find out whether a particular location suits your needs.

Public parks usually offer the lowest rental rates — sometimes as low as $25, which may be refundable if you clean up afterwards. And many parks have pavilions or enclosed spaces so you can shelter yourselves and your guests from the elements. Rates vary depending on the season and day of the week, so do your homework before selecting a site.

Check out these sources for ideas and information about reservation policies and rates:

- ✔ Your local parks and recreation department for municipal parks, gardens, and other facilities

- ✔ Your state parks department for properties owned by the state

- ✔ The administrative office of any National Park Service sites you may be interested in

Many national parks allow wedding ceremonies, but most require permits and nonrefundable deposits. Policies and procedures vary from park to park, too, so be sure to call the specific site to get current information.

- ✔ Your local convention or visitor's bureau, which is useful for information about private and not-for-profit sites

- ✔ Any local historic sites, which often offer their grounds and gardens for weddings

- ✔ Libraries, community theaters, and museums

When you call site offices, ask whether they have any permit requirements (and the fees associated with permits). Be sure to ask about restrictions, too, such as noise limits, maximum number of people, and "clearing out" times. Some sites charge clean-up fees, and some charge extra if you want to reserve the site for a rehearsal. Finally, be sure to ask about restroom and parking facilities; you don't want the unexpected expense of arranging transportation or portable toilets for your guests.

Considering the climate

Rain isn't the only thing you have to worry about on your wedding day. A blistering hot sun can suck the joy right out of the day, too. And wind can wreak havoc with clothing, hairdos, decorations, and table settings. Tents and park pavilions provide shade, and a tent with side panels can mitigate the effects of a too-lively breeze.

In the following sections, I tell you how to best outsmart Mother Nature with tents, other covers, and sources of heating and cooling.

Renting tents

The easiest way to provide cover for your ceremony (assuming the site doesn't have a pavilion or other shelter) is to rent a tent. You can get side panels for any tent style; these can be rolled up to allow for greater air circulation in good weather, or lowered to provide protection from wind, rain, and cold.

Depending on the size and amenities of the tents you're considering — such as heating or air conditioning, temporary flooring, and so on — tent rental can cost you anywhere from around $300 to $10,000 and up.

The following list includes four tent styles you can choose from:

- **Frame tents:** *Frame tents* (also known as *clear-span frame tents*) require minimal staking, so they work well over asphalt and other hard surfaces. These tents have no center poles, so they offer a clear span beneath the canopy.

- **Pole tents:** *Pole tents* have stakes and tension lines at every perimeter pole, so they're a poor choice for driveways, patios, and other hard surfaces. In addition, the stakes and tension lines can present a safety hazard, especially at night; you may want to decorate them with balloons or strings of miniature lights so guests don't trip over them. The canopy is supported with four corner poles, two or more center poles, and smaller poles on each side.

- **Century tents:** *Century tents* are identifiable by the peaks in their roofs. They can be erected over either frame or pole setups. Because of their more elegant silhouette, they're a popular choice for weddings and other celebrations.

- **Pop-up canopies:** *Pop-up canopies* are smaller — usually 10 feet by 10 feet or 12 feet by 12 feet — so you'll probably need several unless your guest list is short. They also usually don't come with side panels — and it can be inconvenient to improvise side panels.

  This style of tent is much cheaper than heavy canvas party tents, and you can hit up friends and relatives to borrow any they have. If the tents you gather are different colors, you can color-code your ceremony and reception: exchange vows under the white canopy, place the gift table and guest book under the blue canopy, serve food under the green canopy, and set out drinks under the red canopy.

Ask friends and family if they know anyone who has a large party tent. If it's in good shape, you may be able to borrow it for your wedding, or the person may allow you to rent it for significantly less than a rental company charges.

Looking at other shelter options

If tents don't turn you on, or if their cost doesn't fit your budget, look for venues that provide shelter. Pavilion rentals at local or state parks usually are quite reasonable — sometimes as low as $50 for the day — and you may get your money back if you clean up the site after your wedding. If you want a more elegant outdoor feel, some parks and gardens also have gazebos for rent.

The main disadvantage to pavilions and gazebos is that the sides are open, affording minimal protection in a shower accompanied by winds and none at all against gusty breezes. They also can get crowded quickly; some are built to accommodate only one or two dozen people.

Look for an outdoor site with indoor facilities you can use in case of bad weather. That way, you don't have to rent tents. (However, keep in mind that you may need to rent chairs and other furnishings for the ceremony — and tables if you combine your ceremony and reception in one location.)

Taking heating and air conditioning into account

Sided tents are relatively easy to heat (assuming you aren't getting married in the Alps in January) with gas or electric heaters. Air conditioning is less effective; you'll suck up a lot of power for only moderate relief from heat and humidity. Of course, to use electric heat, air conditioning, and fans, you need a power source — either a generator (which can be extremely noisy) or nearby electricity and heavy-duty extension cords.

Cords can present a safety hazard, so make sure they're secured under cord covers, flooring, or even duct tape.

On a hot day, help guests stay cool by crafting your ceremony programs into hand-held fans (which can double as favors and save you money). If your budget allows, also hand out ice-cold bottled water as guests enter your ceremony area.

Backyard Nuptials: Getting Married at Home

Many home weddings are a combination of indoor and outdoor functions, and they're appealing for several reasons:

- ✔ You save on deposits and site rental fees.
- ✔ You won't have any problems with conflicting events.

- ✔ You can freely enlist the help of family and friends.

- ✔ You get an intimate ambience that's difficult to replicate elsewhere.

If having your entire wedding day at home sounds like too much work (or too much money), you can follow the example of many couples who looked into home weddings: Have only your ceremony at home, with the guest list limited to immediate family and one or two close friends (who may serve as attendants). Then you can have your reception at another location where things like restrooms, tables and chairs, electricity, parking, and shelter from the elements are all included in the rental price.

Costs for a home wedding can quickly hit the stratosphere. Unless you live in a mansion with a full complement of maintenance, gardening, cleaning, and cooking help, you'll likely have to fork over some significant cash to get your home — or the home you want to use — in shape to handle a wedding.

Here are some potential costs to think about:

- ✔ **Exterior maintenance:** You don't want your guests' first sight to be of peeling paint, crumbling steps, or a sagging front porch. Take an honest look at the home's facade and figure out whether any repairs need to be made before the wedding. If the home needs extensive repairs, it probably isn't a good choice for a budget-friendly wedding.

- ✔ **Facilities:** That half bath on the ground floor of your home can handle only so many visitors, so you may have to rent portable toilets to accommodate your guests. Usually you need one for every 50 guests; more if you plan to party all day long and into the night. And if you have a septic system, you may have to pay someone to empty the tank before your wedding.

- ✔ **Interior cleaning and maintenance:** Cleaning before the wedding (and after) is an absolute must, and if you don't have the time or inclination to do it yourself, you'll have to pay someone to do it for you. You also may need to do some interior repairs, such as fix torn wallpaper or get rid of the bump in the living room carpet that you automatically step over but that could seriously trip up your guests.

- ✔ **Lawn care, landscaping, and terrain:** At the very least, you have to make sure the lawn is mowed several days before the wedding. Don't cut it any closer to the date than that, however, because freshly cut grass can stain shoes (especially pretty white wedding shoes!). Shrubs, bushes, and even trees may need trimming, and flower beds may need weeding. And if your yard is rocky or uneven, or if it has poor drainage, it may not work well for a wedding. You don't want guests to sprain their ankles, and you certainly don't want to wade through standing rainwater on your way to the altar.

✔ **Parking:** If you don't have enough parking on your street, you may need to provide a shuttle bus between your home and a central parking location. Buses can cost $400 or more per hour, and you may need to get permission — and pay a fee — for your guests to use a parking lot.

✔ **Power supply:** You may need to rent a generator to power commercial-grade appliances like coffee urns or to provide power for lights, music, and a loudspeaker or microphone system.

✔ **Tables and chairs:** You may have to rent tables for the guest book and gifts and chairs for your guests — and that can get pricey quickly. Some tent rental companies provide tables and chairs (for a fee, of course). The setup and tear-down ser-vice may cost extra.

Some caterers provide tables and chairs, and their prices may be better than a tent rental company's. Also check out local churches, fraternal organizations like the Elks Club or American Legion, and even libraries and fire departments; they may rent tables and chairs for even lower fees. Ask around and get quotes before you place your order.

✔ **Tent rental:** Backyard ceremonies can be lovely when the weather cooperates; but, of course, it doesn't always behave. So, if your home isn't large enough to accommodate your guests in case of rain, wind, or uncomfortable temperatures, you need to rent a tent to provide some protection from the elements.

You'll likely want to rent a tent for a couple of days. That way you can use the tent for your rehearsal and any day-after gatherings (see Chapter 14). Refer to the earlier section "Considering the climate" for more information on tent rental.

✔ **Trash removal:** You may have to schedule an extra garbage pick-up or pay for your service to take away the extra trash that your wedding generates.

You may be wondering how you can have the home wedding you want without taking out a second mortgage. Just remember that it can be done, but it takes planning, preparation, and legwork. Shop around for the best deals on anything you have to rent. Ask for discounts if you rent multiple items from the same outfit (such as tables and chairs from the tent rental company). Last but not least, enlist family and friends to help with some of the prep chores, and pick their brains for vendor referrals.

Saving Money with Destination Weddings

To most people, having a destination wedding means going to Mexico or the Caribbean. These are certainly popular options (especially for people looking to escape the dreariness of winter), but you can have a destination wedding virtually anywhere. Consider a Great Camp in the Adirondacks, a ski lodge in Aspen, a golf resort in Arizona, or even a glitzy Vegas wedding.

What's the appeal of traveling long distances to a site you'll likely book without ever visiting in person and trusting the arrangements to a coordinator you've never met? Two words: romance and value. What better way to celebrate your own personal fairy tale than against the exotic backdrop of majestic mountains or azure seas? And if you can get both your wedding and your honeymoon for the price of one, what's not to like?

Destination weddings sound great, but because we don't live in the ideal world portrayed by fairy tales and bridal magazines, you have to remember that there are trade-offs to a romantic and cost-effective destination wedding. Consider the following:

- Financial and time constraints likely will severely curtail your guest list; many of your friends and relatives simply won't have the money or time to attend your wedding.

- If you like to be in charge of arrangements, trying to pull all the details together from hundreds or thousands of miles away can be frustrating and time-consuming.

- If you imagine hosting an American-style wedding and reception in a foreign country, you'll probably be disappointed in the results (or appalled at the extra expense).

Destination Weddings For Dummies by Susan Breslow Sardone (Wiley) takes you step by step through planning a destination wedding virtually anywhere in the world on virtually any budget. Like any wedding, a destination event can easily run into the tens of thousands of dollars. But, also like any wedding, you can save a ton of money by shopping around and being flexible with your time frame.

Also check out Chapter 15; much of the information about honeymoon travel applies to planning a destination wedding, too. And if you want to have a small ceremony in an exotic locale and then a bigger celebration back home, flip to Chapter 14 for more information on celebrating with friends and family who can't attend your wedding.

As destination weddings become more popular, venues fill up faster and faster; many are booked more than a year in advance. To get the venue you want for the dates you want, start your search early — ideally 12 to 18 months before your wedding.

If you have your heart set on a destination that fills up quickly and is more expensive than you'd like, schedule your wedding for the off-season to save money. For example, airfares and hotel rates are at their highest in the Caribbean from November to April, but both often are steeply discounted after April 15. In Las Vegas, March and October are the months when conventions descend on Sin City, jacking up airfares and hotel rates. Chapter 15 has more information on off-seasons for various locations.

Resorts and cruises that specialize in destination weddings often give decent discounts when you reserve a minimum number of rooms for your guests. Add those discounts to the destination's slow period, and you can reap significant savings over high-season prices.

Off the Beaten Path: Exploring Nontraditional Sites

Nontraditional ceremony sites are popular with couples who like to take the unbeaten path or who aren't particularly religious or members of a specific church or other place of worship.

As always, the key is matching your tastes with your budget. The options covered here — boats, castles, and historic sites — won't fit every budget, every style, or every vision. But they may get your own creative juices flowing as you decide what you want your wedding to look like.

Ahoy, mate: Finding deals onboard boats

If you live near a lake or river of any size, chances are you'll easily find an outfit that offers dinner cruises — and wedding packages.

Costs can run $50 per person or more, but that often is an all-inclusive price that covers food, drinks, the ceremony, and, of course, the cruise itself. And what could be more fun than having a boat captain officiate your wedding?

For couples on a budget, boat-based weddings offer a number of advantages:

- ✔ You can't go over your budget by inviting too many people, because boats have strict capacity limits (and reputable boating companies carefully adhere to these limits).

- ✔ You have a slim chance of being socked with overtime charges, because the boat returns to its dock on a preset schedule, forcing the closure of the bar and the disembarkation of guests.

- ✔ You don't have to worry about shuttling guests between different ceremony and reception sites. In fact, if your guests' hotel offers a shuttle service, you may even be able to arrange free or discounted shuttle service to and from the dock.

- ✔ Your decoration budget won't explode. There simply isn't enough room on most dinner-cruise boats for extravagant decorations. Depending on how crowded the table settings are, you may not even have room for centerpieces.

As with any other venue, you're more likely to get a price break if you book your wedding for an off-peak time. This may mean a mid-week sailing rather than Saturday at sunset.

Keeping costs down at castles

What better place for your fairy-tale wedding than a genuine castle? And don't think you have to travel to Europe to get that authentic Old-World, regal atmosphere. North America is dotted with impressive castles, many of which make weddings their specialty.

Of course, costs at castles can be over the top. But you have plenty of reasonably priced options, too. Research a variety of castle options around the world at Love Tripper (www.lovetripper. com/castle-weddings/castle-weddingvenues.html).

Holding to your budget at historic places and civic sites

Many exquisite historic and civic buildings are owned by governments or nonprofit groups, so their rental fees tend to be quite reasonable — even as low as $25 per hour in some cases. Some have facilities to host both your ceremony and reception; however, you may be limited in the kind of food and drink you can bring in. Possible venues include libraries, museums, art galleries, and even stately government buildings.

Check with your local chamber of commerce or visitor's bureau; these agencies can put you in touch with historic sites that host weddings and other functions. They may even recommend certain sites based on your needs.

Going Even Further From the Beaten Path

Regardless of what your families may tell you, you can get married practically anywhere. Couples have exchanged vows in group skydives, at fast-food joints, on roller coasters, and in bowling alleys, carwashes, and movie theaters. These are what I call "AP weddings" — they involve sites and themes so unusual that they're reported by the Associated Press and carried by news organizations all over the world.

The cool thing about an AP wedding is the freedom you have to express your individuality. You can integrate any traditional elements you want, toss the ones that don't matter to you, and wrap the whole thing up in something intensely personal — a shared hobby, a favorite hang-out, or a passion for a particular movie. Even cooler is the fact that these offbeat options often cost a fraction of traditional weddings. Imagine having the wedding of your dreams for $2,000 instead of $20,000!

Need some inspiration for your unconventional wedding? Check out Offbeat Bride (offbeatbride.com) or Here Comes the Guide (www.herecomestheguide.com/weddingplanning/region/off-beat). The latter focuses on California weddings, but most of the ideas can be adapted to your area.

Chapter 5

Minimizing Wedding Party Costs

*B*ack in the day (and I mean *way* back — 1,000 years ago or more), the purpose of bridesmaids and groomsmen was to confuse ex-lovers and evil spirits who may have wanted to harm the bride and groom. The wedding party was instructed to wear outfits similar to those of the marrying couple so that malevolent mortals or spirits wouldn't know who to attack. Unless you feel evil spirits are likely to be lurking in the shadows on your wedding day, you don't really need to have attendants. In fact, many couples on tight budgets choose to forgo the traditional wedding party to save money.

Most couples don't think of the costs involved in gathering a group of attendants — partly because, in many cases, the attendants pay for their own attire. But attire isn't the only expense. In addition to pampering and thank-you gifts, you have to include your attendants in your head counts for the rehearsal dinner and reception. And chances are that each of your attendants will bring a date, which adds more folks to your guest list. See Chapter 14 for details on the rehearsal dinner; for now, though, be sure to budget enough money to feed your wedding party and their dates the evening before your wedding.

You also may have to provide attendant bouquets and boutonnieres (see Chapter 8 for info on flowers and alternatives) and arrange transportation between the ceremony and reception sites, which may mean a bigger (or extra) limo or rental car. And you may incur other expenses, such as a wedding party brunch.

I'm not telling you all this to talk you out of having attendants. Just remember that when it comes to weddings, nothing — including having your best friends stand up with you — is truly cost free. If having attendants is important to you, include these expenses in your budget and trim costs in other areas if necessary. In this chapter, I show you how attendants affect your budget and how you can minimize these expenses without sacrificing style or etiquette.

Choosing Members of Your Wedding Party

In the post-engagement glow, you naturally want to share your joy with everyone. If you decide to gather a wedding party, you may even be tempted to include the minor branches of your family tree in it. Curb that impulse, though. It could easily throw your budget seriously out of whack, and skew your wedding dreams to boot.

Even though the maid of honor and best man traditionally serve as witnesses on the marriage license, you can designate anyone you like to fulfill that duty. If you opt not to have attendants in order to save money, ask your nearest and dearest to be witnesses so they still feel included. In fact, in ancient times, everyone who attended a wedding was a witness, and each person had to sign in when arriving at the ceremony; this is the origin of the wedding guest book.

Calculating the number of bridesmaids and groomsmen

When deciding how many attendants you should have, take a look at the size of your wedding. For a small ceremony — 50 guests or fewer — many couples choose to have only a maid of honor and a best man. But you could have two attendants each without looking out of balance with your guest list.

For mid-sized weddings — more than 50 guests, but fewer than 200 — you can have between one and six attendants each, with the number of attendants increasing as your guest list increases. Large and formal weddings (more than 200 guests) often have ten or more bridesmaids and groomsmen, plus additional ushers.

Groomsmen often double as ushers, and the general rule of thumb is to have one usher for every 50 guests. So if you're unsure how many attendants you should have, figure out how many ushers you need; doing so gives you the appropriate number of bridesmaids and groomsmen for your wedding size. Or you can choose to have ushers but no attendants, which will save you money on flowers, gifts, and reception costs.

Deciding on a ring bearer and flower girl

Traditionally, ring bearers and flower girls are most often included in formal weddings, but they make appearances at less-formal ceremonies, too. Child attendants are a good way to include beloved nieces and nephews or children from previous relationships into your ceremony. But keep in mind that expenses are associated with these roles.

 When including child attendants, you need to purchase a flower basket for the flower girl and a ring pillow for the ring bearer. And if you have definite ideas about what you want the children to wear, you may decide to pay for their outfits, too. Depending on the kind of food at your reception and the ages of your child attendants, you may need to arrange for child-friendly meals, which may cost extra. If they're very young, you may want to arrange for child care so they don't disrupt the reception — and, of course, that's another added cost.

 Many couples incorporate four-legged family members into their ceremonies, enlisting the family dog to serve as ring bearer, for example. If you're getting married in a church, this probably isn't an option. But if your wedding is at a park or in your back yard, having a canine ring bearer is an inexpensive alternative.

Outfitting the Wedding Party

Most couples ask their attendants to pay for their own wedding outfits, but many brides who shelled out lots of money for a bridesmaid dress that they never wore again are loathe to put their own attendants in that irksome situation. Especially if they want specific colors and styles, many brides feel they, and not their bridesmaids, should pay. Many grooms feel the same way about rental tuxedos; they don't want their friends to resent paying high rental fees, so they pick up the bill themselves.

However, paying for your wedding party's attire is entirely a personal choice. Most bridesmaids and groomsmen expect to pay for their own, so you don't have to worry about breaching etiquette if you ask them to do so. And, of course, this is the cheapest way to dress your attendants when you're on a budget. Though, if you're set on a specific style and have room in your budget, you and your intended may want to bear this cost yourselves.

Many couples simply give their attendants guidelines as to color and general style, and let them select their own outfits. This approach defuses money issues between you and your friends. Letting your attendants choose their own outfits also gives them the freedom to shop within their own budgets — which may be as tight as your own.

Dressing up your bridesmaids

Your bridesmaids can wear traditional bridesmaid dresses, formal dresses, or cocktail dresses. All these options allow you to get the look you want, no matter how formal or informal you need to go. Bridesmaid dresses usually are more expensive, so if you want to save money, go with formal or cocktail dresses. Costumes also are an inexpensive option.

Gussying up with traditional maid attire

Depending on how elaborate your bridesmaids' dresses are, costs can range anywhere from about $50 to $250 or more. The more expensive dresses are made of satin or silk, and they usually have handcrafted details like beading or embroidery.

But the purchase price is by no means the end of the dress bill. Bridal shops almost always charge extra for alterations, which can run anywhere from $20 to $100. Even if you purchase the dresses at a department store or online, you'll still likely have to pay a seamstress for alterations.

Some department stores offer free minor alterations, such as hemming. If you find attendant dresses you like at a department store, ask about their alterations policy before you place your order.

Procrastination can cost you money. A delay in ordering the dresses can add an extra rush delivery fee to the outfits. So be sure to order bridesmaid dresses (or have your bridesmaids order them) as soon as you decide on a style and color. It's far better — and cheaper — to have too much time for alterations than not enough. Besides, the earlier they have their dresses, the more time they'll have to find the right shoes at the right price.

Increasing your savings with formal gowns or cocktail dresses

You don't have to confine your choices to traditional bridesmaid dresses. Formal dresses often are much cheaper. Plus, your bridesmaid will be able to wear the dress again after the wedding.

You can get great-looking informal or formal dresses by buying at department stores or online retailers, such as Amazon.com or Overstock.com.

If you want a more formal look, check out cocktail or party dresses. To get a less formal look, select simple sleeveless, knee-length dresses for your summer wedding. This choice won't cost you (or your bridesmaids) a fortune, and it allows them to wear the dresses again for any number of summer occasions.

Going dramatic with a costume

Some couples incorporate elaborate themes into their weddings, dressing themselves and their attendants in the appropriate costumes. Costume rentals and purchases can be much less expensive than traditional wedding finery.

If you don't have a local costume shop, look online for ideas and good prices on purchases. Moon Costumes (`www.mooncostumes. com`), for example, has galleries of costume themes, and several of their costumes are less than $50. If you know what kind of costume you want, conduct an online search ("Star Trek costumes," for example) to suss out the best prices.

Some online costume shops offer rentals as well as purchases, but I don't recommend renting from an online retailer. You can't make alterations to a rental costume, and rentals are usually limited to five days, giving you little time to resolve fitting or other issues. If you'd rather rent, stick with a bricks-and-mortar store in your area.

Finding the best attire for the groom's buddies

Unless you're planning a theme wedding, your groomsmen and ushers likely will wear tuxedos or suits. Either option is appropriate; it just depends on the formality of the event and how much you want to spend. Of course, tuxes are the more formal and expensive option.

Opting for tuxes

Most men rent tuxedos because they have few occasions that are appropriate to wear one to, and purchasing a tux can cost $300 to more than $1,500. For that kind of money, a guy can buy a good suit that he can wear again to work or to other more formal functions.

In most areas, a basic tuxedo rental costs between $50 and $100. This price typically includes a vest or cummerbund, a shirt, and a tie or ascot. Measurement and fitting services, as well as cleaning and pressing, will also likely be included in the rental fee. If you have the tuxes delivered (instead of picking them up), you may pay extra. Shoes also usually cost extra.

Some formalwear stores waive the groom's rental fee if a minimum number of tuxes are rented by the groomsmen and ushers. I don't recommend increasing the size of your wedding party just to score a free rental; after all, the other expenses of adding attendants would make that "free" tux quite costly. But if you're already planning to have that minimum number of male attendants, ask the store manager whether he offers such a deal. If he doesn't, look for another store in the same price range that does.

Look at formalwear store Web sites for online coupons or specials. And be sure to ask store personnel about any promotions or specials they offer.

Saving money with suits

Unless you're planning a very formal affair, a good suit is a perfectly appropriate alternative to the traditional tux. The most common wedding suit colors are black, charcoal, and gray. But nothing says that the groom and male attendants can't wear navy or another color of your choice. In fact, you can coordinate suit, shirt, and tie colors to accentuate the color scheme you've chosen for your nuptials.

If you decide to go the suit route, you have many options for dressing your groomsmen. You can

✔ Ask that they wear suits they already own

✔ Purchase or rent suits for them

✔ Ask that they purchase or rent new suits

Men's stores often run two-for-one specials on suits and accessories like shirts and ties, so you can get more value for your money. You can either get two suits for yourself or you can often pair up groomsmen to get the deal.

Ask whether the suit retailer does alterations and find out how much it charges. Simple tailoring, like hemming pants and shortening sleeves, often is free. More extensive alterations, however, may carry an additional charge.

Having fun (and saving money) with costumes

Costume rental prices often are comparable to tuxedo rental costs. Purchased costumes can be quite inexpensive, especially if you search online. See "Going dramatic with costumes" earlier in this chapter and Chapter 6 for costume Web sites to check out.

Costume rentals usually work best when your attendants live nearby because they can go to the costume shop in advance to try on costumes and get a good fit. For purchases, though, you'll probably find better prices online.

Helping the ring bearer and flower girl look as sweet as sugar

The families of the ring bearer and flower girl usually pay for their little one's attire. But, as with your other attendants, if you have very specific ideas about what you want them to wear, consider picking up the cost yourself. Also, if the child's family isn't in good financial shape — and you have room in your own budget — you may want to pick up the tab.

Fortunately, children's wedding attire can be quite inexpensive. Department stores and discount retailers typically have a good selection of lovely dresses for your flower girl and sharp-looking suits for your ring bearer. Renting a tuxedo for the ring bearer may be more expensive than purchasing a suit, so do your research before deciding on one or the other.

 Check out used clothing stores or thrift shops for kids' outfits. These outlets are often chock-full of gently used dresses and suits that their original owners outgrew, and prices are much lower than retail.

Accessorizing: It's all about the bling

As any fashion follower knows, no outfit is complete until you have just the right accessories to create the look you want. But you don't have to go overboard on your budget to create a stylish, pulled-together look for your wedding party. The trick lies in expanding your ideas of how to accessorize your attendants' attire.

Most accessories will be for the women in your wedding party. Men's accessories, at least for traditional weddings, typically are limited to color-coordinated ties and sometimes vests or cummerbunds. Depending on the shirt style, the men also may need cufflinks, but they're less common these days.

Coordinating bridesmaid jewelry

As brides have moved away from the tradition of dressing their bridesmaids exactly alike, they've begun leaning toward matching jewelry. As you can imagine, these jewelry costs can add up quickly. Even a few cultured-pearl necklaces can cost you several hundred dollars or more. Add in matching bracelets and earrings, and you could easily be looking at a four-figure expense.

One way to save is to avoid focusing on earrings or rings as accessories, because they're too easily hidden in photos. If you can't see them, why spend the money? Instead, concentrate on bolder pieces — necklaces, brooches, and bracelets — that stand out much more clearly.

 Consider hosting a jewelry party at your home two or three months before your wedding. The hostess at these parties typically gets credits based on what her guests purchase, and you can use those credits to buy matching jewelry for your bridesmaids. Package the jewelry as your thank-you gift to your attendants to save even more. You also can find great (although not always matching) jewelry at vintage shops, thrift stores, and even garage or estate sales.

Fortunately, you can move the decimal point at least one place to the left and still get a stylish, coordinated look for your bridesmaids. *Illusion necklaces,* made of clear twine and a few colored glass beads or faux pearls, create a cool effect, and you can make them yourself for about $5 a piece with materials from your local craft store. Add coordinating bracelets for another $10 a piece, and you've got a lovely ensemble for an exceptionally reasonable price.

 Before you buy or make costume jewelry, make sure none of your attendants is allergic to low-quality metals. Some people break out in hives or rashes when they wear this type of jewelry — that's definitely *not* a look you want on your wedding day.

Exploring other accessory options for your wedding party

Jewelry isn't the only way to tie your wedding party's look together. You could save some money, for example, by having your bridesmaids carry beaded clutches or evening bags instead of flowers while the groomsmen wear ties in colors that coordinate with the bags. Or you could have the women wear colorful shawls or wraps and, again, coordinate the men's ties with them. You can use inexpensive brooches to pin the bridesmaids' wraps. You also can use affordable costume jewelry pins, which look great without breaking your budget.

The less formal your wedding, the more whimsical you can be with accessories. For a beach wedding, for example, the bridesmaids could carry plastic pails and shovels and the groomsmen could wear beach towels draped over one shoulder — all of which you can buy at a discount retailer for far less than you'd pay for more traditional accessories. Use shell pendants and bracelets (you can buy them or make them yourself) to finish the ensemble.

If you choose accessories that your attendants are likely to use again, they can serve double duty as thank-you gifts — a great way to save money. Plus, you can spend a little more on accessories without feeling guilty; you can get linen wraps, for example, or use better-quality beads for the jewelry. (See the later section "Gifting Your Attendants" for more money-saving ideas.)

Pampering Your Wedding Party

Brides want their attendants to look and feel their best, so bridal spa parties have become popular. But they can be expensive, too. Simple facials and manicures at a salon can cost $100 or more per person; add in professional makeup, hairstyling, pedicures, and massages, and the cost easily reaches into the stratosphere.

The groom and groomsmen usually take care of their own grooming expenses, such as haircuts. However, coed spa parties are becoming more popular, with the men getting manicures and perhaps even facials or massages.

Who pays for these services depends on how adamant you are that your attendants have a specific look on your wedding day. If you insist on every woman having a fancy hairstyle and coordinated makeup, you should pay for those services. If the bridal spa party is just for fun, though, each bridesmaid can pay her own way — or choose not to attend if the cost is beyond her resources. The same rules apply to the male attendants: If you insist they take part, you should build this expense into your budget. If participation is optional, each member can pay his own way.

You can pay for spa and beauty treatments as a thank-you gift for your attendants. Doing so helps you get extra value out of your budget.

Here are some money-saving ideas to help you cut down on the hair and makeup costs:

✔ **If your bridesmaids live near you, have practice parties together to experiment with hairstyles and makeup.** Take pictures of the results you like so you can re-create them on your wedding day. Not only is this fun for the ladies in your wedding party, but it saves lots of money to boot.

✔ **Schedule a makeup party with an independent beauty representative.** For example, you can check with an Avon or Mary Kay salesperson for details. Even if no one purchases the products, you'll pick up useful techniques for your wedding day, and the beauty rep doesn't charge for the party.

✔ **Ask a friend or relative who's a makeup expert to do your bridal party's hair and makeup.** This person doesn't necessarily have to be a professional; an amateur who's great with beauty products also is an option. If a friend or relative is a professional stylist or cosmetologist, she may provide her services for free as a wedding gift.

If you do receive hair and makeup services as a wedding gift, you shouldn't offer a cash tip. However, a personal thank-you gift is appropriate and should be accompanied, of course, by a thank-you note.

If you schedule a spa party, be sure you understand the terms and fees. Many spas and salons include staff gratuities in their pricing, but sales taxes may not be included. Deposits are commonly required, usually 50 percent of the total, and the refund policy may have strict conditions attached. You'll also pay more for a private party outside the facility's normal operating hours or to have the staff come to your home or another location for the party.

Gifting Your Attendants

Your attendants provide support throughout your wedding planning process, so you probably want to show your appreciation for their friendship and commemorate the occasion with a thank-you gift. Gifts are a nice gesture, but don't get wrapped up in the wedding industry hype and go over budget.

Wedding vendors know you want to provide gifts for your attendants, and, not surprisingly, they've turned this tradition into big business. You can find wedding-party gifts that range in price from a few bucks to thousands of dollars — along with the peddling of guilt that so many wedding vendors employ to get you to spend more than you really want to.

You don't have to buy into the thank-you gift hype any more than you have to accept any other overpriced wedding product or service. This gift, like any other that you give, should reflect your knowledge of and affection for the recipient. And, most important, it should fit your budget.

If you decide to give separate thank-you gifts — rather than using accessories or events like a spa day to serve as gifts — try to spend roughly the same amount for each attendant. Here are some ideas for fun, inexpensive gifts:

- **Gift baskets:** You can make these baskets yourself, incorporating any theme you like: bath and beauty, tea time, coffee lover, sports fan, cinema freak, and so on. Get the basket and wrapping paper — and perhaps even some items for the basket — at your local dollar store or discount retailer to keep costs down.

  You can have metal gift baskets engraved for a small cost — usually $10 or less — at places like Things Remembered or even a jewelry store. Or you can get engraved metal key rings to add to the gift basket as a memento of the day.

- **Scrapbooks:** A scrapbook can commemorate your friendship and your wedding if you include favorite photos of yourself and your attendant together, along with a copy of your ceremony program and other mementos from your wedding. Pick up inexpensive scrapbook kits at your local craft store, or look at your local dollar store for photo albums that can accommodate your mementos.

- **A special outing:** If your schedule allows, treat each of your attendants to a few hours of one-on-one time with you — perhaps a lunch, a round of golf, or an afternoon at the mall.

- **Gift cards:** Some people think gift cards are too impersonal, but if you know your best man is never happier than when he's prowling the history section at his favorite bookstore, a gift card may be more appreciated than anything else you could give him.

If you need help thinking of appropriate gifts for your attendants, check out Surprise.com (www.surprise.com). This site scours the Internet for gifts and then categorizes them according to gender, personality traits, interests, and life situations. It also gives you prices and links to the sites that sell the items.

Don't forget your flower girl and ring bearer, if you include these attendants. These little tykes deserve a gift of thanks as well. Some age-appropriate ideas for these special guests include personalized T-shirts, baskets filled with candy or other goodies, and gift cards for things like music downloads or cell phone ringtones.

Chapter 6

Dressing for Your Big Day

. . . .

In This Chapter

▶ Getting a great dress at a great price

▶ Outfitting the groom

▶ Choosing affordable wedding rings

. . . .

The wedding is all about the dress, right? Well, yeah, that stuff about uniting two loving hearts in matrimony, two families becoming one, and building a new life as partners is important, too. But the dress often seems to be the star of the show. Everything else — including the groom's attire — is an accessory.

At least that's the way you may feel when you're trying to decide what you and your betrothed should wear for your wedding and how much you want to spend. The choices — and price ranges — seem infinite and bewildering.

Relax. In this chapter, you can discover the factors that affect wedding dress prices and find out how to avoid common pitfalls at bridal shops. I also help you explore less expensive alternatives to traditional gowns and get ideas for adding your own personal flair to your wedding-day look. You also can check out some options for groom's attire, including traditional and nontraditional tuxedos, suits, and more. Finally, I show you how to find wedding rings that won't strain your wallet.

Looking Like a Princess on a Pauper's Budget

If you flip through any bridal magazine, you may begin to imagine that only the wealthy can afford to get married these days. Featured gowns in these magazines often carry four-figure price tags; when your entire wedding budget amounts to four figures, a $2,000 dress really is the stuff of fantasy.

However, don't despair. Frugal brides-to-be have all kinds of options for realizing their princess-for-a-day dreams on a realistic budget. Thanks to discount bridal stores and the Internet, you can snag your perfect dress at the price you want to pay more easily than ever. I show you how in this section.

Understanding average wedding gown costs

Wedding industry research puts wedding gown costs at anywhere from $800 to $2,500 for the *average* wedding (and the average wedding costs between $20,000 and $25,000).

 These averages are just for the gown. Accessories — including shoes, a veil and headpiece, and underclothing — can add another $200 to $300 to the cost. If you need alterations (most brides do), expect to pay out another hefty sum. And these figures don't include jewelry.

Several factors determine the cost of a wedding gown, including the following:

- ✔ **The designer:** A Vera Wang design costs more than an Alfred Angelo design, which costs more than a little-known designer's gown at a department store.

- ✔ **The fabric:** Both the quality and the amount of fabric play a significant role in determining the cost of a wedding gown. Real silk costs more than silky polyester, for example. And a full, poufy gown that requires yards and yards of fabric often costs more than a simple sheath.

- ✔ **The quality:** Finished seams, linings, and hand-sewn beading and lace accents cost more than ragged seams, no lining, and glued-on accents.

- ✔ **The time of year:** Just like any other fashion, this year's unsold wedding gown models go on sale — usually in November and December — to make room for next year's hot, new styles.

- ✔ **The seller:** You often pay more at bridal shops than at department stores like Macy's or Saks Fifth Avenue. Similarly, you usually pay more at department stores than you do at discount bridal shops, online retailers, or auction sites like eBay.

 Generally, the simpler the gown, the less expensive it is. Lightly adorned tea-length gowns are typically less expensive than elaborately accented, floor-length ones. Those with trains are even more expensive. (See the nearby sidebar for more information on the added expense of going with a train.) Figure 6-1 shows different styles and lengths of weddings gowns.

Figure 6-1: Wedding gown styles.

To train or not to train

Depending on the style of your gown, you may have to decide whether you want a train. Usually, only floor-length gowns require a train, but modern designers have attached tulle or lace trains to street-length dresses as well. Some gowns have detachable trains that fasten to the back (in this case, you may have to pay extra if you order the train). Other trains are sewn into the gown, and you bustle them after the ceremony with buttons or ties. Traditionally, the more formal your wedding, the longer the train. A longer train usually means extra expense, however, because you pay for the additional fabric and detailing.

As with everything else associated with weddings, the very word "wedding" raises the price of a gown. You can pay a premium of 30 percent or more to buy a wedding gown as opposed to an evening gown or dress of comparable quality. Be aware that bridal shops employ a ton of tricks to get as much money as they can out of their customers; they can't rely on repeat business, so they try to make the most of their one-time opportunities. (See the later section "Shopping smarter by avoiding common sales tactics" to find out how to deal with the tactics bridal shops use to raise the price tag on wedding attire.)

Finding a bridal outfit that both you and your budget love

Fortunately, you don't have to deal with traditional bridal shops if you don't want to. You can purchase a formal gown or dress from a department store or clothing chain and still look great. Even if you want a traditional wedding gown, you have lots of options for saving money. For instance, you can make your own headpiece and veil for a fraction of what they cost in bridal shops, and you can avoid the ubiquitous "wedding" markup on shoes by looking for the perfect pair at discount retailers. I discuss these money-saving tips and more in the following sections.

Saving money on the gown or dress

Frugal brides have lots of resources for finding the dress of their dreams at down-to-earth prices. Aside from seeking out discount bridal shops, you can put the Internet, your family and friends, and your creativity to work.

Here are some money-saving avenues to explore as you're searching for the perfect gown or dress:

✔ **Buy a gown online.** The Internet has made finding a deal on a quality wedding gown or formal dress easier than ever. For instance, the Web is home to any number of discount bridal retailers. Check out www.bridalonlinestore.com and www.lilywedding.com, both of which get high marks for quality, value, and service from brides who have purchased from them. Similarly, you can find reasonably priced formal gowns and dresses through department store Web sites like www.macys.com and even Amazon (www.amazon.com).

And, of course, there's always eBay (www.ebay.com), where you can either bid on dresses or, often, use the "Buy It Now" feature for a set price. Many independent and discount bridal shops have stores on eBay, so you aren't limited to second-hand gowns.

Use caution when buying on eBay. Look at pictures carefully, and ask the seller for additional photos if you can't make out details. Always remember to check the seller's ratings and return policies before you place a bid or order.

✔ **Borrow a gown.** Wearing a relative's or friend's gown adds a personal touch to your wedding ensemble. Plus, chances are that your mother, aunt, or best friend will be charmed and honored to loan it to you.

✔ **Rent a gown.** Renting may be a good option if you have your heart set on a designer dress but your budget says "no way." Check in your local phone book for shops that rent wedding gowns or formal dresses. You also can call traditional bridal shops and ask whether they offer rentals. Depending on where you live and what kind of gown you rent, the cost can run anywhere from $100 for dresses that retail in the $300 to $500 range, to $1,000 for dresses with price tags of $3,000 or more. The rental price should include the headpiece and veil, train, crinoline, and other accessories (except shoes and jewelry), and you don't have to worry about cleaning or storing the dress after your wedding.

✔ **Buy a white, ivory, or cream bridesmaid's dress.** Bridesmaids' dresses often cost less than $100, and you can get great styles. Embellish the dress with a colorful sash or wrap, ribbons, or sequins and synthetic gemstones.

Bridal shops have caught on to the money-saving tactic of ordering a white bridesmaid's dress in lieu of a traditional gown. Many of them now either charge an exorbitant fee or require you to purchase at least three (the idea being that you won't order that many unless you really intend to have your bridesmaids wear white). You may have better luck — and better savings — looking online or in mail-order catalogs if you choose this route.

Considering temple-ready gowns

If you're getting married in a church, be aware that some places of worship have strict rules on bare arms, backs, and legs. You may need to take that into account when selecting your dress. Just be sure to avoid putting money down on a gown or dress that you won't be able to wear (at least not without potentially budget-busting additions). You can still have your strapless or halter-type gown; just budget for a bolero jacket, shrug, or wrap to wear during the ceremony. Or look for so-called "temple-ready" gowns that include the wrap or jacket in the price.

✔ **Make your own gown, or have one made.** If you enjoy sewing, or if you have a friend or relative who sews, making your own dress may be an affordable option. Most fabric shops have wedding dress patterns. You also may be able to hire a professional seamstress to make your dress; many talented seamstresses can make designer-looking dresses for far less than you'd pay at a bridal shop.

Cutting costs on the veil and headpiece

You wouldn't think a fabric-covered headband and a wisp of netting could run you hundreds of dollars. But, believe it or not, the average bridal-shop cost for the headpiece and veil is $250.

If you gasped or rolled your eyes at the previous paragraph, take heart: You don't have to shell out that kind of money. In fact, you don't even have to wear a veil if you don't want to. As a reasonable alternative, you can ask your florist to attach fresh flowers to a headband, barrette, or comb. Or consider making your own floral headpiece with silk flowers.

Online retailers like www.veilubridal.com offer steep discounts on all kinds of veils and tiaras; you can purchase plain veils for as little as $30 or $40. You can save money on fancier headpieces and veils online, too — prices can run between $100 and $150, compared with $200 or $250 in a traditional bridal shop.

 Even if you aren't the crafty type, you still can make your own headpiece and veil for around $20 (or less) in materials. You can find do-it-yourself instructions for just about any style of headpiece and veil online. Or follow these instructions:

1. **Cover a plastic headband with fabric (white, cream, or colored to match your color scheme).**

   Secure the fabric with glue, and make sure the fabric seam is on the underside of the headband.

2. **Glue artificial flowers and a few pearl sprays, colored glass beads, or rhinestones onto the headband.**

   Glue guns work well for this step. You can glue each piece individually, or you can run a strip of glue along the headband and attach the embellishments. Either way, be sure to hold the decorations in place for a few seconds to make sure the glue holds.

3. **Glue a length of tulle or other veil fabric to the underside of the headband.**

   The veil can be as short or as long as you like. Most veils fall somewhere between the shoulders and the floor; some even trail on the floor like a train. For a more whimsical look, you can glue ribbons to the back of the headband instead of a traditional veil.

Finding affordable bridal shoes

Even if your gown is floor-length, your shoes will be visible for much of your wedding day — as you walk down the aisle, if you're kneeling at an altar, when you dance, and during the garter toss, for example. So you don't want to wear any old shoes. You want shoes that are attractive, comfortable, and reasonably priced.

You don't have to pay bridal shop prices for your wedding shoes. Instead, after you've decided on your dress, check out discount shoe retailers like the following:

- ✔ Amazon (www.amazon.com)
- ✔ Overstock (www.overstock.com)
- ✔ Payless ShoeSource (www.payless.com)
- ✔ Target (www.target.com)
- ✔ Wal-Mart (www.walmart.com)

You can search these sites by style, size, or color, and they have a variety of wedding-appropriate shoes for less than $30 (compared to an average of $80 for comparable shoes from a bridal shop). Even if you have to pay shipping, you still can save $40 or more. Keep in mind that Wal-Mart has shoes that may suit your bridal outfit, but their site's search function isn't as user-friendly as the ones on the Payless and Target sites. So you may just want to take a trek to your local store instead.

Depending on your style and taste, you can add a splash of color to your bridal ensemble by selecting shoes in a color that matches or complements your wedding colors. Or you can give inexpensive plain white or cream shoes a personal touch by adding colorful bows, sequins, glitter, or ribbons — a cinch with the aid of a local craft store and a glue gun. (Think of Annie Bank's kicked-up sneakers in the movie *Father of the Bride.*)

Cutting back by opting for a nontraditional wedding dress

Only tradition and the wedding industry insist that brides wear an elaborate, expensive, some-shade-of-white gown in the current fashion.

Okay, your family members may raise their eyebrows, or even a ruckus, if you inform them that you intend to wear a nontraditional dress, but it could be fun, right? However, only you can determine whether a potential row with relatives would outweigh the benefits of walking down the aisle less traveled.

You can save a lot of money by ignoring tradition and the wedding industry. Here are some ideas for an elegant, one-of-a-kind bridal outfit:

- ✔ **Go for color.** Choose a cocktail dress, bridesmaid dress, or evening gown in a color that matches your wedding décor. Ruby red, royal purple, and sapphire blue are popular alternatives to white. Opening yourself to a range of colors makes it easier to find a dress that fits your budget and complements your skin tone and body shape.

- ✔ **Shop vintage clothing stores.** Retro is chic, and you can find dresses that impart a unique flair to your wedding. You can stay within your budget by spending just a couple hundred bucks for an evening gown from the 1950s. Other pros: Your dress will be unique, and your guests will have an automatic conversation starter at the reception.

- ✔ **Modify an heirloom dress.** Maybe you have no interest in wearing your mother's wedding gown as is, but what if you added a new skirt to the bodice or a new bodice to the skirt? By doing this, you end up with a unique dress that combines sentimentality with your own taste and style — all at a fraction of the cost of a traditional wedding dress. You can do this with vintage clothing from a secondhand shop, too.

    Unless you're handy with a sewing machine (or have a relative or friend who is), you should hire a seamstress to make the modifications. Just be sure to factor alteration costs into your budget; you may decide another option is better for your wallet.

- ✔ **Have fun with a costume.** Go back to the Renaissance, and walk down the aisle in a richly colored velvet gown (perfect for a winter wedding) or a simple evening gown accented with a velvet cape or cloak. You can find Renaissance gowns at ridiculously low prices. For example, Renaissance Costumes Clothing (www.renaissancecostumesclothing.com) has a burgundy velvet gown, complete with veiled headdress, or a Princess Monaco outfit, also with headdress, each for less than $50. You also can consider renting these types of costumes from a local costume shop.

Some costumes look cheap and cheesy, so be careful if you decide to go this route. Check return policies carefully and order your costume well in advance of your wedding so you have time to look for something else if the costume doesn't live up to your expectations.

Shopping smarter by avoiding common sales tactics

Shopping for a wedding dress is unlike any other clothes shopping you've ever done. For one thing, many bridal shops require you to make an appointment to try on dresses. (However, many accept walk-ins, too, which means, even if you make an appointment, the sales clerks may be busy with walk-ins when you arrive.) When you do walk through the doors, you may be subjected to confusing — and potentially costly — sales tactics.

Here are some common tricks to beware of in the bridal shop along with some solutions so you aren't duped:

- **Charging try-on fees:** Many bridal shops charge fees for trying on their dresses — something no other clothing retailer does.

  Solution: Call ahead and ask whether the shop charges a try-on fee. If it does, move on to the next shop.

- **Bait-and-switch advertising:** Many bridal shops advertise "$99 dresses" or "sample sales" of their merchandise. The problem here is that when you get to the shop, the $99 dresses often are mysteriously gone, and the sample dresses often are stretched, stained, and even torn from having been tried on several times. Naturally, then, the salesperson steers you to the more expensive, good-looking dresses.

  Another dishonest technique is using inflated retail prices before applying a discount. For example, a gown that normally retails for $1,000 may be tagged at $1,100 and then offered at 10 percent off, bringing the price down to $990. So, in the end, you save a whopping $10.

  Solution: Go to the shop when it's convenient for you, not because it's supposedly having a sale. Also, do your research before you shop so you have an idea of what normal prices are.

✔ **Starting with higher-priced gowns:** Think the salesclerks are going to bring out the inexpensive dresses first? No way. They know that many brides buy the first gown they try on. And, because salesclerks work on commission, they have a vigorous incentive to bring out the priciest models first.

Solution: Understate your budget by about 25 percent when you first discuss styles and price with the salesperson. If you've budgeted $500 for your gown, tell her that you want to look at models priced between $300 and $400. And refuse to try on anything priced above your real budget.

✔ **High-pressure sales tactics:** Salesclerks are trained to get you to sign the order form the same day that you try on dresses. They'll tell you your dress will be gone or discontinued if you don't order today, for example. But even if the dress you like is discontinued, chances are you'll be able to find it somewhere — even online — at a lower price.

Solution: Leave your wallet and credit cards at home so you can't give in to the pressure — even if you're tempted.

✔ **Nonrefundable deposits:** Most bridal shops require a 50 percent nonrefundable deposit on any order. So, if you change your mind or the wedding is canceled or postponed, you don't get your deposit back.

Solution: Make your deposit with a credit card. Even though the shop won't refund your money, you may be able to get a refund through the credit card company. Many credit cards won't reverse charges unless they're disputed within 60 days. However, if the shop goes out of business, that 60-day limit may not apply. (And this happens more often than you might think, by the way.)

✔ **Dress substitutions:** Believe it or not, some bridal shops charge brides for the dresses they order and then substitute cheaper dresses when the brides pick up their orders. They can get away with this because of the long gap between ordering and pick-up — often six months. Many brides forget the details of their dress in that time and may never notice that the dress they pick up isn't the one they fell in love with and ordered.

Solution: Take photos of the sample dress you try on and bring them with you when you pick up your dress. This way you can make sure you have the right dress in hand. Keep in mind that most shops won't allow you to take photos until you've placed an order (they don't want you to comparison shop). However, they should let you take pictures after you place an order.

✔ **Hidden fees:** The price on the dress isn't necessarily the price you pay. For example, some bridal shops charge a "rush" fee if your wedding is less than six months away, and many charge extra for plus sizes. Most shops charge a fee to press your gown, and virtually all charge for alterations. For an additional fee, the shop also may deliver your gown to the ceremony site. And the clerk will be happy to complete your bridal outfit, from crinoline to jewelry — at additional cost, of course.

Solution: Before you place an order, ask for an itemized list of any additional charges. Tell the clerk you won't order the dress until you get that information in writing.

✔ **Unauthorized add-ons:** Some shops automatically add the veil and headpiece, shoes, and even slips, crinolines, and other undergarments, to the bill — even when you specifically tell them all you want is the dress.

Solution: Get a receipt for your deposit that clearly spells out what you've ordered — including the dress style number, size, fabric, and delivery or pick-up date. When you go to pick up your dress, refuse to sign anything until you see an itemized list of charges. If you sign before you see the itemized list, you may not be able to dispute any unauthorized charges with your credit card company.

Dapper and Debonair: Dressing the Groom

Grooms traditionally wear tuxedos, but that isn't necessary these days. Even if a bride wears a traditional wedding gown or dress, the groom can wear a suit — as long as the wedding isn't ultra-formal. And, of course, if the bride decides to wear a Renaissance gown (see the earlier section "Cutting back by opting for a non-traditional wedding dress" for more about this option), it makes sense to dress the husband-to-be as a dashing knight or nobleman. In this section, I provide the groom everything he needs to know to decide what to wear on his special day.

Picking out your penguin suit: Wearing a tux

Tuxes come in different styles and degrees of formality, from the super-formal *tailcoat* to the more common *notched lapel coat*.

Morning-coat tuxes usually have waistcoats or vests instead of cummerbunds. Some styles use ascots instead of the more common bow ties. (Figure 6-2 shows different tuxedo styles as well as a business suit.) Unless your wedding is an extremely formal affair, you can choose whichever style you like best.

Most grooms rent their wedding tuxedos, which is much less expensive than purchasing one. Buying a good-quality tux with all the accoutrements — shirt, cummerbund or waistcoat, tie, and cufflinks — costs $500 or more, depending on the designer. Renting a tux of similar quality, with all the accessories, costs about a tenth of the price of buying one.

Figure 6-2: The common tuxedo styles and a typical business suit.

To buy or to rent is your choice. Base your decision both on how much you've budgeted for this wedding item and how much use you expect to get out of a tuxedo. If you're a fixture at charity balls or have season tickets to the ballet, buying a tuxedo may be a better value. However, if the most formal event you expect to attend (other than your wedding) is opening day at the ballpark, renting your tux makes more sense.

Assuming you decide to rent your tux, here are some things to keep in mind:

- ✓ **Rental shop inventory:** Most couples want all the men in the wedding party to wear matching tuxes, with the same shirts, same ties, and so on. So before you commit to renting from a particular shop, make sure it can provide matching items for every man in your wedding party. Otherwise, you may end up having to pay more at another shop to get what you want.

- ✓ **Measurements:** A good rental shop trains its staff on how to take and record measurements to ensure a good fit. Ideally, they even have tailors on staff to make the alterations (instead of shipping the tuxes off-site for the work or ordering from a warehouse). However, if the alterations aren't right, you may have to scramble for alternatives — such as buying a suit at the last minute — that can put a severe strain on your budget.

   Typically, you don't pick up your rental tux until two days before the wedding — Thursday for a Saturday wedding, for example. That leaves little time to find a suitable substitute if your tux doesn't fit.

- ✓ **Package deals:** The tuxedo rental fee will likely include every-thing for the outfit — shirt, tie, cummerbund or vest, suspend-ers, and cufflinks (if needed). Most rental shops also offer shoes, but you may have to pay an extra charge for them.

Many rental shops won't charge for the groom's rental if you reserve a minimum number of tuxedos for the wedding party. I don't recommend expanding your wedding party just to get a free rental (you have to feed those extra ushers, you know), but if you're planning to have five men rent tuxes anyway, ask whether the shop will give you a break on the groom's package.

Considering other clothing options

More and more these days, budget-conscious couples are forgoing traditional wedding attire for more practical garb that they can wear again. If the bride opts for a simple evening gown or brides-maid dress, it's perfectly appropriate for the groom to wear a good suit or even a blazer and dress pants or khakis instead of a tux. In fact, many couples choose to dress the groom and ushers in suits even when the bride wears a traditional gown.

Even if you don't already have a nice suit hanging in your closet, you can take advantage of sales at menswear stores to find one that you can wear for your wedding and then to the office after your honeymoon. You may even find two-for-one deals that offer extra value — two suits you can wear to the office.

You also need comfortable, nice-looking dress shoes to go with your tuxedo or suit. See the earlier section "Finding affordable bridal shoes" for Web sites that offer inexpensive footwear; all the sites listed offer men's shoes as well.

For good-quality men's clothes at really good prices, check out online retailers like Overstock (www.overstock.com) and Amazon (www.amazon.com). These and other sites offer everything from suits, blazers, and dress pants to coordinated shirt-and-tie combos, dress shoes, and even socks. Prices for suits start at less than $100, and you can save anywhere from 10 percent to 35 percent on shoes.

Secondhand clothing stores also can be a good source for low-priced quality men's clothing. Or you can hit the vintage clothing stores and look for a zoot suit to complement the bride's retro gown.

Costumes are options for men, too. You can buy a Renaissance nobleman's costume for less than $100 at www.renaissance costumesclothing.com. Rental fees at your local costume shop may be even lower.

With This Ring: Selecting the Symbols of Your Love

Even though the groom often selects an engagement ring on his own, couples usually consult with each other about their wedding rings. Many couples choose matching rings, but you don't have to. If you want a plain gold band and your betrothed wants something a little fancier, there's no reason you can't both have what you want — as long as you stick to your budget, of course!

Some couples purchase inexpensive rings for their ceremony and then upgrade them later when they have more money to spend. Other couples are appalled at the idea of replacing their wedding bands. Whatever way you decide to go, just be sure that you and your intended talk about your feelings on this topic.

The good news is that it isn't difficult to trim your ring costs. Here are some money-saving options to explore:

✔ **Choose a less expensive metal.** Gold, either yellow or white, is the most common wedding band metal, but you also can get rings in titanium, silver, or platinum. The price curve, from least expensive to most expensive, looks like this: Silver, titanium, gold, and platinum. Keep that curve in mind if you're trying to cut your ring costs. And remember that the material of the ring means nothing; it's the symbolism that's important.

You can get silver wedding bands for as little as $20 a piece. Aircraft-grade titanium is durable, but it isn't as easy to work with for sizing or repair as gold. Prices for gold bands depend on weight: 14 karat gold is less expensive than 18 karat or 24 karat, and 14 karat is harder and more durable, which makes it more suitable for lifetime wear. Platinum runs $300 or more per ring; however, it's very durable and develops a unique patina over years of wear.

White gold is coated with rhodium to make it whiter. With use, the rhodium coating wears away, so most jewelers recommend having white-gold wedding rings recoated every couple of years. This maintenance adds to the long-term cost of a white-gold ring.

✔ **Consider used jewelry.** A good jeweler can adapt heirloom pieces — your grandparents' wedding rings, for example — to suit you and your fiancé(e). If you don't want to use family heirlooms, look in pawn shops and at estate auctions; you may find something you love for a fraction of its retail value. Dusty or dull rings can be cleaned, but make sure you inspect pieces carefully for scratches or other damage.

If you have old, broken jewelry, you may be able to get a jeweler to melt it down and create your wedding bands from it. You'll pay for the jeweler's time and expertise, but you'll save money on the materials. Plus, you'll have rings that are unique to you as a couple.

✔ **Search online.** In the past few years, online jewelry stores have captured more than $2 billion of the retail jewelry market, accounting for 1 in every 20 purchases — a good indication that consumers are happy with the goods and services these retailers provide. Prices at online jewelry stores often are significantly lower than those in their bricks-and-mortar counterparts, too.

As with any online retailer, be sure to check return policies and any guarantees before you buy from an online jewelry store. According to Top Consumer Reviews (www.top consumerreviews.com), Blue Nile (www.bluenile.com), Diamond.com (www.diamond.com), and Mondera (www.mondera.com) rank highest in terms of selection, pricing, and customer service.

You may think that locally owned jewelry shops can't compete on price with the large chains. However, depending on the local store's target clientele, some may be able to. Certainly, some small shops cater to wealthier shoppers, but many are in direct competition for the same people who shop the large chains. Because of this competition, many of these shops may be more affordable with their pricing, and they usually offer superior service, including on-site jewelry designers.

Chapter 7

Hammering Out the Ceremony Details

In This Chapter
▶ Choosing the person to officiate your wedding
▶ Striking the right note with music
▶ Making your ceremony venue festive

Conventional wisdom says that couples have to attend to 1,001 details in any wedding. Your final "detail tally" may not be that high, but you can't afford to overlook certain details if you're on a budget. You'd be surprised at how many engaged couples forget to plan for expenses for the officiant, the music for the ceremony, and decorations for the ceremony site. As a result, many of these couples exceed their budgets before they even put down their first deposits on their weddings.

In this chapter, I give you tips on keeping your ceremony costs in line with your budget, while still having the kind of ceremony you want. The form in Appendix D includes lines for these budget items so you won't forget to plan for them.

Selecting an Officiant on a Budget

If you and your spouse-to-be are members of the same church, temple, mosque, or other place of worship, you may have already decided you want your wedding performed by one of the clergy there. In that case, all you have to do is find out the policies on paying the officiant — and, of course, whether he's willing and available to perform your ceremony.

But if neither of you belongs to a religious group, you're of different faiths, or you think you'd prefer a civil ceremony, you have more legwork to do. The most important thing you need to know is who's authorized to perform weddings in your state. Every state allows clergy members and judges, as well as justices of the peace (in the areas that have this office), to perform weddings. Some states allow other officiants, too, and these others may charge quite a bit less than a minister or judge. (See the later sidebar "Who can perform wedding ceremonies?" for more details.)

However, keep in mind that the definition of "clergy member" can vary from one state to the next. For example, many states allow people who have been ordained online to perform marriage ceremonies, but Arizona doesn't permit marriages officiated by "e-ministers." Other states require officiants who have been ordained online to register before they can legally perform weddings.

 To be absolutely sure your officiant — and therefore your marriage — is legal, call your county clerk's office or marriage license bureau and ask. Make this contact well in advance of your wedding so you have time to make other arrangements if necessary.

Here are some places to start your search:

- ✔ **Your local newspaper:** Check out the wedding announcements section; officiants sometimes advertise their services there.

- ✔ **Your county clerk's office or marriage license bureau:** In addition to knowing who's authorized to officiate weddings, these offices often know who actually offers these services in your area and may provide referrals.

- ✔ **Online:** Organizations like the National Association of Wedding Officiants (www.nawoonline.com) and the National Association of Wedding Ministers (www.aministry.net) offer searchable databases of nondenominational officiants in your area.

 Start your search for an officiant at least six months in advance, especially if you're planning a religious ceremony or have a high-demand date like a Saturday in June. Religious officiants often require premarital counseling sessions or other preparation work (which may or may not be included in their fees) with the couples they marry. And many officiants, civil or religious, are booked several months ahead for popular wedding dates.

Getting the skinny on general costs

After you've determined who you want to officiate your wedding ceremony, you can explore the costs associated with your preference. I help you do just that with the information in this section.

Officiant fees typically range from about $50 to $400 or more, depending on the type of officiant you use and the services he or she provides. Justices of the peace (and, where allowed, county clerks and notaries public) usually have the lowest fees, in the $50 to $100 range. Sitting and retired judges may charge $100 to $200. Clergy fees run the gamut, and are often based on experience. A newly ordained or intern minister may charge only $100, but a more experienced minister may charge $300 or more.

Clergypersons often leave their "fee" up to the couple. If you aren't sure how much of a fee is appropriate, contact the church secretary or administrative office and ask how much couples usually give the officiant.

Some clergy members perform weddings at no charge. Similarly, friends or relatives who get ordained online often officiate for free as well. However, in both cases, etiquette dictates that you offer an honorarium to the officiant. The minimum appropriate honorarium is $100. If the officiant is from out of town, you should consider paying for her hotel room, too. If your funds allow, you may also consider helping to cover some of her other travel expenses.

You can hire a professional celebrant, too. But consider yourself warned: These professionals are usually much more expensive than more traditional officiants, often charging $500 or more. And they may provide services you don't want or need, which doesn't give you a lot of value for your money.

If you get married in Colorado, Pennsylvania, or Wisconsin, you and your betrothed can officiate your own wedding — which is the least expensive option of all. You may have to get a special type of marriage license, so contact your county clerk or marriage license bureau to find out what you have to do if you choose this route.

Breaking down the fees

Officiant fees include different services depending on the type of professional you choose. Those officiants who perform civil ceremonies — judges, justices of the peace, and other public officials — typically charge less because they don't do much more than actually perform the wedding. Clergy fees, on the other hand, may include premarital counseling or planning sessions, the rehearsal, and even travel to and from the ceremony site. These services may cost extra, so you need to understand exactly what your officiant's fees include.

The following questions can help you bring to light extra fees that often aren't included in an officiant's set rate:

✔ **If this is a package fee, what exactly does the package cover?** Write down everything that's included, such as the number and length of planning meetings, maximum mileage, any time limits for the rehearsal or ceremony, and any other services, such as supplying an organist or singers for the ceremony.

If the officiant is responsible for lining up singers or musicians, be sure to note whether the fees for their services are included in your package. Sometimes the package only covers the administrative costs of reserving the organist or soloist, not the performance fees.

✔ **What if I don't want some of the services in your package?** You may not get a discount if you elect not to use some of the officiant's services; in fact, you may be charged extra. For example, some churches charge an extra fee if you choose to use outside musicians, especially if they aren't pros.

✔ **What happens if you can't make the ceremony?** Officiants can get sick or injured or face unexpected family emergencies just like anyone else. Ask about the officiant's backup plan, and, if possible, meet the person who will fill in if the officiant is unable to perform his duties.

✔ **Do you charge extra for additional planning meetings, counseling sessions, or overtime at the rehearsal or ceremony?** You don't want the unpleasant surprise of an extra expense if the rehearsal runs late or you and your spouse-to-be want to meet with the officiant one last time to go over final details.

✔ **Do you charge extra for customizing our ceremony?** Many officiants allow you to choose from a selection of ceremony structures, readings, and so on. Others offer a standard ceremony and charge extra if you want to make changes.

✔ **Do you charge for things like phone calls or e-mail responses?** Some officiants charge on an hourly basis, so the more time they spend with you before and during your wedding, the higher the bill will be.

✔ **Do you require a deposit, and, if so, how much?** Some officiants require a 50 percent deposit, with the balance due the day of the wedding. Others require full payment up front. Make sure you have the terms in writing, and ask for a receipt for any payments you make.

✔ **What is your refund policy?** As with all your wedding vendors, you want to know whether you can get your deposit back if you change your mind about this officiant before the wedding — or if the wedding is postponed or canceled.

Who can perform wedding ceremonies?

Every state allows clergy and judges (and justices of the peace, in states that have them) to perform weddings. Some states allow other officiants, too, and these others may charge quite a bit less than a minister or judge. Here's a list of states that, as of this writing, have other authorized officiants.

Alaska: Salvation Army commissioned officers; marriage commissioners; "deputy marriage commissioner for a day" (if you want a friend or relative to officiate).

California: Marriage commissioners; "deputy marriage commissioner for a day" (if you want a friend or relative to officiate).

Colorado: Couples themselves (check with your county clerk for requirements).

Florida: Notaries public.

Idaho: Designated public officials such as mayors.

Illinois: Certain public officials.

Indiana: Circuit Court clerks; city or town clerks or clerk-treasurers.

Massachusetts: Out-of-state clergy who received a Certificate of Authorization from the Secretary of the Commonwealth; anyone with special one-time authorization from the governor (if you want a friend or relative to officiate).

Michigan: Nonresident clergy; mayors (in their own cities); county clerks.

Minnesota: Clerks of court; court commissioners.

Mississippi: Mayors; local Board of Supervisors members.

New Hampshire: Out-of-state clergy who receive a special license from the secretary of state.

New York: Mayors; city clerks; deputy city clerks; appointed marriage officers.

Oregon: County clerks; deputy county clerks.

Pennsylvania: Couples who obtain a "self-uniting" license; county clerks and their appointed deputies; mayors.

Rhode Island: Court clerks; certain former court clerks; Police Court in the town of Johnston; wardens in the town of New Shoreham.

Vermont: Nonresident clergy who get a permit from the appropriate county probate court.

Virginia: Marriage commissioners.

West Virginia: Court-appointed authorized officiants.

Wisconsin: Couples may officiate themselves if this is part of their religion's "established customs or rules."

Most professional officiants offer contracts that spell out their responsibilities and fees. Make sure the contract also includes details such as the dates and times of your ceremony and rehearsal as well as deposit and refund policies.

The officiant's fee doesn't include the following costs:

✔ **The fee for the marriage license:** You have to pay this fee (which can be anywhere from $10 to $100, depending on where you live) to your local government clerk or marriage license bureau.

✔ **The officiant's tip:** The customary officiant gratuity is $75 to $150, depending on where you live and the breadth of the services the officiant provides for you. (If the officiant performs the ceremony for free, the honorarium counts as the gratuity.)

✔ **The officiant's meal:** If your officiant will attend your reception, you need to budget for the cost of feeding him (and perhaps his spouse).

Remember to include these costs in your budget. You don't want to have to scramble for money to cover them at the last minute.

Hearing the Music of Your Dreams — for Less

Ceremony music is a great way for you to express your personality, tastes, and feelings about the person you're marrying. Unfortunately, it also can cost much more than you'd expect — especially if, like many couples, you focus heavily on the reception music and then add the ceremony music to your budget as an afterthought.

You can have live or recorded music — or a combination of both — for your ceremony. For example, you could play recorded music for 30 minutes before the ceremony, as your guests arrive and are being seated, and then have live music for the ceremony itself.

Some places of worship don't allow recorded music, and others don't allow secular music. Be sure to ask about the venue's music policies and restrictions before you make a deposit.

Generally, recorded music is less expensive than hiring live musicians and singers, and it has the added advantage of predictability; assuming the equipment works as it's supposed to, you'll get the same rendition of, say, "At Last" every time it plays. But live musicians and singers add a certain panache to a wedding ceremony.

Luckily, you can have that extra fillip without breaking your piggy bank. For money-saving tips for both recorded and live ceremony music, read on.

Opting for recorded music

Unless you have a close friend or relative who's an outstanding singer or instrumentalist — and who's willing to share her musical gift for free (or at least in exchange for a free meal at the reception) — pre-recorded music is the least expensive way to have the melodies you want for your ceremony.

Recorded music also may be the easiest way to mix and match music — for example, if you want to walk down the aisle to Pachelbel's Canon in D, have The Beatles' "In My Life" for the solo, and walk back up the aisle to the theme from "Star Wars." If you're asking yourself, "Can I do that?" the answer is of course you can. But you may have to select a nonreligious venue for your ceremony, because some churches, temples, and mosques have fairly strict rules about music. At other venues, though, there are no wedding music rules, so you can choose whatever songs you like.

If your ceremony site is cramped — a gazebo, a boat, or some other small area — recorded music is definitely the way to go. Not only is it cheaper, but it also saves a *lot* of space.

In the following sections, I explain your options for broadcasting recorded music to your audience and tell you how to compile a playlist that your budget will love.

Broadcasting your tunes

Whether you're using a portable stereo or your ceremony site's sound system, be sure to check the sound quality before your big day. You want the music to be plainly audible without sounding tinny or distorted, and you want to make sure the playback system you use is powerful enough to fill the space. A tiny portable stereo probably won't be able to project the music throughout a large chapel, for example, and you'll likely be disappointed — even if you do save money.

If you don't have access to a good-quality portable stereo or a sound system at the ceremony site, consider renting a sound system for the day. This route is especially cost-effective if you decide to have a friend act as the DJ during your reception. In most areas of the country, you can rent the equipment for the entire day for about half (or less) of what a professional DJ costs just for the hours of the reception.

If you decide to hire a DJ for your reception (see Chapter 13), ask how much she'd charge to play the music at your ceremony, too. If she can use the site's sound system and doesn't have to spend time setting up and breaking down her own equipment, she may be willing to do it for a small fee.

Another option: Ask a friend or relative to run the sound system for your ceremony. You won't have to pay him, though you should plan to give him a thank-you gift.

Deciding on a playlist

If you decide to be your own DJ for the ceremony (or you have a friend do the honors), you have to collect the tunes that you want to play. You can shop for wedding music CDs, which usually contain several selections you can use as processional and recessional music as well as a variety of love songs for use during the ceremony. If you're a music buff or have eclectic taste, you also can create your own wedding mix CD, which allows you to include the music you and your affianced really want.

To create your own wedding mix, you can download music from the iTunes store (`www.apple.com/itunes`) to your iPod or MP3 player; costs range from less than $1 for a single song to about $10 for an album. Wedding Music Central (`www.weddingmusic central.com`) has entire ceremony packages starting at less than $20.

Hiring musicians and singers

It would be great fun to walk down the aisle as Yo-Yo Ma renders sweet cello music at the foot of the altar and to look into your betrothed's eyes as Celine Dion sings "My Heart Will Go On." But, even if Mr. Ma and Ms. Dion performed at weddings, I'm pretty sure their fees could in no way be considered budget options.

On the other hand, a gifted cellist and a talented singer from your local high school or college can provide lovely music for very little cost. Some high school and college music programs even have small instrumental and vocal groups you can hire to perform for your wedding; contact the music director and ask if he can recommend any students. Or ask to post a notice on the department's bulletin board, asking interested students to call you to arrange an audition.

The following are some other places to look for ceremony musicians and singers. You can check all these sources and compare the costs and quality of the candidates you find, or you can set a range you're willing to pay and then go down the list until you find someone whose prices match your budget:

- ✔ **At your church or place of worship:** The church organist or pianist may be available to play at your wedding. In fact, he may already have a batch of standard wedding pieces that you can select from for your wedding. Other members of your congregation may have musical talents, too — perhaps a guitarist or clarinetist who could work alone or with the organist or pianist. Don't forget that outstanding singer from the church choir.

- ✔ **Among music teachers and tutors:** Folks who teach piano, guitar, and singing also play piano and guitar and sing. They may be the perfect fit for your ceremony, so don't overlook these musicians.

- ✔ **In your local newspaper:** Musicians often run newspaper ads announcing their services. You also can place your own ad seeking services and setting up auditions.

- ✔ **Online:** Several Web sites offer localized searches for musicians. Start with Wedding Music USA (www.weddingmusic usa.com), which allows you to search for local musicians, bands, DJs, and singers. You also can search craigslist (www.craigslist.org) for the city nearest you; look under Community/Musicians, or post an ad stating what you're looking for (an acoustic guitarist, pianist, and so on).

Whether you choose students, amateurs, or pros to perform at your wedding, always audition the musicians before you hire them. Ask for either a live audition or a recording. If the music you want isn't already in their repertoire, provide sheet music and ask them to play or sing a portion of it; doing so gives you an idea of whether they'll be able to learn the piece(s) in time for your wedding. Auditioning also gives you a chance to assess whether the musicians' skills match the prices they charge you.

You may be able to save money by having the same musicians perform for both your ceremony and your reception, especially if you don't have a long wait between the two events. Alternatively, you could hire one or two band members to handle the ceremony music, and then pay the entire band for the reception only.

Like all other wedding services, prices for musicians and DJs are usually higher in the summer. However, you often can get a price break — perhaps a substantial one — for a weekday or Sunday ceremony, or for a wedding date in January, March, or November. February can be expensive because of Valentine's Day, but you may get a break if you avoid setting your date close to the 14th.

December is a terrible time both to book musicians and to get a price break; private and corporate holiday parties place them in high demand, so the musicians can charge peak rates.

When you're ready to sign up your ceremony musicians, keep the following things in mind. And note that even though I use the term "musician" throughout this list, all these points apply to any singers you hire, too.

✔ **Familiarity with the music:** If the church organist will play at your wedding, you'll only have to provide sheet music if you want her to play a piece outside her repertoire. Give her as much time as possible to learn and practice new pieces (and remember that she may have to transpose sheet music that's written for other instruments). For other musicians, make sure they either know or have plenty of time to learn the music you want them to play.

✔ **Familiarity with the ceremony site:** If you're bringing in outside musicians to play at your church ceremony, or if your ceremony site is something other than a church, make sure the musicians are familiar with the setup. If they haven't performed at your site before, arrange a walk-through to check for things like outlets for electrical equipment.

✔ **The number of hours they'll play:** You need between 30 and 45 minutes of pre-ceremony music, plus the time for the ceremony. Most ceremony musicians charge by the hour, and hourly rates average between $80 and $200. Keep in mind that students' rates usually are about 30 percent lower than the rates for professional musicians. Some musicians charge for a minimum number of hours; a two- or three-hour minimum is typical.

Find out whether the musicians will attend your ceremony rehearsal and whether they charge extra for that. Also, if you're combining, say, the church organist and outside musicians, ask about how they'll rehearse together. And find out whether you'll be charged any fees associated with music rehearsals.

✔ **The musician's attire:** You don't want your musician dressed in a T-shirt and torn jeans at your ceremony. So be sure to talk about what she'll wear, and include this agreement in the contract.

As with all your wedding vendors, make sure you get all the details you work out with your ceremony musicians in writing. The church organist or student musician may not require a formal contract, but you still should have a written agreement noting dates and times for rehearsals and your ceremony, the music you want performed and when each piece should be played (pre-ceremony, processional, and so on), payment arrangements (total charges, deposits, and when the balance is due), and any other special instructions.

Decorating on a Dime

The site you choose for your ceremony (see Chapter 4) affects the kinds of decorations you need. At some venues, you may not need to supply ceremony decorations at all. For instance, you may choose to have your ceremony in the atrium of a hotel that already has trees and shrubs decked out with clear miniature lights — perfect for an evening wedding.

When you're looking at ceremony sites, ask whether the venue provides decorations. Some churches and other locations offer packages that include the rental fee and decorations. Choosing such a package may be less expensive than providing your own decorations. And if you get married near a holiday like Christmas or Easter, the church may already be decorated, so you don't have to provide anything.

You and your spouse-to-be should be the focal point of the ceremony; you don't want to be upstaged by decorations. You also don't want elaborate decorations blocking your guests' view of the ceremony.

If you do want to decorate your venue, you don't have to spend a lot to get a festive, celebratory look. Consider the following low-cost ideas and see whether they spark any of your own:

- ✔ Balloons are an inexpensive way to decorate the entrance of a church or other building; for an outdoor wedding, use balloons to cover a garden arch at the entrance to the ceremony site. Check your local party goods or dollar store for balloons and blow them up yourself; helium is expensive and helium-filled balloons present an environmental hazard when they float away.

- ✔ Simple bows, which you can purchase ready-made or make yourself with materials from your local craft store, serve as lovely pew markers or seat decorations. If your ceremony site allows it, you also can line the aisle with fresh or silk flower petals or wedding confetti.

- ✔ For an evening wedding, place luminarias next to the seats on each side of the aisle. Just be sure to secure them so guests don't knock them over. (See the nearby sidebar "Making luminarias" for more on this do-it-yourself project.)

✔ Wrap pillars in garland (matching one or more of your wedding colors) and clear miniature lights. Or use the garland and lights to decorate the rafters of a gazebo, park pavilion, or garden bower.

✔ For the altar, check into renting potted plants or trees and decorating them with lights and ribbon. Or, if you have a green thumb, save some money and plant some pots yourself. Just be sure to plant them early enough that they have time to grow before the wedding.

Making luminarias

Luminarias are tealight or votive candles placed in paper bags weighted with sand. They're popular Christmas decorations in the Southwest, but they can make a lovely addition to your wedding ceremony, too — and they're inexpensive. You can find all the materials you need at your local craft or dollar store. Depending on your tastes, you can cut designs into the bags or decorate them, or you can simply choose white bags or ones that match your wedding colors.

Chapter 8

Picking Flowers (Or Fun Alternatives)

· ·

· ·

*F*lowers have been an integral element of wedding celebrations at least since the ancient Greek and Roman civilizations thrived, and probably since long before that. In old Athens and Rome, brides wore garlands of fresh herbs or ivy in their hair; it was believed that the fragrant greens kept evil spirits from getting too close to the maiden. The garlands also symbolized fertility, unity, and good fortune for the marrying couple.

Over time, the garland of herbs evolved into a bouquet of flowers. In the 1300s, brides began tossing their bouquets just before leaving on their wedding trips as a way to avoid having their gowns ripped apart by guests who were anxious to grab a souvenir — and, presumably, a bit of the newlyweds' good fortune. (This also is believed to be part of the reason behind the tradition of the groom tossing his bride's garter.)

Like nearly everything else wedding-related, the specific flowers, bouquets, and centerpieces that are favored change with the times. In Victorian times, for example, orange blossoms — either in a headdress or a bouquet — were more or less a required accessory for brides around the world. Today, however, red or white roses are a wedding staple, as are lilies and baby's breath.

 You don't have to limit yourself to these standbys for your wedding. Nor do you have to follow the latest (often most expensive) trends. In this chapter, I show you how to get stunning flowers or other accents to match both your taste and your bank balance.

I also tell you what you need to know to research and hire a florist and help you explore ways to keep your costs down without sacrificing style, elegance, or your credit rating. And if you'd prefer not to have fresh flowers, I give you some information on artificial flowers and other fun alternatives.

Thinking About Your Floral Budget

Fresh flowers are everywhere at most weddings. The bride and bridesmaids typically carry bouquets; sometimes they wear flowers in their hair, too. The men in the wedding party all wear boutonnieres. The mothers and sometimes grandmothers of the happy couple wear corsages. The flower girl's very job may be to carry a bouquet or flower basket, and she may scatter fresh flower petals along the aisle. Flowers also are used as decorations at both the ceremony and reception.

The bill for all these fresh flowers can add up quickly. According to The Wedding Report, an industry research group, the average amount spent on wedding flowers is just under $1,300. Other research indicates that the average price tag for reception centerpieces *alone* is $1,300. Whether you spend this much (or more, or less) depends on where flowers fall on your list of priorities and what kinds of flowers and arrangements you want. (Chapter 1 can help you rank your priorities. Flip there for more information.)

Envisioning the flowers you'll select

Calla lilies, orchids, irises, and gardenias are all popular — and expensive — choices for weddings. But you can get spectacular effects from virtually any kind of flower. So, unless you have your heart set on a certain type, it's smart to look at all your options. As you're reviewing your choices, keep the following elements in mind:

- ✔ **Color:** If you have a traditional white or ivory gown or dress, you can use your bouquet to provide color and dimension to your overall look. Flowers also complement and accentuate your overall color scheme.

You can get carnations, a popular inexpensive flower, in nearly any color you want. Carnations also provide lots of texture, making them a perfect complement to a less ornate wedding gown or dress.

- ✔ **Fragrance:** Some flowers have bold fragrances, and these heady scents could cause problems if you, your wedding party, or even your guests suffer from allergies. Lilacs are beautiful, but they'll detract from your ceremony if they set everyone along the aisle sneezing as you make your way to the altar. Gardenias, some varieties of lilies, and freesia also are, shall we say, exceptionally aromatic. If you like the looks of these flowers but not the scent, consider using artificial versions (which probably will be cheaper than the real thing). Or ask your florist about inexpensive, lightly scented options.

✔ **Maintenance:** Be sure to choose flowers that will hold up well in the environment of your ceremony and reception sites. Some flowers tolerate heat and humidity well and will look lovely at your outdoor ceremony, for example. Others will shrivel up like salted snails if the conditions aren't perfect — which means you'll be paying money for a look you definitely don't want.

✔ **Meaning:** So much of your wedding ceremony is symbolic, and the selection of flowers can be, too, if you want. In Victorian times, the language of flowers was well known: Yellow roses signified jealousy, for example, and lily of the valley suggested happiness. (See the nearby sidebar "Flowery language" for more on the meanings of different blooms — and how to say what you want with an inexpensive flower.) These days, few guests will know what the tulips in your bouquet stand for (love and passion), but you and your spouse-to-be can make this a romantic secret between the two of you. Besides, when they're in season, tulips are much less expensive than, say, calla lilies.

Selecting a style for the bridal bouquet

The true cost of any flower arrangement lies in the labor to create it. However, the types of flowers you choose and the size and style of your bouquet influence its price, too.

If you want to carry a bouquet, you have several styles to choose from. Here's a quick primer on the most popular styles (see Figure 8-1 for examples):

✔ **Biedermeier:** A type of nosegay (see the later entry) consisting of concentric circles of different kinds of flowers (for example, white roses alternating with red carnations). The circles give the bouquet a striped or bull's-eye look. Because of the number of flowers used, Biedermeiers tend to be more expensive than some other bouquet styles.

Flowery language

In the mid to late 1800s, flowers held messages for those who knew the code. Men and women who would never dare say such things aloud could tell each other how they felt by giving a gift of flowers. Here are the meanings of some popular wedding flowers and greens, along with where they fall in the pricing scale:

Baby's breath: Innocence; purity (inexpensive)

Calla lily: Magnificent beauty (expensive)

Carnation: Devotion (general); woman's love (pink); pure love (white) (inexpensive)

Chrysanthemum: Love (red); truth (white) (inexpensive)

Daffodil: Regard; respect (inexpensive)

Daisy: Loyal love (inexpensive)

Fern: Magic; fascination (inexpensive)

Forget-me-not: True love (inexpensive)

Freesia: Innocence; trust (inexpensive)

Gardenia: Secret love; refinement (expensive)

Iris: Passion (yellow) (expensive)

Ivy: Wedded love; fidelity (inexpensive)

Lily of the valley: Happiness (expensive)

Orange blossom: Eternal love; fruitfulness (inexpensive)

Orchid: Love; beauty (expensive)

Peony: Happy marriage (expensive)

Phlox: Our souls are united (inexpensive)

Rose: Love; beauty; joy; passion (price depends on type and time of year)

Color changes the meaning of certain flowers. For a comprehensive list of what flowers of different colors mean, check out `victorianbazaar.com/meanings.html`.

✔ **Cascade:** A waterfall of flowers and greenery. The flowers can be all one kind or varied. A cascade-style bouquet offers an elegant look that works best with more formal gowns and tall or medium-tall brides; cascades can emphasize smaller brides' lack of height. Labor costs make prices on cascades generally higher than some other, simpler bouquet styles.

✔ **Composite:** A technique in which flowers or petals are wired together on a single stem to create the illusion of one large blossom. You can opt for one or more kinds of flowers for this style bouquet. Price depends on the number of flowers you use (which also affects the labor cost).

✔ **Hand-tied:** A dense bunch of flowers wired or tied together or anchored in a holder. This is usually the least expensive bouquet option.

✔ **Nosegay:** A cluster of blooms, all the same length, gathered to form a round bouquet and often bound with ribbon or lace. Nosegays usually have one dominant flower or color. Like hand-tied bouquets, nosegays tend to be less expensive than other styles.

✔ **Pomander:** A ball covered with blossoms and carried by a ribbon. This style of bouquet is commonly used for child attendants, but brides have been known to carry them as well. Depending on the size and the kind of flowers you choose, pomanders can cost anywhere from around $25 to $75 or more.

✔ **Posy:** A small nosegay. Posies are usually quite inexpensive because they don't require as many flowers.

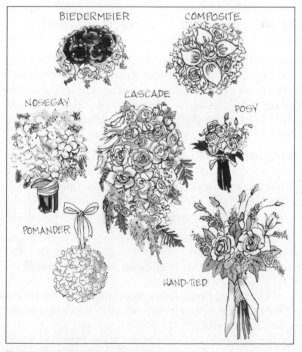

Figure 8-1: Bridal bouquet styles.

Check out bridal magazines and Web sites for photos of various bouquets to see which styles you like. The Knot (www.theknot.com) and OneWed (www.onewed.com) have good representative photos. Also look at nonbridal bouquets for less traditional (and often less expensive) inspiration.

Of course, you don't have to carry a bouquet if you don't want to. See "Considering alternatives to fresh flowers," later in this chapter, for more ideas.

Choosing flowers for the wedding party

Like the bride, the wedding party traditionally carries or wears some type of fresh flowers for the ceremony. The following list shows the most common and traditional options:

- ✔ **Bridesmaids:** Like the bride, the bridesmaids usually carry bouquets; the maid or matron of honor's bouquet is usually a bit larger than the others (but not as big as the bride's).

- ✔ **Male wedding party members:** The groom, his best man and other attendants, the ushers, and the fathers of the bride and groom traditionally wear boutonnieres. This custom dates to the days when a knight wore his lady's colors — in the form of a small scarf or handkerchief — at jousting tournaments.

   The groom's boutonniere usually is one of the colors of the wedding color scheme, and the ushers' or groomsmen's boutonnieres are a complementary color. Boutonnieres for the father of the bride and father of the groom typically are a third color, which distinguishes them from the ushers and denotes their special place of honor.

- ✔ **The flower girl:** The flower girl usually carries a basket of flowers or a basket of petals that she tosses along the aisle. The latter custom comes from old England, when the entire bridal party would make its way to the church behind the flower girl, who strewed petals from a basket along the route.

- ✔ **Mothers and grandmothers:** The mothers of the bride and groom usually wear corsages of different styles. Couples often provide corsages for their grandmothers as well.

The price tag for all these flowers averages about $360 — and that doesn't include the bridal bouquet, altar flowers, or other ceremony decorations.

Boutonnieres from a florist average around $10 a piece, and corsages can run anywhere from $10 to $20 each. But you can get them much cheaper online. Costco (www.costco.com), for example, has a package of 15 boutonnieres and 15 corsages for about $160, which comes to $5.33 a piece. If you don't need that many, you can always use the materials from the extras to make your own bouquets or other decorations. (Remember that places like Costco and Sam's Club charge either a membership fee or a premium of between 15 percent and 20 percent if you're not a member, so these options are most cost-effective if you're already a member.)

Start your search for the perfect wedding-party flowers by looking at what everybody's wearing. Unless you're getting white roses for everyone (white roses go with just about anything), it's nearly impossible to pick out flowers that will work no matter what clothes a person is wearing. After you have the wardrobe nailed down, you can select in-season, locally grown flowers in colors that will look good on each person. And be sure to choose arrangements that are appropriate to your venue and that don't require a lot of labor.

Bridesmaids don't have to carry flowers; like the bride, they can carry pretty much anything. Some brides have their attendants carry small purses, bouquets of antique buttons, or, for a winter wedding, faux fur muffs.

Arranging flowers for the ceremony venue

Ceremony flowers — including altar flowers and floral pew decorations — average $286. But you can trim that cost by doing the following:

✔ **Use inexpensive flowers and greens to fill out larger decorations.** If you're getting married in a church or other large ceremony site, you may want to opt for large floral arrangements for the altar; small arrangements will be lost in all the space. However, because no one but the wedding party will see your altar arrangements up close, you can fill them with inexpensive flowers and greens, such as carnations, ferns, and phlox.

✔ **Share the decorations expense with another couple.** If another couple (or two) is getting married at the same venue on the same day as you and your betrothed, you may be able to share ceremony decorations and split the cost, which could be a huge money-saver. Ask at the church's administrative office or ask the venue's on-site coordinator how to get in contact with the other couple(s); some will make the initial contact, and others will give you contact information. You may have to use mostly white flowers and decorations to avoid clashing with different color schemes, but if you're flexible on this point, you can save quite a bit of money.

✔ **Skip pew or chair decorations.** Guests won't miss them, and you'll save money.

✔ **Grow your own potted flowers or plants for decorations.** Of course, doing so takes some time (and a bit of a green thumb), but it's less expensive than having a florist create displays, and you can enjoy the flowers or plants at home long after your wedding.

✔ **Rely on existing decorations, especially around the holidays.** If your wedding falls around a holiday — Christmas, Easter, or even Thanksgiving — the venue may already be decorated, so you won't have to provide flowers or other decorations. Also, if your ceremony venue is ornate, you can cut back dramatically on decorations and let the existing architecture and artwork shine.

Some brides keep a lid on their floral budgets by moving their ceremony flowers to the reception site. This flower swap is an option, but be aware of the downsides: Some flower arrangements don't travel well, so you may end up with wilted or bruised blooms at your reception. Consider any delays for your guests, too; you don't want them milling around outside the reception hall, griping about the delay while they wait for the flowers to be set up.

Deciding on reception flowers

Traditionally, couples purchase flower arrangements for the head table, the cake table, and each guest table. As you can imagine, this number of arrangements can increase your floral budget considerably. In fact, the Wedding Report indicates that reception flower arrangements average $385; the Bridal Association of America reports that some floral centerpieces alone average $1,272. Of course, the more elaborate your arrangements and the more of them you have, the higher your bill.

The following sections outline some of the most common areas for flowers at the reception.

Centerpieces

The good news is that you don't have to spend a lot of money on floral centerpieces to give your party a chic, elegant feel. Designers today are trending toward streamlined, simple-elegance arrangements. For example, here are some less expensive options you can try:

- ✔ A clear vase with a few blooms, perhaps surrounded by tealights or votive candles

- ✔ A bowl of floating blossoms, petals, or candles, or a combination of the three

- ✔ A pillar candle placed in the middle of the table with flower petals scattered over the tabletop. Just keep in mind that many venues don't allow real flower petals to be placed on their tablecloths because they can stain the fabric; however, you can use artificial flowers or petals.

Many reception venues provide centerpieces, so if your venue offers something you like, don't feel like you have to spend extra money to buy or make your own. By saving money on the centerpieces, you can concentrate your floral/decoration budget on the cake table and head table.

For more alternatives to floral centerpieces, see Chapter 13.

Floral sprays for the head table

Floral sprays are commonly used to dress up the front of the head table; these wide, usually large, arrangements often have a holder in the center for the bride's bouquet. Like bouquets, you can make sprays as simple or elaborate as you care to, but simpler is usually cheaper. To save some money on your spray, choose one that's made of greenery accented with the occasional blossom. You also can use local and in-season flowers, which are less expensive — or even artificial flowers, which are cheaper yet.

Of course, you don't have to use a spray, even if you have a traditional head table. Some couples find that sprays are inconvenient, leaving you and the wedding party little room to enjoy your meal. If you want some sort of decoration, but don't want a spray, consider using ribbons, miniature lights, or big bows on the front of the table.

If your bridesmaids carry bouquets, save yourself some cash and have those bouquets do double duty as head table decorations. Tell your florist what you want to do; he'll design the bouquets so they fit into holders on the front of the head table. If you decide to forego the traditional long head table and either sit with your wedding party at a round table or by yourselves at a small "sweetheart" table, you can use the bridal and bridesmaids' bouquets as centerpieces. Your florist likely will provide small bouquet holders at the ceremony site that can serve as vases at your reception. (Just remember, if you're creating your own bouquets, to include the holders on your supply list.)

Cake table flowers

Some couples choose to decorate their cake table with fresh flowers and petals; others choose to trim the table with greenery and flowers. Because the cake is the focal point, floral and greenery decorations are merely accents; you don't need anything elaborate (and therefore expensive). You can even eliminate this expense if you like.

You can decorate the cake itself with fresh flowers — a small vase of flowers as the cake topper, for example (which may be cheaper than a traditional cake topper), or flowers lining the base or arranged on the top of each tier. If you don't want to fork over the cash for fresh flowers, you can use artificial flowers or other alternative decorations. Most bakers can make frosting flowers in different colors for you, and that option may be significantly cheaper than the fresh-flower route.

Ribbons also are a popular alternative; many brides choose to have their main cake "connected" to side cakes with ribbons in their wedding colors. You can scatter bows and pieces of ribbon on the tabletop, and drape wider ribbons and bows from the table edges to complete the look.

Choosing a Florist

As with all your wedding vendors, you want a florist who's going to give you value for your money, especially if you're on a budget. You want someone who will listen to your ideas, offer sensible alternatives, and stay within your budget.

Some florists admit to jacking up their prices if they sense that the couple or the couple's family has a lot of money. So leave the expensive jewelry and designer suits at home when you meet with florists. Make sure whoever accompanies you doesn't flash a lot of bling, either.

When looking for a florist, start your search by checking in with a local florist who has previously impressed you with reasonable prices and quality products. If you don't have a local florist you like, do the following to find some candidates:

- Ask your friends and family for referrals.
- Check your local phone book.
- Do online searches for local florists at The Knot (www.the knot.com) and My Wedding (www.mywedding.com).

✔ Attend bridal shows. Most exhibitors will have a combination of fresh arrangements and portfolios showing their work.

If you find a florist you like at a bridal show, ask whether he offers a discount for signing a contract that day. You may be able to shave between 5 percent and 10 percent off the price. Just be sure to ask him the questions in the upcoming section first.

When you have a list of potential florists, follow up by interviewing the candidates and getting a written contract. I show you how in the upcoming sections.

Knowing what questions to ask

When you hire a florist, you aren't just purchasing flowers from her; you're also purchasing services. But florists differ widely in the level of service they provide. *Full-service florists* typically consult with you, order and arrange your flowers, deliver them to your ceremony and reception sites, and set them up. *Discount florists* often don't do these things, and that means you have to make other arrangements for getting your flowers to your wedding venue and making sure they're set up the way you want.

It's essentially a trade-off between time and money. If you don't want to add another task to your wedding-day to-do list, paying a full-service florist may be the best choice for you. On the other hand, if your budget is tight, saving a few dollars may be more important to you.

Here are some questions to ask when you're interviewing florists:

✔ **Who will actually be creating my arrangements?** If you aren't interviewing the person who will create (or supervise the creation of) your arrangements, make an additional appointment with that person at a later date; that way, there's less room for misunderstandings about what you want.

✔ **Does your price include delivery and setup?** If not, find out how much extra those services cost, and make sure the charges are included in the contract (see "Getting the details in writing," later in this chapter). If you're responsible for picking up the flowers, make sure that's spelled out in the contract, too. If delivery and setup are included, you may be able to negotiate a lower fee if you decide to do those things yourself.

✔ **Have you decorated my venue before?** If the florist isn't familiar with your ceremony or reception location, ask whether she'll make the time to visit it before your wedding.

If she says no, I suggest continuing your search; you may end up with arrangements that are out of scale with your venue, which is a waste of money.

✔ **How long before my wedding will you deliver and setup the flowers?** You want to make sure your flowers will be delivered and set up before the photographer arrives. Especially if you're having formal photos taken before the wedding, you want to have your bouquet and other flowers ready.

You may have to coordinate with your ceremony or reception site to make sure the florist can get in to set up the flowers early.

✔ **What local flower growers do you work with?** If the florist has business relationships with a variety of local producers, chances are better that your final bill will be within your budget. Why? Because locally grown blooms are less expensive than exotic flowers that have to be shipped from far-away locations.

If, after interviewing your candidates and choosing one, you find that the price is right, you may want to consider using her for several pieces of your wedding plan. Many florists go far beyond flowers in their services; they may offer balloons, streamers, and other decorations as well. Some even rent tables and chairs for events.

Getting the details in writing

Any contract you sign with a florist — and you definitely want a contract — should include the following information:

✔ Detailed list of all the floral arrangements you're buying, including size, color, and number of pieces (for example, three white rose boutonnieres)

✔ Acceptable flower substitutions in case your preferred flowers aren't available; also list any flowers you absolutely don't want

✔ Itemized list of any other items the florist is supplying, such as vases, bouquet holders, balloons, trellises, and so on

✔ Logistical information, including where and when the flowers will be delivered (or picked up, if your florist doesn't do delivery and setup); who's responsible for ensuring site access and how (for example, you'll deliver a key and a permission letter to the florist at least 24 hours before your wedding); and the name and cellphone number of the person who will do the setup as well as a backup phone number for the florist in case there are problems on your wedding day

> ✔ Total cost, including taxes and any extra fees (delivery, setup, and so on)
>
> ✔ Deposit and payment schedule and amounts
>
> ✔ Clear statement of the florist's cancellation or refund policy

Make sure you get a copy of the contract; it should be signed and dated by both you and the florist and should have no blank lines.

Keeping Your Floral Costs Down

Fortunately, it's pretty easy to cut your flower costs. You can save money by purchasing only locally grown flowers that are in season. You can buy flowers in bulk and make your own bouquets and centerpieces. Or you can forgo fresh flowers altogether and use either artificial ones or creative (and low-cost) alternatives. I provide more information on these money-saving tips in the following sections.

Going seasonal

In our global marketplace, you can get pretty much any kind of flower you want at any time of year — for a price. But you can save money by concentrating on flowers that are in season for your wedding.

Some flowers, like roses, baby's breath, carnations, orchids, and calla lilies, are available year-round, and their prices don't really fluctuate much with the seasons. But others are much cheaper in season. Here are some common wedding flowers and the seasons in which they're available in the United States at the lowest cost:

> ✔ **Spring:** Anemones, daffodils, delphiniums, hyacinths, lilies, peonies, sweet peas, and tulips
>
> ✔ **Summer:** Asters, chrysanthemums, daisies, English lavender, forget-me-nots, hydrangea, irises, larkspur, lilies, zinnias
>
> ✔ **Fall:** Asters, chrysanthemums, dahlias, marigolds, zinnias
>
> ✔ **Winter:** Amaryllis, anemones, camellias, Casablanca lilies, daffodils, forget-me-nots, hollies, poinsettias, stargazer lilies, sweet peas, tulips

Nearly all flower prices, and especially prices for roses, go up during the first two weeks of February in the lead-up to St. Valentine's Day. Flower prices also may be higher in the two or three weeks leading up to Mother's Day.

Creating your own arrangements

More and more brides are buying flowers in bulk and creating their own bouquets, corsages, boutonnieres, and centerpieces. The Internet has helped this trend along in two ways:

- ✔ It's easier than ever to find good online deals on bulk flowers
- ✔ You can visit countless Web sites that have videos and instructions on making lovely floral pieces for any occasion

Buying flowers in bulk

You can order bulk flowers from virtually anywhere and have them delivered to your door — in some cases, without even paying extra for shipping. You don't have to go with an outfit you've never heard of, either. Costco (www.costco.com) and Sam's Club (www.samsclub.com) both sell bulk flowers, as do other Internet retailers like Fresh Roses (www.freshroses.com). As of this writing, Sam's Club has 100 or more roses starting for less than $100 including shipping.

Your local florist may be willing to order bulk flowers for you, too. You may even be able to snag close-to-wholesale prices on those bulk orders. If necessary, you may be able to arrange for the florist to store your flowers until you're ready to make your pieces as well. Storage is important, because most flowers need to be refrigerated to stay fresh-looking.

No matter where you buy your bulk flowers from, make sure you give yourself enough time to receive your order *and* make your bouquet, centerpieces, and so on. Depending on the vendor, that may mean placing your order three or four weeks before your wedding. And, when you buy bulk flowers, remember that you're responsible for trimming them and keeping them alive and looking fresh for your wedding. You need appropriate storage space and a block of time to put together your arrangements — two essentials that often convince couples they'd rather spend the money on a professional florist.

Making your own floral projects

Even if you've never so much as arranged a vase of flowers before, plenty of online resources can help you make your own bouquets, centerpieces, and other decorations. The following Web sites can help you get started:

- ✔ Save-on-crafts (www.save-on-crafts.com) has both tutorials and supplies, but you may be able to get less-expensive supplies by shopping at your local craft, hobby, or dollar store.

✔ The Flower Exchange (`www.theflowerexchange.com`) has instructions for making bouquets, headpieces, corsages, and centerpieces.

✔ Do It Yourself Weddings (`www.do-it-yourself-weddings.com`) has photos and instructions for centerpieces.

✔ eHow (`www.ehow.com`) has step-by-step instructions for making bridal and bridesmaids' bouquets and a list of supplies you need for each bouquet. The site also has a selection of how-to videos.

✔ About.com (`weddings.about.com`) provides helpful how-to articles and videos on floral arrangements

✔ YouTube (`www.youtube.com`) has how-to videos from several sources, including Martha Stewart.

If you prefer one-on-one instruction, check with craft stores in your area to see whether they offer classes or seminars; many do. Some craft stores also have instruction sheets for various projects.

The more practice you can get, the better — especially if you've never made bouquets or other floral arrangements before. Use inexpensive artificial flowers to experiment with styles, and when you come up with one you like, take pictures of it so you can re-create it with real flowers for your wedding.

Considering alternatives to fresh flowers

Flowers may be a wedding tradition, but the wedding police aren't going to arrest you if you decide to do something different. In fact, if you or your betrothed suffer from allergies, fresh flowers just may not be practical. That's okay, and quite in keeping with today's trends. These days, more couples are using alternatives as they try to keep costs down while still expressing their personalities in their weddings.

Artificial flowers, of course, are the obvious choice for the allergy-prone bud lover, and today's artificial flowers are a far cry from the tacky plastic creations of days gone by. Craft stores are stuffed to the rafters with an incredible variety of real-looking artificial flowers and greens, perfect for making your own bouquets, centerpieces, and other decorations. If you aren't savvy with flower arranging, you can use the Web sites in the preceding section, "Making your own floral projects," for guidance.

You can make your own artificial flowers, too. At eHow (www.ehow.com), you can find step-by-step instructions, including supply lists, for making things like satin roses and origami flowers.

No rule says that a bouquet — or a centerpiece — has to be made of flowers at all. Brides today are carrying bouquets made of feathers, crystals, candy, antique buttons, and even origami birds.

Try incorporating a hobby into your bouquet and decorations. If you love poetry, for example, you can fashion a bouquet from scrolls of faux parchment paper with some of your favorite lines inscribed in an ink that complements your color scheme. Following the poetry theme, pew decorations could be posies of feathered pens from the dollar store, and centerpieces could comprise notepads, pens, and a small basket so guests can leave notes for you.

Or ditch the bouquet idea altogether and carry a fan, a small parasol, a loved one's Bible, a rosary, or even a fancy clutch or evening bag. Some brides who have a unity candle in their ceremony walk down the aisle with a lit candle, instead of placing it on the altar. Irish custom calls for the bride to carry a horseshoe for good luck (with the open end up, so the luck doesn't fall out); the horseshoe is then hung over the newlyweds' door for continued good fortune. The Offbeat Bride (offbeatbride.com) has a gallery of bouquet substitutes other brides have chosen for their weddings; maybe their ideas will inspire a great idea for you. To see the gallery, go to offbeatbride.com/2009/03/wedding-bouquets#referrer.

You could opt to carry nothing, too, of course. (Talk about saving money!) But many people get nervous when they're the center of attention, and carrying something down the aisle gives you something to do with your hands.

Chapter 9

Capturing It for Posterity: Photography and Videography

*1*f you're like most couples, photography is the one area where you don't want to skimp on your wedding budget. After all, photos (and, if you choose, videos) will be around long after the last morsel of wedding cake has been savored. You may fondly remember your great-aunt Mildred on the rare occasions when you break out the silver-plated chafing dish she gave you as a wedding gift, but only photos can bring back the full glory of your ceremony and celebration. And only videos can capture the sounds and movement of the day.

I'm sure you've heard plenty of the many horror stories of couples who hired cut-rate photographers or videographers — or enlisted the family Ansel Adams–wannabe — with disastrous results. Wedding photos and videos are irreplaceable. If your photographer or videographer doesn't get the shot on the day, it's lost forever. So, if having these photos or videos is important to you, you need to devote an adequate portion of your wedding budget to professionals or skilled amateurs who are sure to deliver beautiful mementos of your big day.

However, you shouldn't blindly pay whatever a professional asks. You can easily save money without sacrificing the quality you deserve. In this chapter, I show you how to choose a photographer and videographer you can afford — where to look, what questions to ask, and what to beware of. I also give you ideas for getting your guests involved and making sure everyone has an opportunity to see the photos they take.

Deciding What Kinds of Photos and Videos You Want

No matter how much you spend to capture memories of your wedding day, it's a waste of money if you don't get the kind of photos or video you want. So before you start interviewing photographers and videographers — even before you set your budget for these professionals — you and your spouse-to-be should talk about what you want to see in your wedding album.

There are no wrong answers here. It's simply a matter of what you prefer. My husband and I, for example, didn't want formal, traditional photos; that wasn't our style. So we hired a photographer from the newspaper I worked for at the time and asked him to chronicle our ceremony and reception as they happened. My friend Jill, on the other hand, has more traditional tastes, so she chose a photographer who was skilled at setting up formal shots.

The same is true for video: You simply have to decide what type of video memories you want to have when the day is done. I chose not to spend the money for a professional videographer, but your priorities may be different. And, depending on what you plan to do with your wedding video — if you intend to post it online, for example, or present copies to friends and relatives — you may decide it's worth the cost to hire a pro.

I provide you with a rundown of the photo and video options in the following sections.

Selecting from the many photography styles

When you and your honey sit down to talk about what you'd like your wedding album to look like, you have lots of photography styles to choose from. Generally, from least to most expensive, your options include the following:

✔ **Candid shots:** These are photos taken as things happen. In fact, the people in the photos often aren't even aware that anyone's taking a picture. If you ask your guests to take pictures during your ceremony or reception (see "Getting Your Guests Involved" later in this chapter), most of them will take candids.

✓ **Photojournalism style:** This style of photography chronicles an event as it happens, without any posed or staged shots. The main difference between candids and photojournalism is that candid shots typically are taken by amateur photographers, while photojournalism denotes a professional. In recent years, photojournalism has become a hot trend for wedding photography. (Bud and I didn't know we were setting a trend!) However, some wedding experts bemoan the lack of formal, posed shots.

✓ **Informal shots:** Some wedding photographers take informal shots of intimate moments between members in the wedding party, such as the bride's mother adjusting the bouquet, the groom and his father talking before the ceremony, or the maid of honor fixing the bride's hair or dress. These shots often are staged rather than spontaneous; that is, the photographer asks the best man to look at his notes for the toast instead of capturing him doing it on his own.

Informals usually are part of a photography package, but you should always ask potential photographers whether they take informal shots and whether they're included in the pricing.

✓ **Traditional style:** Traditional wedding photography comprises the iconic wedding photos you're probably most familiar with: the bride showing off her gown; the bride and groom posed at the altar or other location; and group shots of the wedding party and of the bride's and groom's families. Often these photos are taken at the ceremony site, but sometimes couples prefer to have their formal shots taken in a park or in another setting.

✓ **Portraiture:** This style of photography is the most formal, and the most expensive, option. It involves tons of equipment: lights, backdrops, screens, and often at least a couple assistants to help the photographer get everything just right. In the U.S., portraits seem to be more popular in the South, but they're a tradition for many families across the country. Sometimes a bride has a portrait taken four to six weeks before the wedding; it's then enlarged (usually to 16 inches by 20 inches, but sometimes larger), framed, and displayed at the reception. These bridal portraits can cost as little as $500 and as much as $2,000, depending on the size and the framing.

If you're considering a bridal portrait, remember to factor the extra expenses into your budget. Those expenses may be for more than just the portrait, too: If you want your hair and makeup done professionally, you'll have to budget for those expenses. And, depending on when you order your wedding dress, you may have to pay a "rush" fee to have it in time for the portrait.

You aren't limited to just one style of photography. You can hire a traditional wedding photographer to take formal shots of the wedding party and families, for example, and then hire a photojournalist to shoot the reception — or ask the family shutterbug to get certain shots at the reception. Or you can seek out a photojournalist who also captures posed shots. If you and your betrothed have trouble agreeing on the kind of photos to go with, these options can be good compromises.

Photography contracts often include an *exclusivity clause* — that is, you promise not to hire another photographer for the same event. I'd argue that the ceremony and reception are separate events, so you're perfectly free to hire separate photographers if you choose. But make sure the limits of each photographer's "exclusivity" are spelled out clearly in the contracts.

Considering video options

Unlike still photography, video style lies mostly in the editing, not in how the raw footage is shot. That said, you can choose what you want to have on video. Here are some options, from least to most expensive:

- ✔ No video
- ✔ Video of the ceremony only
- ✔ Video of the reception only
- ✔ Video of the ceremony and highlights of the reception, such as toasts, your first dance, and so on
- ✔ A complete video record of your day, perhaps even including video interviews with or messages from guests and the wedding party

Generally, the more video you have shot, the more it'll cost you; even if the videographer uses a digital camcorder, you'll probably pay for the time he spends shooting and editing.

You can hire a professional videographer or go with an amateur. Pros obviously cost more, but if video is a priority for you, it may be worth the price. On the other hand, if you just want a simple record of your special day, amateur videographers cost less — even nothing, if you have a relative or friend do it. However, remember that you may not get the final product you envision with an amateur; the quality of both the raw video and the editing may be lacking. The following sections outline the pros and cons of professionals and amateurs.

Using a pro

A professional videographer charges anywhere from $1,000 to more than $10,000, depending on what kind of package you buy. The advantage to using a pro is in the quality of the video; it's unlikely a pro will miss important moments, and sophisticated editing can make your wedding video look like an entry in the Sundance Film Festival — a pleasure to watch again and again.

You may find a videographer who charges less than the average for your area, but remember the adage, "You get what you pay for." Like other wedding vendors, the best professional videographers often are booked a year or more in advance, and prices tend to be higher for the most in-demand dates. If a videographer is willing to shoot your Saturday-evening-in-June wedding for less than $1,000, he may not be able to deliver the quality you expect.

Professional equipment is less cumbersome than ever, so you don't need to worry about bulky cameras, lights, and microphones getting in the way. (Of course, this lightweight, high-tech equipment costs big bucks, which is one reason pros are fairly expensive.)

Going with an amateur

If your budget is tight, or if video isn't a high priority for you, you may want to ask a friend or relative to videotape your ceremony and reception for you. You can buy good-quality hand-held digital video cameras for about $250, and these cameras are generally as easy to use as digital still cameras. You may be able to rent one for even less; look in your local phone book for video recorders and players.

With Windows Moviemaker for PCs or iMovie for Apple computers, you can do a fair amount of editing to create a presentation video instead of just settling for the raw footage.

The downside of going with an amateur, of course, is that the quality of the video may be poor — wobbly or jerky, out of focus, or filled with annoyingly unnecessary pans and zooms. The audio quality also may be poor; professional videographers often use wireless microphones to capture vows, toasts, and other spoken moments, but your Uncle Fred's video camera may miss those audio cues and instead pick up the motorcycle roaring by outside.

The less experience your amateur videographer has, the worse your video quality will be. If possible, choose an amateur who makes videography a serious hobby, and pass over the person who's only taken home videos of their children or pets.

A tripod eliminates much of the wobble of hand-held video. For the ceremony, have your amateur videographer set up a tripod in an unobtrusive place where she can capture all or most of the important parts of your ceremony. For example, you might place the camera next to the aisle in the front pew at the church or to one side in back of the altar. Some churches allow you to use the choir area for this; others don't allow any video or photography equipment behind the altar, so check with your officiant or church coordinator.

Be sure to place the camera so it won't get in the way of your still photographer — a tripod is less than romantic when it shows up in the best shot of your first kiss as husband and wife.

Choosing Photographers and Videographers You Can Afford

You can hire a photographer or videographer to fit almost any budget. On the low end, these services generally begin at around $1,000 (that's $1,000 each for a photographer and a videographer). Much of the cost depends on how fancy and extensive you want to get with your wedding photos and videos. Here are the general guidelines to keep in mind:

- ✔ **Photography:** Costs generally increase as the photographer spends more time and takes more pictures at your wedding. Costs also increase as you order more prints (more on this cost in the later section "Negotiating a good deal").

- ✔ **Video:** Costs typically go up as you get fancier with the editing; skillful editing is a time-consuming process, requiring both the equipment and the artistic talent to produce a quality final video. The amount of time the videographer spends with you also may affect the pricing.

Photographers and videographers who work out of their homes or modest studios typically charge less than those with big fancy studios in the heart of town. Remember that those plush carpets and leather couches cost the photographer or videographer money, and he's going to figure those overhead costs into his prices.

In the following sections, I guide you through the process of choosing professionals to capture your wedding on camera, including finding referrals, interviewing candidates, and negotiating a contract.

Beginning your search

When you've decided what kind of photography and video (if any) you want for your wedding, you can start shopping around for photographers and videographers who create the kind of visual memories you're looking for. Most wedding experts recommend that you interview at least three photographers or videographers, but you have to find them first. (I tell you more about interviewing them in the later section, "Interviewing candidates.") You can look for candidates in all kinds of places, but not all of them will yield satisfactory results. I recommend structuring your search in the order of the following sections.

If you live in or near a large metropolitan area, expand your search to the suburbs. Photographers and videographers in smaller communities often charge less, because they have lower overhead costs. Even if you have to pay them mileage to travel to your wedding site, you may still reap significant savings.

Asking family and friends for referrals

Many of the best photographers and videographers don't advertise; they rely on word of mouth to build their businesses. If you know any recently married couples, ask them about their photographer and videographer — whether they were pleased with the results, whether they liked them personally (no matter what you think, personality is important — see "Finding a good match" later in this chapter), and whether they felt they received value for their money. If you feel comfortable doing so, ask the couple how much their photographer and videographer charged and what the prices included.

Searching online

The Internet has made finding professional photographers and videographers easier than ever. Here are some sites to get you started:

- ✔ **Professional Photographers of America** (www.ppa.com): At this Web site, you can search by geographic location, and you also can narrow your search by specialty. If you want to track down a photographer recommended by someone else, you can search by name and studio as well.

- ✔ **Wedding and Portrait Photographers** (www.wppionline. com): This site allows you to search photographers by location and specialty.

- ✔ **Wedding and Events Videographers Association International** (www.weva.com): At this site, you submit your e-mail address and information about your event, and then an association member responds to your request.

Only pros who are members of the organizations listed in these bullet points are included in any searches you conduct on these sites. The upside of this is that members typically are interested in keeping their skills and equipment up to date. The downside is that membership doesn't necessarily mean a particular photographer or videographer is right for you.

One additional Web site you may want to try is craigslist (`www.craigslist.org`). Many local — and affordable — photographers and videographers post ads on craigslist; click on the city or state in which you want to search, and then go to Services/Creative to read ads from local photographers and videographers. You also can post a help wanted ad under Gigs/Creative.

Just as important as knowing where to start your online search is knowing where *not* to look online. Whatever you do, don't look for a photographer or videographer on online wedding advertising sites or print wedding ad "magazines." These outlets have a shady reputation among professionals, and the best candidates don't waste their marketing budget on advertising in these resources. Also steer clear of "featured photographers" on wedding planning sites; photographers often pay tons of money to "earn" this slot, which means they're featured because of their deep pockets, not because of their skill or talent.

Contacting your local newspaper

Most news photographers do freelance work on the side, and many of them are old hands at photographing weddings. A bonus: Local news photographers often are *much* cheaper — and give you more for your money — than traditional wedding photographers. Hiring a news photographer is a good option if you decide you want a photojournalism approach to your wedding pictures. (Refer to the earlier section, "Selecting from the many photography styles," for more information on the photojournalism approach.) Some photojournalists do posed shots, so you may be able to get a mix of styles from one photographer. Or you can hire a less expensive photographer to do your traditional shots.

You may be able to find a photojournalist who's skilled in videography at your local newspaper as well. The idea may seem counterintuitive, but more and more newspapers are expanding their Web sites to include video, which means more and more still photographers are learning the ropes as videographers.

As tempting as it may be to save money by hiring one person to take both still shots and video, don't do it. It's nearly impossible for one person to take both the video and still shots of important moments, and you'll end up disappointed in your pictures, your video, or both.

Checking out local colleges

If your area university or community college has a photography or film program, you may be able to find a student to shoot your wedding at a fraction of the cost of a professional. The trade-off is in experience; there are lots of important moments to capture at a wedding, and if you hire a newbie, you run the risk of her missing some of those shots. On the other hand, students often bring a fresh, creative element that veterans may lack. Depending on the student's equipment and experience, you can expect to pay a quarter to half of what you'd pay a pro.

To find a student, contact the school's department or program office (usually available on the school's Web site) and tell them what you're looking for. They can tell you whether they do this sort of referral and help you arrange next steps.

You should meet student photographers and videographers in person, just as you would professionals. For one thing, you want to gauge how well you and the student will get along on your wedding day. For another, you want to discuss the kinds of shots and overall style you want — and see whether the student listens and understands, or goes off into his own vision of how he wants to shoot your wedding.

Attending bridal shows

Bridal shows are a great place to start your list if you just arrived in town and don't know a soul, but you should never hire a photographer or videographer based solely on what she displayed at one of these events.

Some wedding experts put bridal shows at the top of their "in search of" list for vendors, but they're really a good option only if none of the others listed in this chapter pan out. Why? Because bridal shows only introduce you to what the photographer or videographer considers her best work; they don't really give you the (pardon the pun) full picture of what she would do at your wedding. They only give you an idea of that particular pro's taste and style.

That said, if you're unsure what kind of photos or video would suit you, you can get a feel for the different styles at bridal shows.

Interviewing candidates

Getting the names of possible photographers and videographers is only the beginning of your quest. You still have some homework to do. Here's what you need to do:

- ✔ Review the professional's work.

- ✔ Find out about his experience and what kind of equipment he uses by asking the right questions.

- ✔ Get a feel for the pro's style and personality.

- ✔ Obtain pricing information you can actually use in comparing one candidate with another.

Make sure your interviews include each of these tasks, which I explain in the following sections.

Set up interviews by phone or e-mail, and try to meet at the photographer's or videographer's studio; that's where you're most likely to see a good cross section of the work. Don't try to hire someone over the phone without reviewing the work; you're likely to be disappointed. Besides, you need to meet in person to draw up a written contract to head off any misunderstandings.

Reviewing the work

Never base your opinion of a photographer's or videographer's work on a "best of" portfolio (the kind you're most likely to see at bridal shows, bridal shops, and other marketing locations). Instead, go to the studio and ask to see the albums or videos of entire weddings. You want to get a feel for both the type and quality of the shots.

Don't get carried away by the special effects you may see in many photos or videos — things like sepia tones, star filters, superimposed shots, and the like. Those effects may cost money (and sometimes a lot of it). So when you're reviewing a pro's work, focus your attention on the shot itself, not the fripperies around it.

When reviewing still photography, check the following things:

- ✔ **Exposure:** Seeing many photos that are underexposed or overexposed indicates a lack of skill in different lighting conditions. Processing can correct some of these issues, but you should consider poor exposure a red flag.

- ✔ **Poses:** Do the posed shots look awkward? Do the subjects look stiff or uncomfortable? Even in posed shots, you want your subjects to look relaxed, like they're pleased to be in the moment. If they don't, the photographer's people skills may be lacking.

- ✔ **Framing:** A real pro will never frame a shot where it looks like you have a candelabra sprouting from your head. So pay attention to the backgrounds of the shots. Likewise, remember that the best shots include only what's necessary to complete the scene; a lot of extraneous scenery on the sides or in the foreground is a sure indication of an inexpert shot.

If a photographer refuses to show you albums of complete weddings, walk away and continue your search elsewhere. It's not worth your time to figure out what she might be hiding.

When reviewing a pro's videos, keep an eye on these elements:

- ✔ **Technical quality:** Look for sharp focus, good lighting, and a variety of tight and wide shots.

- ✔ **Audio quality:** Can you hear the celebrant and the vows clearly? If the video contains a musical score, does it overpower the spoken parts?

- ✔ **Storytelling:** Even the best video in terms of technical quality can be painful to watch if the final product seems disconnected. Good videographers spend a great deal of time editing their raw footage to tell the story of a wedding in a seamless, easy-to-follow flow. However, remember that the more elaborate the editing, the more expensive the video is likely to be, because you pay for the time the editing takes.

Many professional videographers post sample videos on their Web sites, and sometimes you'll find testimonials from satisfied clients, too. Be aware, though, that this is a marketing tool, so you're only going to see videos that the pro is particularly proud of.

You'll probably fast-forward through most of the videos you watch, but don't be shy about watching or even replaying the segments that are important to you. Ask to watch two or three videos, so you can get a good feel for what this videographer likes to produce.

Asking the right questions

When you interview photographers and videographers, you need to know a few things before you decide which one to hire. Be sure to ask these questions (in addition to any others that may occur to you):

- ✔ **Who will actually take the photos or video?** Ask whether the person you're meeting with is the one who will be shooting your wedding; if not, ask to meet the person who will be there. For photographers, ask if he'll have an assistant and whether the assistant also will take photos. For videographers, ask how many people will be in the crew.

  For both, ask whether the labor cost for the extra people is included in the package and whether you're expected to pay any other expenses for them, such as mileage or meals.

- ✔ **Is the work you're seeing from the person(s) who will be at your wedding?** Make sure you're viewing samples from the pro you're thinking of hiring — not a collection of the studio's work. You want to see exactly what you'll be receiving.

Don't buy the line that all the photographers or videographers in a studio have the same training. Even if that statement is true, it doesn't mean that Annie's work will have the same look and feel as John's. Personality, talent, and creativity all affect the final product.

✔ **What's the cost structure?** Make sure you understand hourly fees and the prices for prints, albums, and tapes or DVDs. Also be sure to know upfront what is and isn't included in various packages. (See "Negotiating a Good Deal" later in this chapter for more details on costs.)

Ask each candidate whether he offers a no-frills package, and then find out what it includes and what it costs compared to the fancier packages. For photographers, a no-frills package may include unretouched proofs and the negatives; for videographers, it may include a lightly edited version or simply the raw video.

✔ **What will cost extra?** This question allows you to confirm what's covered in packages. Extras may include things like additional prints or tape copies, overtime pay if you ask the pro to stay longer than you contracted him for, parking and travel fees, and special effects for prints or video.

✔ **What kind of equipment does the pro use?** Ask the pro how many cameras he uses and about the format of those cameras (see the nearby sidebar "Understanding photo and video formats"). Also ask about lighting and, for video, microphones. You want to get a feel for how cumbersome the equipment will be and whether it'll interfere with your or your guests' enjoyment of the day.

✔ **How many proofs will you have to choose from?** You generally want to have between 60 and 80 photos in your final wedding album; it takes that many shots to tell the full story of an average wedding and reception. But you want 200 or more still shots to make your final selections from.

For video, ask whether the videographer will cover the entire ceremony and reception, and whether he charges extra if you also want him to cover things like the rehearsal dinner and preparations on the day of the wedding.

Ask whether the photographer/videographer charges extra for taking more pictures or video. Those who use digital equipment typically won't charge more, because they don't have to worry about using up film or tape. But these extra charges could add significantly to your final costs if your professional uses physical film or tape.

Understanding photo and video formats

Technology is a wonderful thing, but it can be confusing when you're deciding which format you want for your wedding. Photographers typically use one (or more) of the following three formats:

✓ **35 mm film:** This format is inexpensive to process, but because the negatives are small, enlargements bigger than 8 x 10 can look grainy.

✓ **Medium format, or 2¼ film:** This format is better for enlargements because the negatives are bigger; you don't lose sharpness the way you do with 35 mm film. Medium format also produces richer colors than 35 mm.

✓ **Digital:** This format has become quite common, and new printers even produce photos that last just as long as traditional film prints.

A photographer's base prices may not differ much among these different formats; after all, the equipment for all of them is expensive. You may save money on actual prints with digital or 35 mm, but, depending on your priorities, you may prefer to pay a little more for the richer colors and better enlargement quality of medium format.

Videographers have four common formats available to them. Betacam and digital video recorders produce broadcast-quality footage. A format called SVHS is the next best thing in terms of quality. And VHS is the standard consumer video format. Generally, VHS is the cheapest option, and Betacam or digital video is more expensive.

✓ **Who owns the proofs/negatives/master tape/raw video?** If the photographer or videographer retains ownership, you have to get all copies through him — and the cost will be significantly higher than if you could make copies on your own. If you own the negatives or raw video, you can shop around for the best deal on professionally made copies. Refer to the later section, "Negotiating a good deal" for more on haggling with the photographer to purchase the original materials.

✓ **How long does it take to get the final prints, albums, or tapes after the wedding?** Don't be surprised if the answer is three or four months; that's pretty common. But be wary if you don't get a firm delivery timeline, or if the timeline seems excessively long.

✓ **What kind of deposit does the photographer or videographer require?** Also find out whether the deposit is refundable (in case you find another pro you like better) and how much notice is required to get your deposit refunded.

✔ **Are you expected to feed the photographer or videographer and assistants?** Believe it or not, this sometimes turns up in the contract, and it definitely affects your budget. If you're paying $20 or more a plate for dinner, a couple extra mouths can add up fast. I'm not saying you shouldn't feed them — if they're spending the entire day with you, you certainly should. But you do need to know how many meals you have to provide and how many people you have to provide them for if you want to stick to your budget.

If you do provide meals for the photographer and videographer (and crew, if there is one), talk to the caterer or the coordinator at your reception site about arranging a less expensive meal for them. You also may want to arrange for the photographer and videographer to eat before your reception officially gets under way, so they'll be available to shoot important moments like your entrance, your first dance, and so on.

Finding a good match

You'll be spending a lot of time with your photographer or videographer on your wedding day, and it'll be much more enjoyable for everyone if you and your professional share a vision of what you want the record of your wedding to look like.

Personality matters, too; you probably won't be happy with the most talented photographer in the world if her personality gets on your nerves. So it's important to conduct your interviews in person; you just can't get a good feel for how you'll get along through e-mail or over the phone.

During your interview, ask the photographer or videographer these two questions to judge whether you've found a good match:

✔ **What do you think are the most important elements to capture at a wedding?** This question isn't so much about making sure she gets the first dance on film as it is about affinities. Some photographers may be more interested in the staging and décor; others may be more interested in the human interaction. If her priorities don't match yours, you probably want to continue your search.

Professionals will ask you for a *shot list,* which is a written note of the photos or scenes you want them to shoot (and, sometimes, what you want them to avoid — especially if you have a camera-hog friend or relative). Even if you choose an amateur, you should prepare a shot list to make sure she doesn't miss important shots.

✔ **What are your favorite kinds of shots?** If you're looking for a traditional feel and the photographer or videographer prefers to shoot offbeat poses or unusual scenes, no one is likely to be happy with the end result.

Comparing packages and pricing

Ideally, of course, every photographer and videographer would offer the same packages so you could easily see who provides the better value. Unfortunately, that's not the way it works. Photography and videography packages can vary greatly, and that can make it difficult to figure out which deal is best for you. Following are two methods to help you make comparison shopping easier:

✔ **Ask each candidate for a list of a la carte prices.** These lists tell you how much each item would cost if you decided to purchase a set number of prints or copies rather than one of the packages. Remember that cheaper packages may not include everything you want or need. Use the a la carte price list to come up with the cost of your own ideal package, and then compare photographers' packages to see which ones come closest to meeting your needs.

✔ **Make a list of the items in each candidate's package and assign a number value — say, from 1 to 5 — to each element.** For example, if having the film negatives is important to you, you'd put a 5 next to that part of a photographer's package. If the leather-covered album isn't a priority for you, you'd put a 1 next to that. Ranking elements in this way allows you to see which candidate offers more of the things that matter most to you.

Negotiating a good deal

Photographers and videographers have to eat and pay their bills just like anybody else, so most of them structure their pricing to ensure that they can cover their expenses (including investment in equipment) and be reasonably compensated for their time, talent, and expertise. Still, you may be able to negotiate certain aspects of the contract.

Know the going rate for your area before you open negotiations. This information helps you judge how reasonable a given pro's prices are and can give you an idea of how much of a price break you may be able to get.

Some areas that may be open to haggling include the following:

- **Getting a lower rate for an off-peak wedding date:** If you're getting married on a Saturday in June, you can't expect a break on rates, because this is high-demand time for all wedding vendors. But for a Thursday afternoon in August or a Saturday morning in January, you may be able to negotiate a lower rate because it's less likely that the photographer or videographer will be able to book a gig at his full price. (Refer to Chapter 3 for more on choosing off-peak wedding dates.)

- **Buying a la carte services instead of a package:** Most wedding photographers and videographers have a variety of packages to choose from; very few offer a la carte pricing up front. However, if the packages don't meet your needs or your budget, ask about picking and choosing the services you do want. For example, you may hire the photographer or videographer for the ceremony only, instead of for the entire day.

- **Purchasing the negatives or master video:** You may pay a premium for these originals, because many photographers and videographers earn a good portion of their income from selling prints and copies of the video. However, if you can negotiate the purchase of the originals, you'll still likely save money in the long run; if you have the negatives and master video, you can make your own copies for a fraction of the price. Plus, you don't have to worry about tracking down the photographer or videographer years later if your own prints or video copies are lost or damaged.

If you do buy the negatives or master video, be sure to store them properly. Heat and moisture can damage film, videotapes, CDs, and DVDs. Keep them in a cool, dry place, preferably in a fire-safe container. You also can keep them in a safe-deposit box (and you may be able to deduct the rental fee on your income taxes if you itemize).

- **Buying the photography proofs:** You can save money on prints by arranging to buy the photography proofs and using them to fill gaps in your wedding album or to send mementos to family and friends. The proofs won't have the same fully polished look of retouched prints, but most professional proofs are good enough.

- **Combining orders:** Your photographer or videographer may be willing to offer a discount if you place one large order instead of having friends and relatives all place their own separate orders.

Ask if your photos or video will be posted online. Many pros offer this feature, which allows your family and guests to look through the photos (or get a preview of the finished video) and decide whether they want to buy copies. If you're offered a discount for combining orders, you can then send the link to your friends and family along with a deadline for placing an order with you.

✔ **Getting a discount for cash.** If you can pay cash, ask for a discount. When you pay cash, the photographer or videographer doesn't have to pay the fee that credit card companies charge businesses for each transaction, and he doesn't have to wonder whether a check will bounce. Just remember to get a receipt for any cash you hand over.

✔ **Buying albums elsewhere.** If a package includes a photo album, ask how much the price would drop if you bought your own. You can always tell the photographer that you don't care for the album choices he offers. Many retailers carry lovely photo albums at a fraction of the price of traditional wedding albums from the photographer.

When you negotiate a contract with any vendor, remember that the worst that can happen is that he'll say "no." Give the photographer or videographer a chance to explain why something isn't negotiable; it may give you a better idea of whether others might be willing to give in a little. If, for example, the response is, "I don't negotiate," you may be able to find a better deal elsewhere. But if the response is more about the pro's own costs, it may not be reasonable to expect a price break from him or any other candidate.

Getting Your Guests Involved

Your guests are going to take pictures whether you ask them to or not, so why not take advantage of the additional record of your wedding?

Many couples provide disposable cameras at the reception to encourage their guests to take photos. Often the problem is that the guests take the cameras with them, and the happy couple never gets to see the pictures.

You have a couple of ways around losing out on the cameras. You can ask a member of your wedding party to be in charge of collecting them at the end of the reception. (You'll likely still lose some, however, because not every guest will stay until the very end). Or you can ask your guests to have the film developed and post the pictures online so everyone can see them.

With photo-sharing sites like Flickr (`www.flickr.com`), Shutterfly (`www.shutterfly.com`), and Kodak Gallery (`www.kodakgallery.com`), you and your guests can share photos for free. The Kodak site even lets you order prints and specialty items like photo mugs, T-shirts, and other keepsakes.

You also can ask your guests to share their photos by lending you the memory cards from their digital cameras. If you have access to a laptop computer, you can assign someone to download the memory cards right at the reception; then you don't have to worry about keeping track of which memory card belongs to whom or about having to return the cards to their owners. Alternatively, you can appoint someone to collect the cards and make sure each one has the owner's name and address. After you have the photos, you can post them online and invite your guests to view them.

Here's one caveat about having your guests take photos: Especially in dimly lit sites, multiple flashes can ruin the shots your professional photographer or videographer is trying to take. Ask your guests to refrain from taking flash pictures during your ceremony.

At the reception, try setting up a photo corner — maybe even with a fun backdrop — where your guests can flash away without interfering with the pros.

Although lots of digital cameras also have video capabilities, I don't recommend encouraging your guests to take their own video of your ceremony or reception. For one thing, it's difficult enough to keep snapshot-happy guests out of the photographer's way; you don't want to have to police your guests' behavior around the videographer, too. For another, inexpert video is just plain painful to watch. So, unless you want amateur videos of your wedding posted on YouTube, don't encourage your guests to take video. (Some probably will do it anyway, of course.)

Chapter 10

Putting It in Print: Invitations, Programs, and Miscellany

Many couples are surprised at how much wedding invitations can cost, and especially at how quickly seemingly small extras — like having your return address printed on the back flap of the envelope — can add up.

The average cost for 100 invitations is around $225 to $250. If you choose an expensive printing option, such as engraving or hand calligraphy, costs can easily shoot into the $1,500 to $2,000 range.

Fortunately, couples looking to save money on their printed materials have plenty of options. In this chapter, I explain those options and give you ideas for trimming costs on every piece of printing you need for your dream wedding.

Invitations should be mailed six to eight weeks before the wedding, so start your search for the perfect, affordable invitation at least three or four months in advance. See Chapter 3 and Appendix A for more on getting your wedding planning timeline in order.

Shopping for the Best Deals

You have many more purchasing choices for invitations than your parents did. But that can be a double-edged sword. Sure, you can order invitations and all the accessories you want for a song, but you may sacrifice quality. Worse, if you go with a catalog or Internet company, you may not find out about a problem until you have your invitations in hand.

Regardless of where you buy your invitations, the pricing structure is usually a la carte. That means you pay a base price for invitations and envelopes, and virtually everything else — from special printing processes to inserts — costs extra.

Here are some things to keep in mind when you're comparing vendors and prices:

- **Buy for the number of households, not the total number of guests.** Forgetting this guideline and ordering twice as many invitations as you need is a common mistake, and one I made myself. Most of your guests will likely be couples, so you need only one invitation per address. The exception is when you invite an adult who lives at the same address as a couple (your college-age nephew, for example, who still lives at home). In that case, the couple receives one invitation, and the other adult guest at the same address receives a separate invitation.

- **Round your order to the next lot size.** Invitations are usually sold in lots of 25, 50, or 100, and the price per invitation is usually lower for larger lot sizes. If your guest list has 130 people, order 150 invitations. You'll save money in the long run because you'll have extra invitations if you need them; if you have to go back and order extras, you'll pay a hefty fee because the company likely will treat it as a new order.

- **Extra envelopes cost extra.** Don't assume that the printer will throw in extra envelopes; most of them, including catalog-based and online print services, charge extra. It's worth it, though, because who hasn't made a mistake once or twice in writing an address? Order enough envelopes to cover your guest list, plus an extra pack of 25 (the way envelopes are typically packaged).

Skip the foil-lined envelopes, especially if money is tight. They're a nice detail, but they add to your costs. Besides, your guests will never miss them.

The following sections list the pros and cons of various types of invitation sources.

Bricks-and-mortar print shops

The main advantages to working with a local print shop include the following:

> ✔ The shop probably does a *lot* of wedding printing, so its employees can help you choose styles and even wording.

> ✔ Such shops usually let you take sample books home for a few days so you and your spouse-to-be can look over different invitation styles at your leisure.

The biggest disadvantage to traditional print shops is price. Most charge full retail for paper stock and special printing requests. However, they may offer price breaks on packages — if you purchase your thank-you notes at the same time as your invitations, for example, or if you order a certain quantity.

Mail-order catalogs

Catalog companies cater to virtually every budget, although most of them are owned by the same parent company — a printing giant called Taylor Corporation. Not coincidentally, Taylor also owns many of the major invitation brands, including Carlson Craft, Celebration, and Royal.

Just because many companies are owned by Taylor doesn't mean you'll pay the same price everywhere. You can find the same Taylor-made invitation in a mail-order catalog for half the price that a retail shop charges. You can find these deals in the following Taylor-owned catalogs: *Wedding Invitations by Rexcraft, Current,* and *The American Wedding.* Check out www.catalogs.com to order free copies of these (and other) catalogs.

The variety in pricing is the biggest advantage of using mail-order. The main disadvantage is that you can't see and touch the product unless you order samples, which may cost you. Timing also may be problematic, depending on whether you can fax proof changes instead of mailing them. And, if you aren't sure how to word your invitation, you won't have a store employee to help you.

Web sites

The Internet has exploded with printing sites in recent years. Again, Taylor Corporation owns most of the major ones, but as with mail-order catalogs, pricing is all over the board.

Some sites have virtual design studios that let you experiment with different papers, ink colors, and type styles, which is nice if you're looking to create something that really complements your wedding vision. And as with mail-order catalogs, some will send you physical samples, although you may have to pay for them. You can approve proofs online at many of these sites, too.

Here are some sites worth checking out:

- ✔ Custom Shots (www.customshots.com) lets you upload photos to personalize your invitations.

- ✔ eInvite (www.einvite.com) has hundreds of invitation styles, including an eco-friendly category. Some styles run less than $1 a piece.

- ✔ IndianWeddingCard (www.indianweddingcard.com) has unique, handmade paper invitations at a fraction of the cost you'd pay for handmade paper in the U.S. Even though the invitations are handmade in India, you will have a two-week maximum shipping wait.

- ✔ Wedding Invitations 411 (www.weddinginvitations411.com) uses Carlson Craft invitations (a brand owned by Taylor) and offers styles starting at less than $1 per invitation.

Be sure to check prices carefully. Some Web sites (and catalogs) list prices "per 100" invitations, and others list them "per 50," making straight price comparisons a little challenging. After all, $67.50 looks pretty good compared with $98 — until you discover that you only get 50 invitations in the first instance and 100 in the second.

Some sites let you design e-mail invitations, which are much cheaper than traditional printed invites (and, of course, they're eco-friendly). Etiquette mavens look down their noses at this, but unless you're having a formal wedding, you can ignore traditional etiquette on this point.

Choosing an Invitation Style to Fit Your Budget

Etiquette dictates that your invitation reflect the kind of wedding you're having; that is, the more formal your wedding, the more formal your invitation should be. Beyond this rule of thumb, though, you have free rein in choosing invitations. It comes down to your budget and your style. I can't help you figure out your style, but I can show you how your choices — in everything from paper to printing process to inserts to the very size of your invitation — affect your finances.

Picking out paper

You have literally hundreds (perhaps even thousands) of paper possibilities to choose from. Wedding invitations come in all colors these days; you aren't restricted to basic white or cream. You can have royal blue paper with white or silver ink, or pale green paper with maroon ink, or . . . well, you get the idea.

The factors that influence the price of paper stock include

- **Weight:** Paper *weight,* which affects the price more than any other factor, is measured in pounds. Generally, the higher the poundage, the thicker the paper — and the more expensive it is. (As a baseline, the plain white paper you use in your computer printer or office copier is typically 20-pound stock.)

  Vellum is one exception to the general higher-weight-equals-higher-price rule; this sheer paper, often used to protect lettering on an invitation from the other envelope contents, can be more expensive per sheet than standard 20-pound paper.

  Wedding invitations should be on paper that's 80-pound or heavier. Lighter-weight papers look and feel cheap and amateurish — not the impression you want to give your guests. Heavier paper has a rich, indulgent feel that tells your guests they're being invited to a truly special event.

- **Composition:** The materials used to make the paper affect its price. Pulp paper is generally the cheapest; linen paper, with its cotton content, is more expensive. And paper with recycled content may cost more than regular paper.

- **Finish:** *Finish* is the surface texture of paper. Fancy finishes, like shimmery effects, usually bump up the basic cost.

- **Artistic edging:** Invitations with rough-cut or beveled edges are typically more expensive than straight-edged ones.

- **Texturing:** Textured papers don't have the smooth feel of the paper you use in your home printer. Some textured papers are actually made from woven fibers, and they, of course, are usually costlier. Some embed seeds or other elements to get a different texturing effect. Others, like faux parchment, are less expensive than the real version.

- **Manufacturing method:** How a paper is made also affects cost. Handmade papers like rice paper and *yuzen* (a silk-screened Japanese paper) are substantially more expensive than mass-produced papers.

- **Shipping:** Believe it or not, you can order unique, imported papers from countries all over the world. Not surprisingly, these papers are usually pricier than more traditional stock, and international shipping can cost a bundle.

Comparing printing process costs

How your invitations are printed affects the price almost as much as your paper choice. Fortunately, the days when wedding invitations were considered gauche if they weren't engraved are long gone. Today, you can get lovely printing from a variety of methods without paying a small fortune.

Whether you make your invitations or have them done professionally, select a printing process that works with the paper you choose. Digital printing works best on smooth paper, for example; it doesn't work well with textured paper. Most catalogs and professional printers note which printing processes are available for various paper types. Or ask at your local copy center or office supply store for do-it-yourself advice on matching printing and paper.

Common printing processes, from least to most expensive, include the following:

- **Digital printing:** These days, you're as likely to encounter digital printing as you are offset printing (see the next bullet). Computer technology allows for more precise resolution and color matching, in hues just as vibrant as offset printing.

  Short of using your own computer and printer (see the later section "DIY: Indulging Your Creativity (And Saving Money)" for details), digital printing is the most economical option. It works best on smooth or lightly textured paper; text and designs often don't transfer well to heavily textured stock.

- **Offset printing (lithography):** Many printed materials you see are created through *offset printing,* or *lithography.* An inked plate or *roller* transfers the text or design to the paper, creating a flat (not raised) printed image. Materials that use more than one color of ink are more expensive because each color of ink requires its own plate. Offset printing works well with either smooth or textured paper, and it's one of the less expensive options available.

- **Thermography:** *Thermography* involves a combination of ink, resin, and heat to create raised lettering that looks the same as engraving at a much lower price. Thermography is the most popular option for wedding invitations today. Aside from the lower cost, thermography allows you to choose different ink colors (engraving works best with black ink, not so well with other colors), so you can combine the level of formality you want with your own flair.

- **Foil stamping:** Like engraving, *foil stamping* involves etching the text or design onto a copper plate. The "foil" is a special material that's applied to the paper, and the heated copper plate is placed on top of the paper, stamping the foil into the paper. The result is similar to the now-rare letterpress process, but foil stamping offers a much wider range of type styles.

Because of the customization, foil stamping is comparable in price to engraving. It's usually used for formal weddings and with heavily textured paper.

✔ **Engraving:** *Engraving* is the oldest form of printing. Paper is sandwiched between an etched copper plate and an inked plate; the etched plate forces the paper onto the inked plate, creating raised lettering on the front of the paper and dimples, or "bruises," on the back. Engraving is expensive because the copper plate has to be custom-etched and can be used only once; in fact, you may be given the copper plate as a keepsake.

If you're having a very formal wedding and your guest list is quite long (more than 250 people), engraving may be both appropriate and cost-effective. For smaller weddings, engraved invitations can cost anywhere from $100 to $500 more than other printing methods, depending on inserts and other options.

✔ **Calligraphy:** Handwritten calligraphy is a lovely choice for wedding materials, but it's quite expensive — which is why most couples use it only to address their invitations (typically both the inner and outer envelopes). You can expect to pay $1.50 to $2.50 per invitation (in addition to the cost of the invitations themselves); however, you may be able to find a calligraphy student who will do it for less. Computerized calligraphy is also a cheaper option — about $1 per invitation — and allows you to match the printing on the envelopes with the printing on your invitations.

Including inserts (or not)

Wedding invitations used to be elaborate, seven-piece collections: the invitation itself, an inner and outer envelope, a response card and return envelope, vellum or tissue paper inside the invitation, and a reception card. You still can purchase this kind of set, but etiquette no longer demands it except for the most formal weddings.

Inserts cost extra. The base price for invitations typically includes only the invitation and mailing envelope. Everything else has an additional fee, including services like having your return address stamped on the back flap of the outer envelope. Plus, the more inserts you stuff into your invitation, the more expensive postage is likely to be (see the later section "Adding postage" for more on factors that affect mailing costs).

Here are some ways you can keep costs under control without violating any rules of etiquette:

- ✔ **Skip the reception card.** If your ceremony and reception are at the same site, simply have the printer add "Reception immediately following" in the lower left corner of the invitation. If the reception is at a different location, you can say something like "Dinner and dancing, 7 p.m., Highland Country Club." If guests need a map or driving directions, print them on lightweight paper (or even do it yourself on your home computer) to keep the postage weight down.

- ✔ **Give guests alternatives to RSVP.** Some wedding experts estimate that only about 30 percent of guests use response cards to let you know whether they'll attend. So you can ask them to respond via e-mail or on your wedding Web site instead. You can put this information on a simple card, and you save on postage because the invitation itself will be lighter and you won't have to provide stamps for the response envelopes.

- ✔ **Use postcards for RSVPs.** If you want to include response cards, postcards are a good option: They don't require envelopes, and postcard stamps are about 15 cents cheaper than regular first-class stamps.

The U.S. Postal Service decides every year whether to raise its postage rates in May. But you can buy "forever" stamps at the current price and use them no matter what the new rate is, thus saving yourself a few bucks.

- ✔ **Determine whether you really need to provide maps and driving directions.** If most of your guests are local, you probably don't need to provide maps or driving directions to your ceremony and reception locations; the name of the site and an address are sufficient. The exception is if your site isn't well-known or is difficult to find.

  For out-of-town guests, maps and driving directions are a thoughtful touch. But you don't have to make them fancy. Simple (and inexpensive) options include

  - **Providing the information on your wedding Web site.**

  - **Having copies made at your local copy center or office supply store.** Stores like Staples and FedEx Office (formerly Kinko's) have high-quality black-and-white and color printers, and copies cost a few cents each.

- ✔ **Resist the urge to tell your guests where you're registered for gifts.** Registry cards are tacky, no matter what kind of wedding you're planning, so don't order them. Instead, list registries on your wedding Web site, or let family and friends spread the word on where you're registered.

Adding postage

Even if you stay within your budget on your invitations, you may experience sticker shock when it's time to mail them. Contrary to what you may have heard, weight isn't the only factor that affects postage costs. Even if your invitations weigh less than an ounce, you'll have to pay extra if your invitations:

- ✔ Are oversized or perfectly square

- ✔ Are addressed along the shorter dimension instead of the longer one

- ✔ Contain anything that makes the surface uneven

- ✔ Have wax seals, ribbons, or other unusual elements on the outer envelope

Check out the U.S. Postal Service Web site (www.usps.com) to see whether you need to adjust your postage budget.

Creating Programs and Other Materials

Invitations aren't necessarily the only printed materials you need for your wedding. Couples commonly provide save-the-date cards, programs for the ceremony, place cards for meals, and napkins emblazoned with wedding bells or rings, the couple's names, and the date. And don't forget about thank-you cards. Expenses for all these things can add up quickly. But you can find easy ways to keep costs down and still communicate effectively with your guests. I show you how in the following sections.

Sending save-the-date cards

Unless you're planning a destination or holiday wedding, or the majority of your guests are from out of town and need to make travel arrangements, save-the-date cards aren't necessary. And even under those supposedly required circumstances, you can accomplish the same goal by sending out an e-mail. It's free and eco-friendly.

Getting your guests with the program

Ceremony programs are quite common these days. They list the order of the ceremony and all the participants (usually identifying how the participant is connected to the couple, as in "friend of the bride" or "groom's brother").

You can order programs from your printer, but that's likely to be expensive. You don't need anything fancy; a simple 8½-x-11 sheet folded in half is perfectly acceptable. Design your program on your home computer and make inexpensive copies at your local copy center or office supply store.

Microsoft Office has free downloadable templates for their Word program; go to office.microsoft.com and look through the Templates tab. Or you can purchase complete do-it-yourself wedding kits, available from stores like Target and Wal-Mart as well as countless online retailers.

With a little creativity, you can turn your ceremony program into a keepsake favor for your guests (and forgo traditional favors at the reception to save money.) One couple I know created fans, using heavy card stock and colorful plastic handles, with the ceremony program on one side and a personalized crossword puzzle on the back. The puzzle encouraged socialization during the reception, as guests consulted one another on the answers to the clues. For more creative, do-it-yourself ideas, see the later section "DIY: Indulging Your Creativity (And Saving Money)."

Showing guests to their seats

Some couples include pew cards in their printed materials so that ushers will know who's to be seated in the front rows. This is usually reserved for very large or formal weddings.

More common are place cards for the reception, and they're a good idea even if you have a buffet dinner because they encourage mingling and prevent guests who don't know many other people from awkwardly looking for a place to sit.

Again, you can have place cards professionally printed or you can make them yourself. All you need is a good quality card stock that stands on its own when folded. Or you can use miniature photo frames as both a place card and favor; just print the guest's name and table number on a piece of paper and place it in the frame.

If you hire a calligrapher to address your invitations, ask her how much she charges to do place cards. You'll have to provide the paper, but your place cards will have an elegant look, and the cost may be comparable to having them printed.

It's a napkin! No, it's a souvenir!

At one time, personalized paper napkins were pretty much a given for any wedding, and they're still quite a common accessory. They aren't terribly expensive, either. Depending on the size and how elaborate you get with the design, you can find them as low as $25 for 100 or upwards of $75 for the same quantity.

Under certain circumstances, you want to provide paper napkins — if you're serving appetizers or nuts and mints, for example. But there's no rule that says the napkins have to be personalized. This is strictly a matter of choice and your budget priorities.

Saying thank you to your guests

The one etiquette rule you *can't* ignore is the one that requires handwritten thank-you notes after the wedding. Partly this is because my mother would be appalled if I advocated anything less, but mainly it's because, no matter how casual your wedding is, it's still a special occasion, and special occasions demand a special effort in the way of thank-yous. The good news: You don't have to have special wedding thank-you notes printed up. A package of notecards from your local stationer or drugstore will do just fine.

DIY: Indulging Your Creativity (And Saving Money)

Except for napkins, which don't work well on home printers, you can make virtually all your printed materials yourself, if you choose. Printing design software is affordable and makes designing unique materials easy; check out Target (www.target.com) or Staples (www.staples.com) for software packages, or look at your local Costco or other warehouse club for better prices.

If you have a PC with Internet access at home, you can download free templates for all kinds of wedding materials from Microsoft's Web site (www.microsoft.com). If you use an Apple computer, you can get the Microsoft templates if you purchase Microsoft Office for Mac.

Office supply stores carry a variety of quality papers, as do many online sites. To make shopping around easier, start with price comparison sites like Nextag (www.nextag.com), which also offer reviews of products and sellers. Laser printers, which are relatively inexpensive, create clean, professional-looking printing. If you don't own a printer, you can save your designs to a CD or flash drive and take it to your local copy center for printing.

Homemade invitations and other materials also let you express your personality and creativity in ways you just can't get from the pros. You can create one-of-a-kind materials with stamps, stencils, paints, and pencils — even ribbons and dried flowers, if you choose. Find materials at your local craft store; you may even be able to take a free crafting class there.

Although most supplies for doing your own printing are inexpensive, ink cartridges for your printer are not. Depending on how much printing you do and how elaborate you get with color, ink can easily swallow up any savings you may expect from doing it yourself. Even if you purchase less expensive (and more eco-friendly) refill kits, you still can shell out a lot of money for ink. Another potential issue is getting a good imprint on paper if you're using an inkjet printer. Inkjet printers don't work as well as laser printers, especially on textured paper; laser printers produce a better imprint.

Online printers like PrintRunner (www.printrunner.com) or iPrint (www.iprint.com) allow you to upload your design — or even create your own using the site's tools — and order the number of invitations you need. Prices start at less than $1 per invitation, which may be less expensive than buying multiple ink cartridges.

The main downside to doing it yourself, of course, is time. If other commitments are slopping over the edges of your already-full plate, paying a pro may be a good investment for your sanity.

Part III
Celebrating with Your Guests

The 5th Wave   By Rich Tennant

Okay — let's get one of the parents.

"I don't care how kitschy it is, I still would have rather had a professional photographer."

In this part...

After the vows are exchanged, the party begins! In this part, you discover how to throw a terrific wedding bash without breaking the bank. I help you figure out the costs associated with various reception sites and uncover ways to keep those expenses under control. I also show you less expensive options for feeding and entertaining your guests.

You may have other events surrounding your wedding, too, so this part includes a chapter on prewedding and postwedding get-togethers, including the rehearsal dinner, gift-opening parties, and receptions for those who can't make it to the actual wedding. And, if you're planning a honeymoon, this part includes ways to make your romantic escape an affordable one.

Chapter 11

Selecting the Reception Site

. . . .

In This Chapter

▶ Sizing up your chosen reception sites

▶ Picking from among the many types of reception venues

▶ Organizing transportation to and from your wedding venues

. . . .

*T*he perfect party doesn't just happen. And what is a wedding reception but a fabulous party marking a most special occasion? A successful party requires the right combination of space, atmosphere, and menu. These items are the foundation for all the other elements of your reception.

In this chapter, I share tips on all things reception venues, from choosing the right space to accommodate your guests to comparing fees and charges at the different kinds of venues. I also provide a checklist of amenities to make sure your guests are comfortable and well cared for. Finally, I address the practical issue of moving yourself and your guests from your ceremony to your reception.

You can save money — and make your wedding day more convenient for your guests — by combining your ceremony and reception sites. See Chapter 4 for information on ceremony sites that can serve double duty.

Matching Sites with Your Guest List

Just as a few dozen guests can seem insignificant in a massive cathedral, a too-large or too-small reception site can suck all the energy and fun out of your post-ceremony celebration. Most wedding experts recommend that you come up with an estimated head count before you start shopping for reception venues, but you can work it either way.

If, for instance, you love a particular site, you can resolve to limit your guest list to fit that site. However, keep in mind that limiting your guest list can be tough (see Chapter 2 for tips on setting your guest list). The easier option may be to figure out how many people you expect to fete and then go looking for sites that are big enough (or small enough) to fit your head count.

Large spaces can be "sized down" in several ways, but you can't make a small space bigger. If you're torn between a site that's a bit too big and one that may squeeze your guests, you need to decide whether you're willing to pay more for a bigger site or trim your guest list to fit a smaller one. Larger venues often have higher minimum-charge requirements; you may have to commit to paying for 200 guests, for example, even if you only intend to invite 175.

How much space you need depends both on how many people you're hosting *and* what activities you're providing. A cocktail reception, for example, requires less space than a sit-down dinner, and a buffet dinner with dancing requires more space than a tea-and-cake reception. Table 11-1 offers further guidelines for matching square footage with the expected activities of your reception.

Table 11-1	Per-Guest Space Estimates
Reception Type	*Square Feet per Person*
Cocktails, dancing, and passed hors d'oeuvres (some seating)	6–8
Cocktails, dancing, and hors d'oeuvres stations (some seating)	12
Sit-down dinner and dancing	12–13
Buffet dinner and dancing*	15–16

Buffet dinners typically require more space per person than sit-down dinners because you need room to set up the buffet and plenty of space for your guests to maneuver easily between their tables and the food stations.

Finding the Best Venue for Your Reception

Reception sites come in all shapes, sizes, service levels, and price ranges. Unfortunately, figuring out which site offers the best value can be tricky, because services, amenities, and pricing structures vary widely among the different kinds of sites.

Word-of-mouth may be the best way to come up with ideas and recommendations for reception sites. Ask friends and relatives for suggestions; between attending business functions and other weddings, they're sure to have firsthand knowledge of at least some of the possibilities in your area. Plus, their experience is a handy guide in gauging whether a particular venue is worth considering. After all, if friends had a lousy meal there, you probably don't need to spend your precious time looking at it yourself.

Even though food and drinks constitute the major portion of most couples' wedding budgets (see Chapter 12 for food and drink details), more goes into a successful reception than just a great meal. The ideal reception site is capable of attending to all your guests' needs for the day. So, regardless of the type of facility you choose, pay attention to the following amenities when you're scouting potential venues:

- ✔ **Acoustics:** If a site can host more than one event at a time, find out whether the reception rooms are adequately sound-protected to prevent audio bleeding from other events.

- ✔ **Bathrooms:** Check out these important facilities to make sure they're clean, convenient, and plentiful enough to accommodate your guests. If the site hosts more than one event at a time, determine whether there are enough bathrooms to go around.

- ✔ **Coat check:** Ask whether the venue has a place for guests to check their coats (or at least a secure place to hang them). If the venue does offer a coat check service, find out whether you can cover the expense for your guests so they don't have to pay (and figure this cost into your budget). A coat check service may not be critical for a summer wedding, but for other seasons, it's an amenity that means a lot to your guests.

- ✔ **Parking:** Estimate whether the venue has enough parking for your guests and whether the site offers valet parking. If it does have a valet service, is the fee included in your rental contract or do you or your guests have to pay extra?

Read on for a primer on what you can expect from several of the most common reception venues. Keep in mind that you can work around virtually every shortfall for every potential site if the benefits outweigh what's lacking.

Church fellowship halls

If you've already decided to have your ceremony in a church or other place of worship, one of the most common — and least expensive — options is to have your reception in that church's fellowship hall immediately following your ceremony.

Some of the pros of using this type of venue include the following:

✔ You often can use the hall for free or for a small clean-up fee, especially if you're a member of the congregation.

✔ You don't have to rent tables and chairs.

✔ You can bring in outside caterers without being slapped with a surcharge (see Chapter 12 for more on catering).

✔ You don't have to provide transportation to a separate location for yourselves, your wedding party, or your guests.

You may run into a few of these potential downsides, however:

✔ Fellowship halls tend to be pretty Spartan, requiring a lot of decoration to create an inviting atmosphere.

✔ Some houses of worship have restrictions on the hours their halls can be used, the noise levels, and the serving of alcohol.

✔ Fellowship hall policies may prohibit the use of candles, birdseed (for throwing in lieu of rice), or other elements you may want to include in your celebration.

You can work around some of these cons. Consider borrowing decorations from church members who've recently hosted weddings, for example. Instead of a cocktail reception, you can have a brunch, which is perfectly appropriate (dry!) for a fellowship hall. Besides, cheaper food and beverage choices, such as those available for brunch, may allow you to expand your guest list. As for prohibitions on candles and the like, you can brainstorm with your betrothed and others for alternatives (such as electric candles, for example) — assuming those prohibited things aren't high on your priority list, of course.

Hotel ballrooms

After church weddings and receptions, hotel ballrooms are the next most common venues for nuptial celebrations. As with church celebrations, you often can have both your ceremony and reception at this type of venue.

The pros of hosting your reception at a hotel include the following:

✔ Some hotels waive the ballroom rental fee if you agree to a minimum food-and-beverage charge.

✔ Nearly all hotels give you breaks on room rates for you and your out-of-town guests.

✔ Tables, chairs, place settings, and linens are usually included in the package. Some even throw in centerpieces and wedding arches (for those who have ceremonies at the venue). Most have a range of color options so you can at least complement, if not match, your wedding colors.

✔ They often have on-site wedding coordinators who make sure your reception goes smoothly. The good news is that you usually don't pay extra for this service.

✔ If you have both your ceremony and reception in the hotel, you'll save money on transportation.

✔ Hotels often can recommend other local wedding vendors, such as entertainers, florists, and bakers. However, be careful, because some try to steer you to vendors who pay a "commission" to get on the hotel's preferred vendor list.

Some potential pitfalls of celebrating in a hotel ballroom include the following:

✔ You may be competing with other events, including other wedding receptions, at the same time as yours. Multiple events can mean problems with service, noise carryover between reception rooms, and crowded parking lots, coat check facilities, and restrooms.

✔ You may have to use the in-house caterer, or pay a hefty surcharge to bring in an independent one. (Chapter 12 provides more catering information.)

✔ You may end up paying hidden fees. Some fees that are commonly excluded from the price quote (but are noted in the fine print) include mandatory gratuities for the staff, cake-cutting fees, and even sales taxes.

You may be able to save yourself some legwork — and money — by calling your local convention and visitors bureau and asking for hotel recommendations for your reception. The bureau may even send out a sort of "request for proposals" to potential sites, essentially opening up your reception to bidding. This strategy is particularly effective if you have lots of out-of-town guests; after all, the primary purpose of a convention and visitors bureau is to fill hotel rooms.

Include in your search hotels that cater to business travelers. They often have the same reception facilities as hotels that cater to other clientele, but, unlike other hotels, weekends tend to be their slow times. You may be able to get a deal for your Saturday evening wedding that no other hotel would think of offering.

If your town hosts a lot of conventions, competition for reception space, caterers, and other services can be stiff. So the earlier you start looking for an appropriate site, the better your chances of getting the one you want on the date you want.

Banquet halls

Banquet halls specialize in wedding receptions and other food-oriented events, so usually they prohibit you from bringing in outside caterers or alcohol. Bakers are the exception; most halls allow you to hire an outside baker to make your wedding cake.

Here are some pros of going with a banquet hall:

✔ Because they specialize in events like wedding receptions, they have lots of experience in setting up rooms to improve traffic flow and efficiently serve food and drinks.

✔ Many have in-house wedding coordinators whose services are included in the package price and who stage-direct your reception to make sure everything happens when it should.

✔ The décor in halls is usually attractive and tasteful, but it's neutral enough that it doesn't clash with any embellishments you want to add.

The following are some of the not-so-great points of banquet halls:

✔ Prices can be significantly higher than with other venues, and you may not have as much negotiating power as with other sites.

✔ The food and service at these venues may be mediocre.

✔ Depending on the facility, yours may be only one of several events taking place at the same time, which can make you feel less special on your wedding day.

Clubs

Country clubs offer some of the poshest facilities around. Despite popular belief, you may not even have to be a member to use these sites. Some clubs open their reception doors to anyone; others only require that a member — who may be a mere acquaintance — sponsor your reception. (In essence, that person promises to pay in the event that you stiff the club.)

You may be able to have both your ceremony and reception at a country club, thus cutting down on transportation and other costs.

Most country clubs have terraces or patios that can accommodate a ceremony setup.

Municipal-owned clubs usually are much cheaper than private clubs, and they tend to have less restrictive policies on bringing in outside caterers and alcohol. Other inexpensive options include civic clubs, such as the Elks, Junior League, and Lions, or military clubs (if you or a relative is serving in or has retired from the armed services). Remember, though, these clubs usually aren't as fancy as private clubs, and some may require a good deal of decoration to look appropriately festive.

Food and beverage costs may be significantly higher at country clubs, and most won't allow you to bring in outside caterers. A price difference of even $2 or $3 per person can raise your total bill substantially, so be sure to weigh the extra cost against your other wedding priorities.

Restaurants

Restaurants can be an excellent alternative to some of the other venues that I mention in this section. Many have private dining rooms that can accommodate groups of 50 or more; some even have stunning views of city skylines or natural landscapes. Decoration costs are minimal, and you can treat your guests to really excellent food. Best of all, the same menu that costs $45 per person at a hotel or banquet hall may run you $30 or less at a restaurant. However, most restaurants charge a mandatory gratuity (usually 18 percent) for large parties, so be sure to factor that into your budget.

The main downside of opting for this type of venue is that most restaurants aren't equipped to handle dance parties. So, if you really want to do the Macarena with your guests until the wee hours, a restaurant probably won't work for you.

Considering Transportation

If your ceremony and reception are being held at the same location, you don't have to worry about paying for additional transportation — unless you just can't bear the thought of pulling up to the site in your everyday car.

However, if you have separate ceremony and reception sites, you have to decide how to get from one to the other. And this applies not just to you and your new spouse, but perhaps to your wedding

party and even your guests, too. Hiring a limousine is the traditional solution. But you're limited only by your creativity — and, of
course, distance.

In this section, I help you weigh the costs and benefits of limou-
sines, buses, and alternative modes of transportation.

Hiring a limousine service

Depending on where you live, limo rentals average between $65
and $100 an hour for a standard six-passenger car. If you want
a specialty limo — a Rolls Royce, for example — the price can
leap to $200 or more per hour. Party limos, such as the 20- to 30-
passenger stretch Hummer, can run you thousands of dollars for a
three- or four-hour rental — the minimum at most limo services.

When you're figuring out how much you want to spend on a limo
service, keep these things in mind:

✔ **How the rental fees are calculated:** Most services have a
three-hour minimum rental, so even if you only use the limo
for an hour, you pay for three. Other companies charge in
15-minute increments, so if you go over the contracted time
by even a few minutes, you'll pay a hefty overtime charge.

Find out when the clock starts (and stops) ticking on your
rental. Some companies start counting down from when the
limo leaves their garage; others don't start the clock until the
limo arrives at your site. It may be a difference of only a few
minutes, but it could cost you dearly in overtime fees.

Weigh the minimum cost against your actual usage of the limo
service. If your reception site is only a five-minute drive from
your ceremony site, you may decide it isn't worth paying the
three-hour minimum — especially if your guests won't even
see you drive up.

✔ **Extra amenities (and the associated fees):** Some limos are out-
fitted with leather interiors, wet bars, televisions, and even red
carpets. All those special touches cost extra, so be sure you
know how much you're paying on top of the standard rate.

✔ **Hidden costs:** The following are some hidden costs to be
on the lookout for. When you shop around for prices, ask
whether the limo service charges any extra fees, such as the
following:

• **Fuel surcharges:** When gas hit $4 a gallon in 2008, many
limo companies added fuel surcharges to their standard
rates to recoup some of the expense. However, even

though gas prices dropped significantly in the following 12 months, not all companies dropped this extra charge.

- **A mandatory tip for the driver:** This tip is usually 10 percent to 20 percent of the total bill.

- **Per-stop fees:** These fees are usually charged for multiple pick-up and drop-off locations; fees range from $15 to $30 per stop.

✔ **Deposit, cancellation, and refund policies:** Most companies require a 50 percent deposit to hold the make and model of limo you want for the date and times you specify. Find out when you have to cancel to avoid a service fee. Also determine how you go about getting a refund if the driver is late or doesn't show up at all.

Many limo rental companies offer wedding packages that include streamers, "Just Married" signs, and even Champagne for the happy couple. If the package is a flat rate, you may want to go with it and save yourself the potential worry of incurring overtime fees with a traditional hourly rental.

Arranging bus transport for your guests

At most weddings, guests are left to find their own way from the ceremony to the reception; there's nothing wrong with expecting them to do so at your wedding, especially if money is tight.

However, couples who can afford it like to offer their guests the option of provided transportation — especially if many of their guests are from out of town, or if the reception site is difficult to find or has limited parking facilities.

In most areas, buses are the most efficient ways to transport lots of people. Average charter rates for a full-sized motor coach are about $90 an hour; most charter bus companies have a five-hour minimum, which is appropriate for most weddings. Some companies charge a mandatory gratuity for the driver (usually 10 percent); if this fee isn't included in the rental price, plan to pay it directly to the driver at the end of his shift.

To find charter bus services, skip the Internet and look to your local phone book first. Many of the sites you'll find on the Web are actually brokers, not charter companies. So they often tack on a hefty commission — sometimes as much as 40 percent — to hook you up with a local company.

Exploring alternative options

The most obvious (and generally the cheapest) alternative to hiring transportation is to let your attendants and guests arrange their own. But if that route doesn't appeal to you, you have plenty of other options. If your reception site is on a lake or river, you could arrange to arrive in a boat, for example.

Brides and grooms before you have made their way from the ceremony to the reception via

- ✔ Horse and carriage (may be more expensive than a limo)
- ✔ Antique or classic car (least expensive if you can borrow a friend's)
- ✔ Motorcycle (due to safety concerns, not advisable if you don't have your own)
- ✔ Inline skates (quite inexpensive, though possibly too strenuous when wearing wedding togs)
- ✔ Tandem bicycle (quaint and budget-friendly)
- ✔ Pedicab (generally less expensive than a limo)

Choose whatever mode of transportation appeals to you (and fits your budget). Just remember that, with all the excitement and commotion of the day, comfort and convenience may be your highest priorities.

Chapter 12

Feeding the Hordes

*M*ost people have deeply ingrained preconceptions about what a wedding reception should look like, and these preconceptions can cause you to spend more than you really want to. But don't worry; you have hope in your corner. Budget-conscious couples are finding creative ways to throw memorable parties without spending a small fortune. It's a matter of coming up with the right combination of timing, place, formality, and size to craft a celebration that everyone will enjoy.

In this chapter, I show you how various options can fit into your budget, how you can save money on food and drink (and where you shouldn't try to scrimp), and how you can express your sense of style and taste with outside-the-cake-box ideas.

Setting a Food Budget

Food (and alcohol) represents the single biggest expense for virtually any wedding, and you may be shocked when you first begin researching caterers in your area. Prices on the coasts and in large metro areas are higher than in smaller cities or in the middle of the country. Even so, you can expect to pay anywhere from $20 to $300 *per guest* just on the food. Alcohol and the cake, of course, are extra.

In general, food and alcohol (if you choose to provide it) take up between 40 percent and 50 percent of your total wedding budget. So, if your wedding budget is $5,000, plan to devote between $2,000 and $2,500 to your catering bill.

The factors that have the biggest impact on your food budget are

- ✔ **The number of guests you have:** Of course, as your guest list grows, your catering bill increases proportionately. If you want to invite a bigger crowd, be sure you're ready to choose a less expensive menu.

- ✔ **The kind of food you serve:** As you probably expected, a fancier meal is going to cost you more than a simple one. So, if you want to wow your guests' palates, be prepared to invite fewer people.

- ✔ **The way you serve it:** Buffet-style meals can be much less expensive than sit-down meals, so if you're looking to cut costs, consider setting up a buffet instead.

When you're figuring out your budget, you have a choice of starting with the number of guests you want to invite, the kind of food and service you want, or the amount of money that's in your estimated budget (see Chapter 2).

To decide where to start, break out the list of priorities you and your betrothed identified for your wedding (see Chapter 1). Would you rather have a fancy, formal meal for 50 people, or would you rather invite more of your friends and family and go with a less expensive, less formal menu to accommodate the extra people? (See the following section, "Adjusting the Formality Dial," to see what different meal options can look like.)

There's no right or wrong answer here; it's entirely up to you and your spouse-to-be. If you're willing to pay $5,000 for your reception, for example, and you have your heart set on a formal prime-rib-and-lobster dinner, chances are you'll have to pare your guest list down to the bone. On the other hand, if you want a big, boisterous celebration, $5,000 will pay for one heck of a barbeque.

Adjusting the Formality Dial

Generally, the less formal your reception, the lower your food bill will be. But you don't have to sacrifice style and elegance to limit your spending — you only have to broaden your idea of what a stylish and elegant wedding reception looks like. In the following sections, I help you do just that by explaining the many meal options you have.

Sophisticated and relaxed: Daytime receptions

Daytime celebrations tend to be less expensive for a number of reasons:

- ✔ Demand for reception sites is lower, so rental the fees are typically lower.

- ✔ Food is less expensive, in much the same way that you spend less on an entree at a restaurant during the lunch hour than at dinnertime. (Of course, portions are usually smaller at lunch-time, too.)

- ✔ You aren't expected to provide much in the way of alcohol (see the later section "Answering the Alcohol Question" for more on serving adult beverages).

- ✔ Entertainment isn't as expensive, because there's less demand. Plus bands or DJs often can book an afternoon and evening gig for the same day (see Chapter 13).

- ✔ Often, the event won't be as lengthy.

Even though daytime functions are less expensive, they can be among the most sophisticated events you'll encounter. Plus, because the food is less expensive, you get more for your money. In this section, I tell you what you need to know to throw a successful brunch, tea, or garden party.

Of course, you aren't limited to brunch, garden parties, and teas. You also can have a lunch reception that's formal or informal or indoors or out; no matter what, your costs will be significantly lower than the same event in the evening. Have a picnic, a clam-bake, or a potluck meal to keep food costs down.

Let's do brunch!

Brunch, which is usually served between 10:30 a.m. and 1 p.m., combines breakfast foods and light lunch fare. These menus are among the least expensive catering options. You can provide a variety of specialty buffets — for example, a fruit and salad bar, finger sandwiches, and a sweets buffet — along with made-to-order omelet and pasta stations and perhaps a carved meat station.

You can have a traditional wedding cake, too, if you like. Or you can choose something lighter, such as sponge cake and fruit compote, cookies, pies, or sweet fruit crepes.

Offer a coffee bar, juices, and soft drinks. If you want to serve alcohol, stick with mimosas and bloody marys. Because they're mixed, the alcohol for these drinks doesn't have to be high-quality.

Entertainment for a wedding brunch doesn't have to be elaborate, because these types of weddings often don't include dancing. Instead of a DJ or dance band, you can use recorded music or hire a small band, harpist, or pianist to play background music.

Decorations for a brunch should be light and sparse — not nearly as elaborate as for a formal dinner. And, of course, limiting your decorations saves you money. Stick to centerpieces on the tables and some decorations for the head table, cake table, and gift table; a few fresh, in-season flowers along with ribbons or streamers will suffice for the latter tables.

You can do a straight breakfast reception (which usually is served from 9 a.m. to 11 a.m.), but you run the risk of feeling rushed — and having sleepy guests — if you have the ceremony immediately before the reception.

With a brunch reception, you can have the ceremony at 10 a.m. or 10:30 a.m., which means that you (and your guests) can set the alarm for a less ungodly hour that morning.

Brunch fare can cost less than half — even as little as a third — of a full dinner menu. Depending on where you live and the caterer you use, you may be able to keep your per-guest cost to around $10 to $15 for a brunch.

Meet me in the garden

Garden parties (which can be held indoors) usually are afternoon affairs, starting after 1 p.m. and ending around 4 p.m. The key advantage here is that no one expects you to provide full meals during this time frame. Instead, you can offer light appetizers — either butler-passed or at stations — which are far less expensive than a full buffet or sit-down meal. In fact, you may be able to afford more expensive appetizers, like bacon-wrapped scallops or handmade mini ravioli, because you don't have to worry about providing a meal, too.

Traditional wedding cakes work well at garden parties, but other dessert options are just as good. Less expensive options include fancy cookies, chocolate truffles, parfaits, and tarts.

Coffee, tea (iced and hot), lemonade, and soda all go well with light afternoon fare. Alcohol, if you choose to provide it, can be limited to beer, wine, and a signature drink like Planter's Punch or apple martinis; no one will remark on the absence of a full bar at this kind of function.

As with brunches (see the previous section), entertainment and decoration requirements are minimal with garden parties, which can save you a bundle. Depending on the venue and the kind of appetizers you offer, your cost per guest can be around $15 or less.

You're invited to tea

Afternoon teas are classy affairs that are similar to garden parties but have an emphasis, naturally, on tea. They usually run from 2 p.m. to 5 p.m. However, "high tea," which has a larger menu, traditionally is served at 5 p.m. A traditional English afternoon tea consists of scones with cream and strawberries, fruit tarts, finger sandwiches, and petit fours. You can have a traditional wedding cake, too, but you can get by with a smaller version because so much of the menu is sweet; some guests won't have cake at all, and those who do will likely prefer smaller portions.

Alcohol is seldom served at tea receptions, except for Champagne for toasts. Coffee, lemonade, and soda round out the drink menu. Entertainment usually consists of background music — classical or light jazz — and can be recorded or live. And decorations usually take an understated slant — decorous small centerpieces, for example, and perhaps a few flowers or petals on the dessert table. Catering expenses for an afternoon tea can be less than $10 per person, depending on the site and the extent of the menu.

Other daytime celebrations

If you want to keep things casual, you have several options. Picnics are among the least expensive meals to host, for example. You can provide hot dogs and hamburgers and enlist family members and friends to provide signature dishes. Limit decorations to tablecloths and balloons, and have a sheet cake, cupcakes, cookies, or other desserts in lieu of the traditional tiered wedding cake.

Other casual daytime options include

- A clambake, with corn on the cob and a variety of salads

- A luau, with pulled pork (or a whole roasted pig, if you prefer), tropical fruit salad, rice or poi, banana bread, and sweet potatoes

- A lunch spread, with meat and cheese platters, rolls, raw veggies, potato chips, dips, and cold salads

With any of these menus, you can feed 100 people for $500 or less. Check out restaurant suppliers or club warehouses like Costco or Sam's Club to get deals on bulk foods, and hit party supply stores for paper goods and decorations to fit your theme.

A sweet affair: Dessert receptions

Dessert receptions are a great way to satisfy couples with a sweet tooth, and they also help you get around big food bills. Usually held later in the evening — starting between 8 p.m. and 9 p.m. — these functions focus on a plethora of sweets, such as truffles, tortes, cheesecakes, and crème brûlée. Like cocktail receptions, dessert receptions are shorter affairs, typically lasting only two hours.

Coffee is a given at dessert receptions; you can even provide a coffee bar with different flavors (don't forget the decaf). Other typical beverages include tea (iced and hot) and soda. Alcohol is usually limited and often available only in specialty coffee drinks.

The potential disadvantage to dessert receptions is finding a site that isn't booked for a traditional dinner reception.

However, keep in mind that you don't need a dance floor or formal seating, so you probably can use a smaller meeting room or restaurant. Not only are these venues more cozy for a dessert reception, but they also may be cheaper. Per-guest costs for dessert receptions are typically between $10 and $20.

Cocktail receptions: A social alternative

If you and your intended aren't big on dancing and you're beer or wine buffs, a cocktail reception may be just the right function to celebrate your wedding. Cocktail receptions emphasize mingling and socializing rather than entertainment, so you can use inexpensive recorded music or an inexpensive DJ. If needed (depending on the size of the room and the number of guests), you can rent a microphone and loudspeaker for announcements and toasts. Decoration costs are minimal, too; you can use simple candles as centerpieces and decorate the guest book, gift, and cake tables with ribbons and artificial flowers or petals.

Alcohol will consume the biggest part of your budget with this type of reception, because you'll be expected to provide a relatively full bar. You don't have to provide top-shelf liquor; recognizable brands are fine (although they, too, can add up to a significant bill). On the other hand, your food costs are limited to appetizers and the cake (or other dessert option).

Even though your beverage menu is more extensive, you don't have to provide that full bar for as many hours as you would during a dinner reception. A typical cocktail reception lasts two hours — usually 5 p.m. to 7 p.m. or 7 p.m. to 9 p.m. — compared with four hours for the average dinner reception.

A two-hour cocktail reception with light appetizers may cost $20 to $30 per person — but you don't have to pay for the $20-per-guest meal on top of the cocktails.

Formality at its finest: Dinner receptions

Dinner receptions, which usually begin between 6 p.m. and 7 p.m. and end between 10:30 p.m. and midnight, are typically the most formal and most expensive option. The expensive nature of these events is due to the fact that, in addition to expecting a full meal (as opposed to only appetizers or light fare), your guests also expect alcohol and entertainment — two big expenses. (Alcohol is covered later in this chapter; see Chapter 13 for info on keeping entertainment costs down.)

Another reason dinner receptions can be so expensive is because etiquette usually forces couples to include a beginning cocktail hour, complete with alcohol and hors d'oeuvres. Even though etiquette says you need a cocktail hour, if your budget can't withstand the added expense, feel free to do without.

You can keep your food expenses down by choosing a buffet-style dinner, which is generally cheaper than a sit-down meal. Buffet dinners are cheaper because labor costs are lower. For sit-down meals, you need one server for every 20 to 25 guests; for buffets, you need one server for every 50 to 75 guests. Plus you don't have the labor of preparing individual plates for each guest.

Here's the lowdown on what you generally get with these two options:

- ✔ **Buffet service:** With a buffet dinner, you can offer your guests a wider variety of main and side dishes often at a lower cost per guest. For example, a typical buffet offers at least three main dishes and three or four side dishes.

- ✔ **Sit-down dinners:** With a sit-down dinner, guests usually have their choice among one or two meat entrees and a vegetarian option. Side dishes typically are the same for each entree.

Having an international affair with ethnic cuisine

Selecting an ethnic theme is a good way to keep both food and alcohol costs down. Italian, Mexican, and Chinese buffets are usually cheaper than buffets that offer beef, pork, and chicken entrees. For sit-down dinners, give your guests a sampler plate of ethnic cuisine (which eliminates the need for choosing similarly priced entrees).

Limit alcohol to drinks that fit with the cuisine. If you've chosen an Italian theme, for example, offer Chianti and limoncello. For Asian cuisine, offer sake and Asian beer. Serve wine and Greek ale with a Mediterranean meal, and margaritas and Mexican beer with enchiladas and chimichangas.

To make sure your food budget doesn't explode with a sit-down dinner, choose entrees that are the same or nearly the same in price. For example, you may give guests their choice of pork medallions, chicken, or pasta primavera, all of which may be priced at $14.95. But if you offer, say, prime rib at $25 a plate and chicken at $14.95, and 90 percent of your guests choose the prime rib, your budget could easily shatter.

You can save money on either a buffet or sit-down dinner by decreasing the number of courses. If you have a cocktail hour, for example, you don't really need a soup or salad course at dinner.

Selecting a Caterer to Cook for the Crowd

The food is arguably what your guests will remark on the most at your reception. So, no matter what kind of reception you decide to have, you want the food to be as memorable and plentiful as your budget allows. Choosing a caterer to provide this all-important feature of your big day can be a challenge, and the price tag can induce something akin to heart failure if you aren't prepared for the shock.

The following sections outline the basics of selecting a caterer, starting with knowing what you're expected to pay for. I also offer tips on asking potential caterers key questions so you can make an informed decision.

Knowing what you're paying for

Some reception sites require you to use their in-house caterer; others allow you to bring in outside caterers. No matter which way you go, you need to understand what you're paying for. And that's not always easy, because there are lots of charges and fees that you don't know about until you're presented with the final bill. Of course, these hidden fees are in addition to the standard fees you expect.

Caterers generally charge on a per-guest or per-meal basis. Many of them offer a variety of choices within specific price categories. For example, you may be able to choose one of three kinds of salad, up to three entrees from a list of six, and so on — and whatever you choose will cost so much per guest.

In addition to the per-guest charge, here are some expenses that you may not expect:

- ✔ **Cake-cutting fees:** Most often charged by hotels and reception halls, this fee can add $1.50 or more *per slice* to your cake cost.

- ✔ **Catering surcharges:** Sites that allow you to bring in outside caterers may charge your caterer a surcharge of 7 percent to 15 percent for the privilege of using the facility. Most caterers pass these surcharges along to their customers, so you end up paying that extra money.

- ✔ **Corkage fees:** Sites that allow you to bring in your own alcohol don't often let you do so for free. They charge you for opening the bottles and serving the drinks — a fee that can be as high as $10 per bottle.

- ✔ **Mandatory gratuities:** This fee typically is 18 percent of the total food and beverage bill.

- ✔ **Sales tax:** In some areas, the sales tax on catered affairs may be close to 10 percent — adding nearly $500 to a $5,000 food and beverage tab.

You can't negotiate away sales taxes or mandatory gratuities, but some of these other fees may be open for discussion. For example, you may be able to negotiate a cap on catering surcharges or corkage fees. If you can't negotiate a better deal, weigh these costs against the alternatives; you may find that, even with the corkage fee, you can save money by providing your own alcohol.

Keep your priorities in mind, too. If having that fabulous caterer from across town is high on your list of must-haves, perhaps you'd rather adjust other areas of your budget to account for the surcharge.

Get every detail in writing *before* you sign a contract or make a deposit. Make sure any verbal promises are noted in the signed contract, too. Keep written records — a journal of conversations and copies of e-mails — of any changes or promises made after you sign the contract. These records provide you some insurance in case the person you deal with stops working at the facility before your wedding day; you can show the new staff member the details you worked out and thus stand a better chance of getting the deal you planned for.

Asking caterers the right questions

Whether you're going with an in-house caterer at a hotel or an independent outfit, you need certain information to help you make a final decision. The best way to get the information you need is to interview potential caterers. Here are some questions you should ask every caterer you're considering:

- **Do you offer taste tests, and is there a charge for them?** Some caterers offer free taste tests for groups of potential clients once or twice a month; others make individual appointments, but charge a small fee (which makes sense, because they incur costs in preparing the food). If a caterer tries to tell you a taste test isn't necessary, look for another professional.

- **Do you specialize in specific cuisines or menu types?** Some caterers have the popular Italian buffet down to a science, which is great if you want Italian food. If you want a sit-down Mediterranean dinner, though, look for a caterer that specializes in that cuisine.

- **Where is the food prepared?** It's particularly important to ask off-site caterers where they prepare the food, because it may affect your choice of reception sites. If the caterer prepares all the food at her own kitchen and only needs to set up serving areas, you don't have to worry about whether your reception site has adequate kitchen facilities. But if some or all the food needs to be prepared on-site, you need to make sure your reception site has the proper facilities.

- **How do you charge for servers, and how many do I need?** Find out whether the labor charge is included in the caterer's price, or whether the caterer charges a mandatory gratuity based on the total food and beverage bill. Buffet dinners require fewer servers than sit-down dinners; ask whether the cost of additional staff for a sit-down meal is included in the price.

✔ **Do you provide alcohol/bar service, and how is the cost calculated?** Some caterers charge per drink; some charge per opened bottle; and others charge an hourly rate per guest. To avoid paying more than you budgeted for, make sure you understand the price structure as well as the types and brands of alcohol that will be served.

Even though etiquette warns against cash bars at wedding receptions, budget-conscious couples (and those who want to put an extra brake on overindulgence) often choose this option. Even with a cash bar, though, you have some expenses. Most caterers, whether in-house or independent, require you to pay a minimum gratuity for the bartenders. Often, an extra charge kicks in if bar receipts don't meet a preset minimum.

✔ **What are your policies on deposits, cancellations, and final payments?** Get these policies, along with the due dates for deposits and cancellation notices, in writing.

Managing Menu Choices

Your menu should generally reflect the formality and overall theme of your wedding. You can get away with more elegant food in a casual setting, but too-casual food in a formal setting comes across as miserly. You don't want to serve hot dogs and cold cuts at an elegant banquet hall, for instance. Beyond that, though, you have pretty wide latitude in menu options. (Refer to the earlier section "Adjusting the Formality Dial" for examples of matching your menu with your venue, time of day, and budget.)

Here are some considerations you should keep in mind when choosing your menu:

✔ **Tastes:** You may love pan-seared marlin, but what if your guests aren't big on seafood? Be sure to provide a variety of foods (while staying within the same general per-guest cost) so all your guests can find something they like. Be especially careful when you're serving ethnic cuisine.

✔ **Dietary needs:** If any of your guests are vegetarian, vegan, diabetic, or otherwise restricted in their diets, try to take those needs into account. If you know of any food allergies among your guests (nuts, eggs, and so on), find out whether the caterer can accommodate those special needs too. And, as always, ask whether the caterer charges for special requests.

✔ **Ages:** If children will attend your reception, ask whether you can order special meals for them. You may even want to arrange for them to eat first; hungry children can easily disrupt special moments at the beginning of your reception.

✔ **Seasons:** Rich, hearty dishes hit the spot in the fall and winter; light fruit salads and crisp veggies are refreshing in the summer. Matching your menu to the season helps strike the right note for the reception — and it may even save you money, because, like flowers, in-season foods are less expensive.

No matter what kind of reception you have, you should be able to incorporate any special needs into your menu without breaking your budget. Ask your caterer for ideas on cost-effective ways to accommodate your guests' needs and preferences.

Variety is the key to pleasing the greatest number of guests. Even with a sit-down meal, you can offer a choice of entrees so your guests can find something they like. And you can do it without wrecking your budget.

Answering the Alcohol Question

Alcohol: To serve or not to serve? This is a tricky question for many couples. After all, alcohol is expensive, it's a potential party-wrecker, and it can raise liability concerns.

Forgoing alcohol altogether is always an option, especially if you, your fiancé(e), and most of your guests are nondrinkers (or if you're committed to saving big bucks on your nuptials). If you don't include alcohol, you can use sparkling cider for the toasts and provide a full range of soft drinks, coffee, tea, and juices. Even this full range of beverages is *much* cheaper than a beer-and-wine bar.

Most couples choose to provide at least some alcohol at their receptions. If you fall into this category, read the following sections to find out how alcohol is priced, to discover tips for keeping costs down and overindulgence at a minimum, and to understand how much legal responsibility you may bear for your guests' actions after they leave the reception.

Understanding how you pay for alcohol

At most reception sites, you pay for bar service either by the opened bottle or by a flat per-person-per-hour rate. Some charge by the number of drinks poured, which makes it financially imperative that you tell the waitstaff to leave half-full glasses alone (see "Keeping a lid on drunkenness" later in this chapter).

No matter which way you pay, alcohol is likely to represent a big chunk of your per-guest cost. Plan to spend between $10 and $45 per guest on the bar bill. In addition to the alcohol charges, you'll most likely have to pay mandatory gratuities for the bartenders, and you may have to pay sales taxes. (See "Selecting a Caterer to Cook for the Crowd" earlier in this chapter for more on catering fees.)

If the venue or caterer allows you to supply your own alcohol, you can save a ton of money by purchasing cases of wine and liquor and kegs of beer from wholesalers or discount clubs like Costco and Sam's Club. The venue or catering employees serve the drinks, but you get to keep any leftovers.

Some reception sites don't allow you to bring in your own liquor or outside bar services. And those that do allow these options often charge a *corking fee,* which is really just a penalty for not using the on-site service. Be sure to ask about policies and fees when you're scouting reception locations, because the corking fee may eat up any savings you'd realize by providing your own alcohol.

Slashing your booze bill

Traditional etiquette says that if you serve alcohol at your reception, it's tacky to ask your guests to pay for it. However, budget-conscious couples often defy traditional etiquette and provide a cash bar. In some circles, having a cash bar won't raise a single eyebrow; in others, it's considered a serious breach of manners. If you're considering a cash bar, be sure to weigh potential social consequences against your budget constraints.

If your funds won't cover a full open bar and you don't want to forgo alcohol or have a cash bar, consider these options to keep costs down:

- ✔ **Serve only beer and wine.** This common compromise doesn't violate any etiquette rules. As a variation, you can serve beer, wine, and a signature drink. This variation gives your guests more drink choices but still keeps expenses down.

- ✔ **Close the bar during dinner.** At many receptions, the bar is open for the cocktail hour, closed for dinner, and reopened for two to three hours after the meal. This pattern reduces overall consumption. And most guests won't even notice that the bar is closed while they eat because, well, they're busy eating. Besides, if you decide to have Champagne for the toasts, the staff will serve it to your guests at the end of the meal.

✔ **Give the caterer a consumption or dollar limit and ask to be alerted when your guests approach it.** The bartenders can keep a running tab, and then you can decide whether to continue serving above and beyond the cap you set. If you choose this option, be sure to build a cushion into your preset limit; if your budget is $750, for example, set the cap at $500. That way, you can gracefully accommodate your guests without fretting about the extra expense.

✔ **Close the bar an hour before your reception officially ends.** Alcohol consumption usually slows down after dinner because people are full and busy dancing. (Consumption is highest during the cocktail hour.)

✔ **Offer fewer choices later in the evening.** For example, try switching from a full bar to beer and wine only after dinner. Another option would be to offer only coffee drinks — with Irish cream, Kahlua, or other liqueurs — after dinner. You also can save by closing the bar as dinner is winding down.

✔ **Don't offer Champagne.** If you aren't a big fan of Champagne (and many people aren't), skip the bubbly and let your guests raise glasses filled with the beverages of their choice when it's time for the toast. Alternatively, serve *only* Champagne — especially for a brunch or afternoon reception.

✔ **Serve more affordable liquor.** Even if you have a full bar, you don't have to provide top-shelf liquors. Opt for recognizable brands, but don't feel compelled to provide "only the best" (which often translates into the priciest).

✔ **Skip the cocktail hour before dinner.** Offer coffee, tea, and soft drinks for early arrivals at the reception site, but hold off on opening the bar until about 15 minutes before dinner is served. Most people drink less during and after a meal, so your consumption costs will be lower.

Keeping a lid on drunkenness

Unfortunately, overindulgence at wedding receptions isn't just a stereotype. Sometimes an open bar seems like an invitation to drink as heavily as possible, and the results are never enjoyable. (Brawls make your wedding memorable — just not in the way that you hoped.) Plus, hearty drinkers can seriously inflate your bar bill.

Follow these tips to keep the flow of alcohol at reasonable levels:

✔ **Pass the drinks.** Instead of letting your guests line up at the bar, have waitstaff circulate with trays of wine, beer, and signature drinks. This touch of elegance controls both costs and consumption because you can limit how frequently the servers circulate through the crowd.

✔ **Make your guests ask for refills during dinner.** It's easy to drink too much when someone continually tops off your wine glass every time you take a sip. Tell servers to hold off on refills until they're requested. Remember, lower consumption means lower costs.

✔ **Tell servers not to clear half-full glasses.** Clearing glasses that aren't empty is a huge money-waster, because a guest whose drink is gone when she returns from the dance floor will go to the bar and get another one — and, of course, you have to pay for all those extra drinks. Besides, there's an even chance that, if your guests finish that half-full glass, they'll decide they've had enough.

Considering liability issues

Liability laws regarding serving alcohol vary from state to state and even from city to city. Ask the caterer and reception site manager about liability insurance, and check with your local government and state liquor authority about your potential liability.

In some areas, you and your caterer could be held at least partly responsible if a guest at your wedding overindulges and is involved in a car accident after your reception.

Also ask the caterer what kind of training the bar and waitstaff has in recognizing the signs of intoxication and how they'll handle it if any of your guests exhibit those signs. Intoxication isn't a pleasant issue to bring up, but it's important, especially if you could be sued for damages as a result of serving alcohol at your reception.

Making Your Cake the Star

The cake is, traditionally, the centerpiece of the wedding reception. It gets its own table. Guests and the wedding photographer incessantly snap its picture. It's the focal point of the cake-cutting ceremony. And many guests feel it's inappropriate to leave a reception until the cake is cut.

Unfortunately, all this attention means the cake is expensive, too. The average wedding cake costs about $550. Add in fondant decorations, cake-cutting fees, and multiple tiers with different flavors and fillings, and you could easily spend $1,000 or more for your cake.

However, if you know what drives up the cost of wedding cake (besides the word "wedding," which increases the cost of everything), you can figure out how to keep your cake expenses under control. And if you aren't excited about traditional wedding cake, you have a range of lower-cost options to choose from.

Creating a multitiered masterpiece isn't the same as baking a birth-day cake at home. It takes real skill and care to set up the elaborate mountains of cake and frosting you see in bridal magazines. And the higher the cake, the higher the price: A four-tier cake that serves 100 people costs more than a three-tier cake with the same number of servings.

In this section, I tell you about the average cake costs, give you tips on selecting a baker, and offer some less-expensive alternatives to the traditional tiered cake. Figure 12-1 shows some traditional wedding cakes and some less-expensive options.

Figure 12-1: Dessert options for your reception.

Getting the skinny on average cake expenses

Most bakeries and pastry chefs charge by the slice for wedding cakes, and the cost per slice depends in large part on the amount of labor involved in decorating and setting up the cake.

For about $1.50 a slice, you can get a small tiered white or choco-late showing cake along with a sheet cake for serving your guests. For around $5 a slice, you can get a two- or three-tiered cake in standard flavors like white, chocolate, carrot, or lemon. Cakes with lots of tiers, unusual fillings or flavors like red velvet, and lots of confectionary decoration can run $10 a slice or more.

The following sections help you navigate the many factors that go into wedding cake pricing.

Decorating factors

When it comes to cake decorations, the most important thing to remember is that fancy, detailed decoration takes time and skill — and time and skill cost money. Even the type of frosting can add to costs, mainly because of the labor involved. This section aims to help you control these costs.

Fondant, a concoction of sugar, corn syrup, and gelatin, gives cakes a shiny, smooth finish. But getting that smooth, silky finish takes a lot of time and manual labor. Usually, the cake is made, frozen, iced with fondant, frozen again, and topped with another layer of fondant to get the tops and sides perfectly smooth. All that labor means higher costs for you — an average of an extra $1 per slice.

Fondant is pretty, but it doesn't taste very good. Opt for old-fashioned buttercream frosting. This type of frosting is much less labor intensive, is a lovely ivory color (when the baker uses yellow butter instead of expensive imported white butter), and is more pleasing to the palette. And the best part is that it's much cheaper than fondant. Whipped cream is another inexpensive option. It's not as sweet as buttercream frosting, so it's a nice complement to cakes with sweet fruit fillings.

Fondant and sugar decorations in shapes of things like flowers and strands of pearls also add to the labor and cost of a cake. To cut these costs, consider asking your baker to decorate with fresh flowers, ribbons, or strings of faux beads from your local craft, party, or dollar store; you can save a lot on your baker's bill and still have a beautiful, unique centerpiece for your reception.

Setup and delivery factors

Delivery and setup fees can add $50 to $100 or more to your total cost, depending on the distance from the bakery to your reception site and how complex the setup is. Generally, these fees are lower if your cake display is simple; however, some bakeries charge a flat rate regardless of distance or setup difficulty. Ask about the deliv-ery radius, too; the baker may charge extra if your site is outside a certain range, because of the extra travel time and fuel costs.

Other cost-adding factors

How many ways can you bump up the cost of a wedding cake? They're almost endless. Here are some of the most common "extras" that add significantly to the price:

- **Multiple flavors and fillings:** The trend lately has been to make each tier a different combination of cake and filling flavors. This adds to the labor, which in turn can add $0.50 to $1 to the per-slice cost. Stick with standard flavors and fillings to keep costs down.

- **Nuts and dried fruits:** Adding nuts and dried fruits is another way to break from the traditional white wedding cake, but it's also another way to add up to $1 per slice. Besides, if any of your guests have nut allergies, this option can cause problems. Buck the trend and opt for cream filling and simple frosting adornments.

- **Caterer's markups:** Some caterers, hotels, and reception halls have their own pastry chefs, but many don't. So when they suggest you purchase your cake through them, they outsource the job and then charge you a hefty markup — sometimes as much as 30 percent. Compare the caterer's or venue's per-slice prices with independent bakeries before making your decision.

- **Cake-cutting fees:** If you dodge the caterer's markup by hiring your own baker, you'll likely encounter a cake-cutting fee, usually a minimum of $1 per slice. You may be able to negotiate a lower fee; if you can't, be sure to factor this cost into your budget.

Selecting a baker

Price, skill, and service can vary widely among bakeries, so it's important to do some comparison shopping before you hire a baker.

Because they don't have the staff to set up dozens of cakes every Saturday, smaller bakeries often do only a handful of weddings per day. So their slots fill up fast. To make sure you get the vendor you want, start your search early.

Here are some tips to help you in your quest for the perfect baker:

- **Ask to see a portfolio of the baker's work.** Even the smallest bakeries should have a photo album of wedding cakes they've made. Look for pleasing decorations and professional setup. Even in amateur snapshots, you should be able to see whether the cake display looks good.

✔ **Find out how many wedding cakes the baker or his staff set up on a typical day.** Large bakeries may deliver a dozen or more cakes per day, especially at the height of the wedding season. That's not necessarily a bad thing, but you do want to know whether your cake display will be left unattended for hours before your reception. If so, move on to another baker, because long periods of inattention could be disastrous. Ask when your cake will be delivered (you want it set up no more than two hours before your reception) and how the staff will coordinate with the reception site to make sure the display is protected from accidental damage.

If your wedding is on a weekday, a Sunday afternoon, or a holiday weekend, ask whether the bakery slaps you with a surcharge for overtime. Some bakeries don't regularly provide delivery and setup staff on these less traditional wedding days, so you may have to pay extra.

✔ **Ask for a breakdown of fees.** Some bakeries charge a flat per-slice fee plus delivery and setup, and others break down their fees for each component — cake flavor, filling, fondant, decorations, and so on. Either way, get a written estimate that identifies what's included for the quoted price. Also find out about deposit requirements and refund policies.

✔ **Request a taste test.** Most bakeries let you try different cake flavors before you decide which one you want. However, many only offer taste tests on days when they're baking wedding cakes. Some may charge a nominal fee.

✔ **Ask who's responsible for non-confectionery decorations.** If you want to use fresh flowers, ribbons, or other decorations, find out the logistics of getting those decorations to the baker for setup. Some bakers coordinate with your florist; others ask you to make sure the florist delivers the cake flowers to the right place at the right time. If you're providing ribbon or other decorations, plan to drop them off at the baker's shop a few days before the wedding — and be sure to get written confirmation that you've delivered them.

Cutting your cake costs

Many brides and grooms have come up with creative — and tasty — ways to keep their wedding cake costs under control. Some choose "regular" cakes instead of traditional wedding cakes; many grocery store bakeries and even discounters like Wal-Mart have delicious and beautifully decorated cakes that cost far less than a traditional wedding cake. Here are some other ideas to keep cake costs down:

✔ **Save the cost of building a tiered cake, but still have a beautiful display.** For example, instead of paying your baker to set up an elaborate tiered cake, have her make several round cakes. You can then place one on a tall cake stand and the others at varying heights on the table (to achieve visual depth). For extra decoration, run ribbons in your wedding colors from the central cake to the side cakes. While a tiered cake may cost $400 or more, a selection of nicely decorated rounds may cost less than $200.

✔ **Ask your caterer or reception site coordinator whether she has an in-house pastry chef.** You may find that it's less expensive to have your caterer supply your cake if it's done in-house. (If the caterer contracts with an outside bakery, you'll pay a markup.) With an in-house pastry chef, you'll save on — or be able to negotiate away — delivery and setup fees and the cake-cutting fee that most companies charge when you bring in a cake from another baker.

✔ **Check out cakes at places like Wal-Mart, Costco, Sam's Club, or even your favorite grocery store.** You can get cakes of different sizes (and different flavors) and then display them on a multilevel dessert tray or cake stands of varying heights. Your costs may be half — or less — the expense of a traditional wedding cake.

✔ **Hire a cake-baking/decorating instructor.** Check out your local community college or craft store to see whether either offers a cake-decorating class; if so, the instructor may be willing to create your cake at a significant discount from a traditional baker.

✔ **Use small cakes as centerpieces.** Instead of one big, elaborate cake, have your baker make a small cake for each table — or purchase them from your favorite grocery store. Buy glass cake stands from your local dollar or discount store, or shop thrift stores and garage sales for inexpensive and unique cake plates. Small cakes require less labor to decorate, so the per-slice cost can be 30 percent to 50 percent lower. And, after the wedding, you can donate the extra cake stands to a non-profit thrift shop (and possibly deduct the donation on your income taxes).

✔ **Bypass the groom's cake.** I guarantee your guests won't miss it. Another option is to purchase a birthday cake from your favorite grocery store bakery — minus the "Happy Birthday" message, of course — to use as your groom's cake. You'll avoid the inevitable wedding markup if you go this route.

✔ **Order enough cake for only three-quarters of your guests.**
Some people will leave before the cake is served, and others
just won't have dessert. This option is especially helpful if you
plan to have a sweets table in addition to the cake.

✔ **Ask the caterer to cut smaller slices.** A 2-inch slice is still a
substantial dessert portion, and you'll get more servings out
of your cake.

Plan for you and your new spouse to personally serve trays of cookies or biscotti to your guests after dinner and before the cake is
served. It's a nice way for you to ensure that you greet each of your
guests and thank them for being there. Plus, cookies are less expensive than wedding cake, and many people prefer to have a small
cookie instead of a big piece of cake, especially after a heavy meal.

Some bridal experts recommend having your baker make only the
top tier of your cake — the one you'll cut into — and decorating a
Styrofoam dummy for the rest of the tiers. The idea is that you can
save money by having sheet cakes (which don't require the same
labor-intensive decoration) to serve your guests. Your guests probably won't know the difference, but this tactic doesn't always save
you money. After all, you still have to pay for the materials and
labor involved in decorating the dummy cake, and you have to pay
for the sheet cake as well. In some cases, a real tiered cake can be
significantly less expensive.

However, you *can* save money if you have a small "show" cake
for cutting and a sheet cake for serving to guests. Ask your baker
about price differences so you can decide whether the savings outweigh your vision of a grand edifice of a wedding cake.

Looking at low-cost alternatives

Of course, no law exists that says you *have* to have a traditional
wedding cake. Other dessert options can be significantly cheaper —
as little as half the per-serving cost of cake — and more fun and
unique.

Some simple, low-cost alternatives include the following:

✔ Cheesecake

✔ Chocolate fountain with fruit, pretzels, and potato chips for
dipping

✔ Cookies, bars, and brownies

✔ Cupcake trees

✔ Ice cream novelties

✔ Mini tarts

✔ Pies

Grocery-based bakeries and independent shops can make delicious desserts for virtually any budget; you just have to communicate your wishes and budget limits to the baker. The baker may even have ideas beyond the options listed here.

To save even more money, consider enlisting the help of friends and family to create your dessert buffet. Building and decorating a traditional wedding cake takes skill and experience, and well-meaning friends who offer to "do your cake" may get in over their heads. But cookies, tarts, and pies don't require specialized decoration or setup, and they lend a wonderful homemade touch to your celebration.

You can serve alternative desserts in any number of ways: as a dessert buffet, as centerpieces on your tables, or as butler-passed treats. For ice cream desserts, a self-serve freezer or staffed ice cream bar work best.

Cupcakes in lieu of the traditional wedding cake are trendy, but they aren't always cheaper. Remember that much of the cost lies in the labor, and elaborately decorated cupcakes are just as labor-intensive as a traditional cake — and maybe even more so. If you want cupcakes, consider simple colored frosting instead of elaborate details to keep costs down.

Chapter 13

Arranging Entertainment and Preparing the Venue

- -

In This Chapter

▶ Getting in the groove with music

▶ Saving money on your entertainment costs

▶ Decorating on a dime

- -

*L*ots of things go into a memorable wedding, but couples and guests don't always have the same perspective on what really matters at a reception. Various surveys over the past decade have shown that couples tend to put the highest priority on food and drink, but guests tend to remember the entertainment first, food second, and decorations last.

Interestingly, couples and guests' views align more closely *after* the wedding: Within a week after their receptions, 78 percent of brides say they wish they'd put more emphasis on choosing their entertainment, and 81 percent of guests cite entertainment as the most memorable element of a wedding.

This chapter focuses on getting the best entertainment and decoration values without sacrificing style or fun. After all, the important thing is not how much you spend but how what you do spend helps everyone have a good time.

Using Music to Set the Tone for the Reception

Your DJ or band leader is more than an entertainer: He's the master of ceremonies for your reception. He makes sure the entire event flows smoothly, covers all the elements (your first dance, the cake cutting, and so on), and involves your guests.

So, whether you choose live or recorded music, you want an emcee who knows how to make a party go.

Aside from personal preference, your budget may dictate whether you hire a DJ or a band. DJs usually are less expensive than a band, but make sure your DJ is skilled in keeping things moving so your guests don't get bored. Even though bands typically cost more, good ones get the crowd fired up and keep the dance floor filled.

You don't have to hire a DJ or band for your reception, because no rule says that you have to even offer dancing. For a brunch, tea, or cocktail reception, for example, you may only want background music, in which case a friend or relative can be in charge of making sure the CDs or MP3 player keep playing. (See Chapter 12 for details about these and other kinds of receptions.)

If you do decide to hire a DJ or band, read on, because in the following sections, I give you the lowdown on choosing a music professional who's a good match for you and your reception.

Enlisting a DJ

DJ rates vary widely depending on the market and the DJ's experience, equipment, and showmanship. For a four-hour reception, you may pay anywhere from $400 to $2,000 for a professional, but the general range is between $100 and $300 an hour — again, depending on several variables. The following sections help you choose a DJ and understand how payments work.

Selecting a good match

The DJ's personality and professionalism — or lack thereof — can have a bigger impact on how you remember your wedding than any other single factor. That's because the DJ sets the tone for the party.

She can be a polished emcee, imperceptibly guiding the timing and flow of the event, reading the crowd to decide whether they're in the mood for a slow dance or the Electric Slide, and making sure all the high points are covered. Or she can be ineffectual and unable to gain the guests' attention. Worst of all, she could be an obnoxious boor, helping herself too frequently to the open bar, making ill-timed and ill-mannered jokes, and generally turning off your guests and prompting them to leave early.

The latter situation shows why it's so important to meet potential DJs in person. You want to assess the DJ's personality, her speaking style (not just the quality of her voice), her attitude toward her job, and even her attitude toward weddings and marriage. (Refer to the later section "Asking the right questions" for more information.)

Ask to see video of the DJ at a wedding. You don't want a compilation or fancily produced video, just footage of the DJ directing the show. Pay attention to both the newlyweds' and the guests' reactions, and get a feel for the energy and "vibe" of the reception. Seeing the DJ in action helps you gauge how well she'll fit in with your vision for your own wedding.

Understanding what you're paying for

To avoid unpleasant surprises, make sure you know what's included in a DJ's quoted price and what costs extra. You may not be able to negotiate away extras, but at least your budget won't crack under an unexpected strain.

A typical wedding DJ package should include

- ✔ At least one consultation to plan your reception
- ✔ A customized music list
- ✔ At least four hours of music
- ✔ At least one audio mixer
- ✔ At least one microphone
- ✔ Multidisc CD player(s)
- ✔ Setup/tear-down time

If a package doesn't include these things, you may be dealing with an inexperienced DJ. In that case, ask lots of questions about the DJ's equipment and music library to make sure he can handle the gig. If either the equipment or music selection seems inadequate to you, look for another DJ.

Items that usually cost extra include

- ✔ **Overtime:** The DJ's overtime charges may be either time-and-a-half or double time. Overtime for a $100-per-hour DJ, for example, may be between $150 and $200. Find out when overtime is triggered — some DJs start the OT clock if they go 15 minutes over the contracted time, and some give you a 30-minute grace period. You may have to pay overtime fees in cash; this policy should be spelled out in your contract.

- ✔ **An assistant:** The cost for an assistant may or may not be included in the package. If it isn't, make sure you know how much you're paying for the assistant and how much overtime for the assistant costs (see the preceding bullet).

- ✔ **Meals and drinks:** Some DJs ask that they (and any assistants) be fed before or during the reception. You can arrange with your caterer to provide box lunches and bottled water or soft drinks.

Common sense dictates that the DJ shouldn't drink alcohol at your reception. After all, he's supposed to be a professional, and you're paying him to entertain your guests, not party with them. Unfortunately, DJs have been known to overindulge at weddings. So make it clear to your DJ that the bar is off-limits at your reception. If he argues with you, find another DJ.

✔ **Mileage:** You'll usually only encounter this extra fee if the DJ is traveling a long distance to spin at your wedding. Find out whether your DJ charges for mileage and how much he'll charge.

✔ **Additional time:** You may pay for additional time if the DJ also is handling your ceremony music and has to attend the rehearsal, for example.

✔ **The tip:** Tips are generally required for DJs. The average tip is $50 to $100. (See Chapter 2 for more on which vendors usually get tips.)

As with any vendor, make sure the terms of your contract are in writing before you hand over a deposit. Check out the later section "Asking the right questions" to find out more about deposits.

Hiring a band

Bands are generally more expensive than DJs; hourly rates can easily range from $450 to $750. As with DJs, though, actual rates vary widely, particularly in large metropolitan areas, which can support more live bands. So make sure you do your research before settling on a band.

The bandleader should be able to act as emcee for your reception, the same way a DJ does. So personality matters. Even if you're familiar with the band, make a point of interviewing the leader in person so you can decide whether his style meshes with yours. (The later section "Asking the right questions" provides some tips for successfully interviewing the bandleader.)

Some bands may try to impress you with slick music videos. But keep in mind that the skills required for making a high-quality video don't necessarily translate into a good live performance. If you haven't heard the band in person, ask for an audition. Or ask for a video of the band actually performing at a wedding; raw, unedited footage gives you the truest sense of how the band acts and sounds in front of a live audience.

In the upcoming sections, I help you determine the type of band music you'd like to have at your reception, and I also tell you what's included in an average wedding band package.

Getting the sound you want

Cover bands, which typically play a variety of music from a variety of artists, are the most popular for weddings. Some cover bands specialize in certain types of music, such as '80s tunes or country music. Others have a more general repertoire and play everything from Nat King Cole to Carrie Underwood.

Specialty bands can really bring a theme wedding to life. A calypso band is a great choice for a beach wedding, for example. A jazz trio, a swing band, or a Big Band group can provide just the right musical ambience for a cocktail reception. And karaoke bands are increasingly popular for weddings, because guests get to choose songs and serenade the newlyweds.

Keep your guests in mind when deciding on a particular style of music. If your friends and family don't even sing in the shower, a karaoke band probably isn't the best choice for a fun, memorable reception. Similarly, if most of your guests are into current music, a 1950s cover band will likely flop, too.

Knowing what's included — and what's not

Wedding band packages may vary a great deal, so it's important to understand what the quoted price includes and what you have to pay extra for. In this section, I give you a general idea of what is and isn't covered, but be sure to check with your prospective band before signing anything.

The package price for the average wedding band will likely cover

- ✔ At least one consultation to go over your music list and other details

- ✔ The musicians' playing time (excluding overtime)

- ✔ Amplifiers and other equipment

- ✔ Sheet music

- ✔ Emcee services (including microphone and loudspeaker)

- ✔ Setup and tear-down time

Even though setup and tear-down is usually included in the price, you may be charged extra if your reception site presents significant extra labor — if the band members have to carry their instruments and equipment up several flights of stairs or across the equivalent of a football field, for example. Be sure to discuss any potential setup issues at your first meeting to avoid an unexpected expense later.

The list of extras — which come with additional price tags — may include the following:

✔ Overtime fees (which may be charged if you want the band to play for five hours instead of the standard four, or if your reception goes past the closing time specified in your contract)

✔ Meals and drinks for band members

✔ Backdrops or stage lighting

✔ Additional microphones for karaoke, toasts, and so on

Make sure you have the contract details in writing before you give the band a deposit.

Asking the right questions

If you're like most people, your wedding is the only occasion when you'll hire a DJ or a band. Your lack of experience in this department can make interviewing candidates a little intimidating. But if you know what questions to ask, you can feel more confident that the entertainer you select will deliver what you want — and what you expect — for the price that fits your budget.

Here are some things you need to know, whether you're interviewing DJs or live bands:

✔ **Who will actually be performing at my reception?** If you're going through an agent or company for DJ services, make sure you get to speak with the DJ who will be at your reception, and ask whether that person is guaranteed to be there. For bands, ask which band members will be at your reception, and, of course, whether they're guaranteed to be there.

DJs sometimes bring assistants, and the typical wedding band has five members, so be sure to budget for all of them to be included in your meal count for the caterer.

✔ **Do you take breaks during the evening?** DJs don't usually take breaks, but bands typically split a four-hour reception into three sets, with roughly 15-minute breaks in between. If a band or DJ does take breaks, find out whether they provide recorded music (and the equipment to play it) during those breaks. Experienced pros provide recorded music during breaks because they know that guests tend to leave when the music stops. If your candidate doesn't provide break music, I suggest looking elsewhere.

✔ **What kind of experience do you have?** Ask how long the DJ or band has been performing at weddings and how many weddings they do in a typical year. Lack of experience isn't necessarily a deal-breaker, but your reception may not flow quite as seamlessly as it would with a seasoned pro.

✔ **What was your favorite wedding gig like?** This question gives you a chance to find out what a DJ or band really enjoys about doing weddings and provides a natural springboard to talking about what you do and don't want for your reception. This type of chat is an easy way to gauge whether this performer is a good fit for you.

✔ **When and how would you go over the details of my reception?** The DJ or bandleader should meet with you a couple weeks before your wedding to confirm your music list, the roll of people to be announced, your expected toasts, and the special moments you've chosen, such as the cake cutting and special dances. You can meet in person or talk over the phone, but you may prefer the face-to-face meeting if your instructions are complicated or if you have more questions. This final meeting should be included in the quoted price.

✔ **Have you performed at my reception site?** If the DJ or band isn't familiar with the site, ask for a list of setup requirements; you can then consult with the venue to find out what it provides. This question opens the discussion to any special needs the DJ or band may have, such as extension cords for outdoor venues or hand trucks for moving equipment over long distances.

✔ **Do you provide any additional services?** Some DJ companies offer slide shows, video services, and even live video monitoring of the dance floor and moments like the cake cutting. These services typically cost extra, so make sure you know what the fees are before you sign a contract.

✔ **Do you have insurance?** Professionals should always carry insurance that covers accidents involving themselves and others. For instance, find out who's responsible for medical bills and other damages if the performer is injured at your reception site. Similarly, discuss what happens if one of your guests trips on the DJ's power cord and injures himself.

✔ **How much of a deposit do you require, and when does it have to be paid?** Most DJs and bands ask for a 50 percent deposit. Few will hold the date unless you put down a deposit — especially if your wedding date is at the height of wedding season. Be sure to find out whether deposits are refundable. Policies on this vary, and the closer you get to the wedding date, the less likely you are to get the full deposit back.

If you like a DJ or band but aren't quite ready to put down a deposit, ask whether you can have "right of first refusal" for your wedding day. That way, if someone else wants to book the same day and time, the DJ or bandleader will call you and ask whether you're still interested. If you are, you have to pay the deposit; if not, you just say, "No, thank you," and the DJ or band can then book the other client.

✔ **What happens if you don't show up?** This may sound like a rude question, but it's a vital one. You want to find out whether the DJ will provide a replacement if she gets sick, or whether the band has a backup in case a member is injured in an accident. And, last but not least, if somebody just doesn't show (a horrifying thought, I know, but it does happen), who should you contact and what happens to your deposit?

Pay attention to the questions the DJ or bandleader asks you, too. Pros will want to make sure they understand your tastes and desires; they'll make an effort to learn a little about you and your fiancé(e). Candidates who seem more interested in telling you what they play or reminding you of what a great deal you're getting may disappoint you on your big day.

After you get the answers to the questions in the preceding list, ask for a detailed written estimate that spells out what's included in the fee, the deposit policies, and any additional services you may be charged for, such as overtime, mileage, extra setup costs, and so on. And, of course, be sure all this information is included — along with specific dates and times — in any contract you sign.

Trimming Entertainment Costs

Entertainment is an important expense that you don't want to scrimp on, but that doesn't mean you can't save a little cash along the way. In this section, I show you how your wedding date and time can save you big bucks, and I also provide some other tips for cutting your entertainment costs.

Choosing a budget-friendly wedding date and time

Like anything else wedding-related, the easiest way to cut your entertainment expenses is to get married at an off-peak time: a weekday afternoon or evening, a Saturday in November or January, or a Sunday in June. (See Chapter 3 for more information on selecting an off-peak time for your wedding.)

Even DJs and bands that do a lot of weddings often perform at other functions, too, so you may run into nonwedding conflicts with your date. High-demand times for these entertainers include the winter holiday season, graduation parties in June and July, and social dances in the fall and spring. Friday and Saturday nights are, naturally, the most likely to be booked first.

The time of your reception matters, too. Many DJs and bands book two events on high-demand days: one in the afternoon and one in the evening. Afternoon events typically end by 5 p.m., and evening events usually don't start until 7 p.m. The time in between allows the performer to move and reset his equipment.

Events that end later than 5 p.m. or begin earlier than 7 p.m. are called *crossovers,* and they can be significantly more expensive than a typical afternoon or evening gig. It makes sense from the performer's point of view, because if you plan to end your reception at 7 p.m. or start at 5 p.m., you eliminate the DJ's or band's ability to book another paying gig that day. So it's only fair that you compensate the performer, at least partially, for that lost potential income. You can save yourself the extra expense by scheduling your reception to end by 5 p.m. or to start no earlier than 7 p.m.

Saving a bundle with some helpful hints

Beyond choosing a frugal wedding date and reception time (see the preceding section), you have several other options for keeping your entertainment expenses down. Here are a few:

- ✔ **Have your DJ or band do double duty.** Hiring one DJ or band for both the ceremony and the reception may save you some money in your overall budget, especially if you don't have a long gap between the two. Ask whether the band's singer is willing to be the soloist for your ceremony, or whether the DJ is willing to run the music for you. Find out what the extra service would cost, and then compare it to the cost of using separate services (including things like buying a gift for a relative or friend to sing at your ceremony).

  Some places of worship don't allow you to bring in outside music or musicians. Be sure to check with your ceremony site before building this potential savings into your budget.

- ✔ **Rent a sound system and enlist a friend to emcee.** You can rent equipment for around $300; the price likely will include a multidisc CD player, a mixer, two speakers, and a wireless microphone. To find a rental company, look under the Audio Visual Equipment category in the phone book.

If you decide to go this route, make sure the speakers are powerful enough to fill the space at your reception. Even though small speakers can put out wonderful sound, you may need extras to make the sound big enough for your reception hall. The rental company should be able to help you determine the number of speakers to use.

✔ **Rent a karaoke machine.** A package with all the bells and whistles — an extensive song list, several microphones, a projector and monitor so guests can sing along, and even tambourines — can cost less than $1,000 (including delivery fees) for a Saturday evening in big cities. Weekday prices usually are cheaper except during December, when holiday parties drive up demand. Ask a friend to emcee for the reception highlights and be in charge of the karaoke sign-up sheet.

To ensure variety and the best experience for your guests, a karaoke package should have a minimum of 5,000 songs to choose from.

✔ **Buy or rent an MP3 sound system.** This type of system is a great way to customize your music list and save money. You can rent a system for around $200 a day, or you can purchase one for around $750 — and have it to use in your newlywed home, to boot. Some of these systems work best in smaller rooms, but customers on review sites report using them for large outdoor events and being quite satisfied with the performance.

Creating a Party Atmosphere with Reception Decorations

Ask any seasoned party thrower and she'll tell you that there are three main ingredients to a great party: entertainment, which is covered earlier in this chapter; food and drink, which I discuss in Chapter 12; and décor, which is the focus of this section.

Depending on the site you choose, you may not need much in the way of decoration. But even if you intend to transform a plain meeting hall into an elegant party room, you can do it without straining your budget.

To get started, take some snapshots of your reception site and ask the site manager for a floor plan. These materials can help you decide where you want to focus your decorating and visualize how the site will look when you're done dressing it up. They also can help you identify decoration ideas that won't work as well.

In this section, I help you determine the best centerpieces and other decorations for your wedding reception.

Deciding on centerpieces

Floral centerpieces are the most common choice for wedding receptions (see Chapter 8), but they're by no means the only option. In fact, you have nearly unlimited alternatives that often are much less expensive — and more fun for you and your guests.

 If you choose floral centerpieces, keep costs down by opting for simple, smaller arrangements with a few in-season flowers and lots of greenery (which is usually less expensive than blooms). Figure 13-1 shows some floral centerpiece designs.

Figure 13-1: Some floral centerpiece options.

When it comes to centerpieces, keep in mind that it isn't how they look but how they affect your guests' experience that is important. Your wedding reception is a social occasion, and your guests want to talk and make eye contact with each other. A bulky centerpiece that blocks the line of sight across the table is awkward and irritating. Instead, go for something that won't stifle the "feast of reason and flow of soul."

Many reception halls provide centerpieces at no extra charge; they're often included in the setup fee. For example, the venue may provide you with centerpieces of mirrored tiles and tealights in frosted glass holders — a simple and elegant arrangement that doesn't interfere with guests' eye contact or conversation.

As noted earlier, centerpiece possibilities are virtually endless. The following sections represent just a few fun and inexpensive ideas that may fit both your vision and your budget. Figure 13-2 provides illustrations of some of these ideas.

Figure 13-2: Inexpensive centerpieces.

Going seasonal

You don't have to use a particular season as a theme throughout your wedding to make good use of seasonal items in your table decorations. For example, you can turn a simple glass bowl and a candle that matches your color scheme into several different centerpieces depending on the season. The following are just a few of the many options you have:

✔ **In the winter:** Fill the bowl with pine cones and a few sprigs of holly or mistletoe and then place the candle in the center.

✔ **In the fall:** Use the same display but choose small gourds and colored leaves or fall flowers like asters or mums instead of pine cones and holly.

✔ **In the summer:** Place your candle in the center and then fill the bowl with real or wax fruit. Lemons, limes, and oranges are especially colorful and summery.

✔ **In the spring:** Scatter colored glass stones or pastel-colored crepe streamers around your candle. Just be sure the candle won't burn down far enough to ignite the paper.

You can get most of these materials from your local craft or dollar store, and the total cost will be around $5 per centerpiece. Not bad!

Another option that you can adapt to any season: Wrap empty boxes in paper, ribbons, and bows that match or complement your wedding colors, and stack a few in the middle of each table.

Opting for edible arrangements

Edible centerpieces are gaining popularity, partly because they're different from the usual floral centerpiece, and partly because they can be much less expensive. Here are a few suggestions, but don't be afraid to let your imagination off the leash:

✔ **Give guests dessert up front.** Fill a tiered serving tray with mini cupcakes, fruit tarts, bite-sized pieces of cheesecake, cookies, or other sweets. You can do this in addition to or in lieu of a traditional wedding cake. Keep in mind that it may be cheaper to have sweet-filled centerpieces and a small wedding cake for cutting.

✔ **Make snacking easy.** Fill glass serving bowls (provided by your caterer or reception site, or purchased from your local dollar store) with candy or snack mix and colorful plastic scoops. Or have the caterer provide appetizer platters for each table.

This centerpiece idea could save you money by doubling as favors for your guests. Simply leave treat bags at each place setting and guests can dip up some goodies to take home. (See Chapter 17 for more fun and inexpensive favor ideas.)

✔ **Go for the at-home feel.** Make the food the centerpiece by asking the caterer to serve the meal family-style. Most caterers set condiments or serving chargers in the middle of the table for family-style serving. This serving style is a good way to promote conversation among your guests; it's difficult to remain silent when you're passing platters of food around the table.

Giving guests something to talk about

Many couples create photo collages for their receptions, showing themselves growing up and during their courtship. It's easy to
turn this idea into an unusual (and inexpensive) centerpiece by
creating photo pyramids. It's a great conversation starter for your
guests. For a broader personal touch, consider using photos of the
couples in your wedding party, including attendants, parents, and
grandparents.

Follow these steps to make your own photo pyramids:

1. **Make copies of the photos you want to use.**

   Office supply stores and retailers like Wal-Mart make
   copies for a few cents each.

2. **For each centerpiece, collect three boxes of different sizes.**

   The largest should be about the size of a shoe box. The
   smallest should be about the size of a wristwatch box — no
   smaller, because smaller boxes won't provide enough support for the photos.

3. **Cover each box with wrapping paper or fabric that
   complements your color scheme. Then stack the covered
   boxes three high, with the largest at the base and the
   smallest at the top.**

   Glue or tape the boxes together so they don't move.

4. **Glue or tape your photos to posterboard that's cut to fit
   the photo.**

   Placing your photos on the posterboard helps to prevent
   the photos from curling and sagging, so don't skip this
   seemingly unnecessary step.

5. **Arrange the photos around the tiers formed by the
   stacked boxes, and tape or glue them in place so they
   don't fall off.**

   If you want, you can place the photo pyramids on Lazy
   Susans to allow guests to easily look at all the pictures. You
   can get plastic Lazy Susans at your local dollar or discount
   store and dress them up with ribbon or with the same
   wrapping paper or fabric you use for the boxes.

If photo pyramids seem like too much effort, try this adaptation:
Buy three 8 x 10 photo frames per table, fill them with your favorite
prints, and arrange them in a triangle in the middle of the table.
You can get inexpensive frames at your local dollar store. To add
flair and texture, purchase a mix of styles. Also consider using multiple smaller prints in the frames.

Putting favors in the center spot

Many couples save money by having their favors do double duty as centerpieces. Here are a couple quick ideas:

- ✔ Use clay flower pots (paint them with your wedding colors), rocks, and branches to create "favor trees." Then you can hang your favors on the branches with ribbon or fishing line. Get artificial dried branches, as well as floral foam to secure them, at your local craft store.

- ✔ Place your favors around a grouping of pillar candles of varying heights.

- ✔ Buy glass cake plates from your local dollar store and arrange the favors on them; drape ribbons or beads over and around the cake plate to add color.

Flip to Chapter 17 for ideas on inexpensive favors and more ways to make them do double duty as part of your décor.

Choosing other decorations

Centerpieces aren't the only decorations you want for your reception. You also want to consider sprucing up the entryway, the cake and gift tables, the guest book table, and perhaps even the walls and ceilings, depending on the existing decoration of the venue.

Here are some inexpensive options to dress up your venue:

- ✔ **Balloons:** Choose balloons that go with your color scheme, and then group them in bunches at the corners of your gift and cake tables. You can string a series of balloons along the front of your head table, too, instead of having a floral spray.

- ✔ **Ribbons, bows, and streamers:** Bring out your wedding colors by draping coordinating ribbons, bows, or crepe streamers along table tops or around the edges of tables.

- ✔ **Miniature lights:** If your venue has lots of pillars, railings, or potted plants, create a festive atmosphere by stringing them with miniature lights. Clear lights go with any color scheme, but you also can find them in solid colors, too. Wrap them in lengths of tulle from your local craft or fabric store.

If your timeline allows, shop for miniature lights immediately after Christmas. At this time, you probably can get them for half or a quarter of the regular price. If that won't work for your schedule, ask friends and family if they have lights you can use.

What about the walls and ceiling? If your site is a reception hall, don't worry about dressing up the perimeter; your guests will be focused on the food and entertainment and probably won't even notice if you drape the chandeliers with ivory cloth that matches your gown.

Chair bows and covers are lovely accents, but they're a lot more expensive than you may think. Many reception halls charge you $2 to $3 for the covers, plus another per-chair fee for ironing and installing them. If you're planning on 100 guests, you could easily spend $500 or more just on chair covers, which may not fit well in your budget or your list of priorities.

If your site is less upscale, though — say a park pavilion or a meeting room — you may want to consider ways to soften fluorescent lights or cover wall decorations that can't be moved (such as trophy cases and portraits of club leaders). Some sites provide *pipe and drape* — a system of poles and cloth — for an additional fee (although you may not have a choice of drape colors). You may be able to rent pipe and drape from another vendor as well. You can attach balloons, ribbons, and streamers to the drape if you feel as if it needs dressing up.

Soften harsh fluorescent lighting by attaching cloth or closely grouped streamers to the overhead fixtures. Be sure to let the material sag several inches below the lights; this creates a pretty draping effect and prevents the material from getting too hot.

Chapter 14

Making the Most of Prewedding and Postwedding Events

*W*ith all the focus on the ceremony and reception, it's easy to forget that your wedding encompasses a whole collection of activities. The rehearsal dinner, of course, is near the top of that list, but you may end up planning several other events as well. For instance, you and your intended may want to have special get-togethers for your respective attendants, parents, and siblings. You also may want to invite family and guests to a day-after gathering — a great way to spend a little more time with people you may not see very often. And you may want to travel back to your hometown a few months after the wedding to see the people who didn't attend.

None of these functions is free, naturally. But in this chapter, I share tips for stretching your wedding budget to include these expenses.

Keeping Costs Down for the Rehearsal Dinner

Traditionally, the groom's family pays for the rehearsal dinner — a get-together the evening before the wedding for the bride's and groom's immediate families, attendants and their spouses or

significant others, and others integrally involved in the ceremony
(such as the officiant, soloist, or readers, if they're friends or relatives). These days, though, the bride and groom are just as likely
to pay for the rehearsal dinner, and keeping these expenses under
control is a vital part of sticking to your wedding budget.

Like your wedding and reception, your rehearsal dinner can be
as lavish and expensive (or as modest and inexpensive) as you
want. Costs range from $10 per person or less to as high as $250
per person, or even more. Your cost depends on three things: the
number of guests, the location, and the menu.

Considering the guest list

Depending on the size of your families and wedding party, you can
easily have 30 or more people at your rehearsal dinner. At $10 a
head, you're looking at a $300 bill, and when money is tight, that
$300 may as well be $3,000.

Just as it's tempting to invite everyone you've ever considered a
friend to your wedding, you may be inclined to include everyone
who's in town to your rehearsal dinner. But if Cousin Millie and
Uncle Frank aren't part of the actual ceremony, consider leaving
them off the guest list for this event. Limit the invitees to immediate family — parents, siblings, and perhaps grandparents — and
those who have a role to play in the ceremony (including the officiant, if appropriate). See "Feting Out-of-Town Guests," later in this
chapter, for ideas on getting together with guests who won't attend
the rehearsal dinner.

Keep attendance from ballooning by issuing invitations to those
who should be at your rehearsal dinner. If it isn't a formal affair,
your invitations don't have to be formal; a verbal or e-mail invitation is enough. If you want to send professionally printed invitations, check whether your printer offers a discount; some do when
you order rehearsal dinner invitations along with your wedding
invitations.

Choosing a location

The least expensive option is to host your rehearsal dinner at
home — either your home or, if you don't have room for a hefty
crowd, the home of a friend or relative. In warm weather, you can
set up a party tent in the backyard and decorate it with Japanese
lanterns or party lights and balloons.

If you don't have enough outdoor space, look into renting a pavilion at a local park. Rental fees usually are quite reasonable — often $50 or less — and you may even get your deposit back if you clean up the site after the dinner.

Another option is to rent a clubhouse. Apartment complexes and mobile home parks often have meeting or party rooms that tenants can reserve for a small — often refundable — deposit; if you don't have access to one yourself, see if any local friends or relatives can reserve such a facility. Or you may be able to use facilities at your church or local firehouse.

Restaurants are, naturally, the most expensive sites for rehearsal dinners. Even if you choose a relatively inexpensive buffet, the cost per person can easily top $20. See the next section, "Planning the menu," for tips on keeping costs down if you decide to hold your rehearsal dinner at a restaurant.

Don't obsess about (or spend money on) floral decorations or flashy centerpieces for the rehearsal dinner. If you want to dress up a clubhouse or meeting room, use inexpensive balloons and streamers. The rehearsal dinner is a much less formal affair than your wedding, so it doesn't require the same level of decorative detail.

Planning the menu

Food and drink are the major expenses for a rehearsal dinner. If you're having the event in a home or rented space rather than in a restaurant, you can keep those costs low by planning a simple menu. Some inexpensive options include the following:

- ✔ A cookout with burgers, hot dogs, chips, salads, soda, and beer
- ✔ An Italian buffet with lasagna, breadsticks, salad, soda, and Chianti
- ✔ A pizza party
- ✔ An informal cocktail party with hors d'oeuvres, soda, beer, and wine
- ✔ A potluck dinner (ask only in-town guests to bring a dish; out-of-town guests can bring wine or soda if they want)

Does a local friend or relative make a fabulous signature dish? Ask him to cater your rehearsal dinner in lieu of buying a traditional wedding gift. For our backyard rehearsal dinner, my fiancé's sister and brother-in-law provided their famous barbequed chicken, and his mother made her signature macaroni and potato salads. We supplied beverages, fresh veggies and dip, and all the tableware, for less than $100.

Bachelor and bachelorette parties

Traditionally, the honor attendants (best man and maid or matron of honor) organize bachelor/bachelorette parties and either pay for the party themselves or arrange for the rest of the bridal party to chip in. When funds are tight, though, it isn't uncommon for everyone — including the bride and groom — to pay their own way. If you're in this situation, remember to budget for your last outing with your pals.

Remember, too, that you don't have to have a stereotypical final fling. Maybe you and your buddies would rather play a round of golf or spend an evening watching your favorite movies together, which may be more meaningful and easier on everyone's wallet.

Don't feel bad if you decide not to hire a professional caterer for your rehearsal dinner. Out-of-town guests especially may appreciate a home-cooked meal; they'll be eating plenty of restaurant food during their stay.

If you choose to have your rehearsal dinner at a restaurant (or to bring a caterer to your home or rented dining space), you can keep costs down by simplifying the menu. Choose a buffet instead of a sit-down dinner, limit (or eliminate) alcohol service, and skip extras like hors d'oeuvres. Opt for self-serve platters of cookies or brownies for dessert.

 When you investigate restaurant locations for your rehearsal dinner, find out whether the site charges any fees in addition to the food. Most restaurants add a gratuity of around 20 percent for large groups. Some charge a rental fee for private dining rooms, and some require a minimum food bill that you pay regardless of how many people actually attend your dinner.

Hosting Gatherings for Your Wedding Party

Some religious traditions stipulate that men and women have separate wedding-party get-togethers. However, even many nonreligous couples find that segregated activities help them recharge and refocus in the hours leading up to the wedding.

In this section, I offer some ideas for getting the women and men in your wedding party together — separately.

Bridal brunch

Bridal party brunches — hosted by the bride on her wedding day — are popular in some circles. A brunch is a nice way for the bride to relax with her attendants and female family members in the midst of the hectic wedding day schedule. It's also an opportunity for the bride to thank her attendants and relatives for their wedding help and to present them with gifts before the ceremony.

Such brunches can be expensive. Some wedding experts insist that the bridal brunch be an elegant affair, with elegant decorations and elegant food in an elegant setting. A champagne brunch at the best restaurant in town can easily run $30 or more per person. Add in decorations and perhaps transportation and your brunch bill can begin to rival costs for the rehearsal dinner.

Of course, you don't have to get all fancy to have a good time with your bridesmaids. Consider these alternatives to an upscale brunch:

- **A spa party:** See Chapter 5 for more on this idea.
- **A casual lunch the day before the wedding:** You also can dine the day of, if you're having an evening ceremony.
- **A sleepover party the night before your wedding:** This sleepover can double as your bachelorette party.

If you prefer the idea of a bridal brunch, go for a more casual feel to minimize costs. Host it at your home or a friend's or relative's house. Set out a selection of pastries and fresh fruit and serve coffee, tea, and juice. If you want to include alcohol, make pitchers of mimosas (orange juice and champagne) or bloody marys. You can use a less expensive champagne brand for the mimosas because it'll be mixed with the orange juice.

Groom get-together

What about the guys? Although their traditional get-together is the bachelor party, some grooms like to plan a special wedding-weekend outing with their buddies, father, and father-in-law-to-be — a round of golf, perhaps, a game of hoops at the park, or some other activity that helps everyone relax and puts the stresses of wedding planning aside for a few hours.

If you want to arrange this kind of activity for the male members of your wedding party and your respective families, etiquette dictates that you pay for it (just as etiquette dictates that the bride pay for the brunch for her half of the wedding party). As with the bride's brunch, though, you can choose to host a less expensive guys' outing — say, lunch at your favorite sports bar. If funds are especially tight, you may opt to worry less about etiquette; tell the guys how much the planned activity costs and give them the option of declining.

Any of the activities in this section can double as a bachelor party — which may be an attractive option if money and time are scarce.

Feting Out-of-Town Guests

When people travel to your wedding, it's natural to feel an obligation to entertain them. This is one reason that so many couples end up spending a small fortune on the rehearsal dinner: They expand the guest list to include all their out-of-town guests rather than just the wedding party and immediate family.

You have other options to include these important people — as well as local guests — and these options can be much less expensive than a full-fledged party. Consider the following:

- ✔ **Arrange activities for the day before or the day of the wedding.** If time allows, plan a softball game, a board game party, or some other inclusive activity. Make attendance optional; your guests may have other ideas for their free time. And keep the formality dial at 0; remember that your wedding is still the main event.

- ✔ **Invite them for coffee and dessert after the rehearsal dinner.** This gives you a chance to socialize without all the commotion of your reception and keeps food and beverage costs on a short leash. It also provides a nice balance between time with your immediate family and the wedding party and time with friends and family who you may not see often.

- ✔ **Host a day-after brunch or picnic.** Depending on travel arrangements (yours and your guests'), a next-day brunch or picnic may be the perfect way to wind down your wedding weekend. This should be a casual affair — comfortable clothes, not-too-fancy food, and a relaxed atmosphere. (See the nearby sidebar, "Sample day-after menus," for inexpensive food ideas.) Limit spending for this function to no more than $100; after all, it's an extra, not the main event.

  Make the day-after event a gift-opening get-together for all who want to attend. Lots of guests enjoy seeing the happy couple open their gifts, and the activity provides natural conversation starters. Ask your honor attendant or a family member to keep a list of the gifts you receive and who they came from; this is essential when it's time to write thank-you notes.

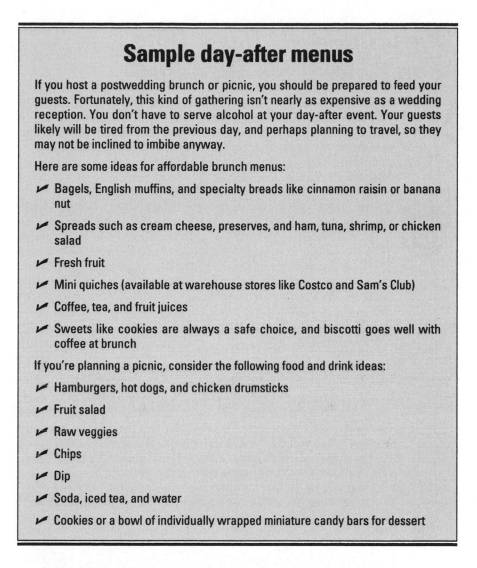

Sample day-after menus

If you host a postwedding brunch or picnic, you should be prepared to feed your guests. Fortunately, this kind of gathering isn't nearly as expensive as a wedding reception. You don't have to serve alcohol at your day-after event. Your guests likely will be tired from the previous day, and perhaps planning to travel, so they may not be inclined to imbibe anyway.

Here are some ideas for affordable brunch menus:

- Bagels, English muffins, and specialty breads like cinnamon raisin or banana nut

- Spreads such as cream cheese, preserves, and ham, tuna, shrimp, or chicken salad

- Fresh fruit

- Mini quiches (available at warehouse stores like Costco and Sam's Club)

- Coffee, tea, and fruit juices

- Sweets like cookies are always a safe choice, and biscotti goes well with coffee at brunch

If you're planning a picnic, consider the following food and drink ideas:

- Hamburgers, hot dogs, and chicken drumsticks

- Fruit salad

- Raw veggies

- Chips

- Dip

- Soda, iced tea, and water

- Cookies or a bowl of individually wrapped miniature candy bars for dessert

Tell your guests as soon as possible about any extracurricular activities on your wedding weekend so they can make their travel arrangements accordingly. You don't want to spend the next few years hearing great-aunt Sally lament that she would have loved to attend your gift-opening get-together if only she had known about it in advance.

Partying with Those Who Can't Make the Wedding

Unless you're very fortunate, not everyone you invite will attend your wedding. This is especially true if guests have to travel a long distance, or if your wedding is on a high-traffic weekend like Memorial Day or another holiday. Hosting a postwedding get-together is a great way to celebrate with those guests who were unable to attend your wedding.

If your budget limits your dream wedding to only a few dozen guests, a postwedding celebration can be the perfect way to include all those you had to leave off your guest list. Host a party after you return from your honeymoon (or a few weeks after your wedding, if you delay or skip the honeymoon) and invite those who didn't make the cut for the actual wedding. Call it a housewarming party or a newlywed party — whatever you like. Just remember to follow two etiquette rules: Don't expect your guests to bring gifts (you didn't invite them to the wedding, after all), and don't decorate in a wedding theme.

Even if you don't get married in your hometown, you still can plan to celebrate with your hometown friends. Ask one of those friends to host a cocktail reception a few months after your wedding, or plan a get-together at a local restaurant. This takes a little extra effort and planning, of course, but you'll avoid the wedding markup. Plus, you don't have to include this in your wedding budget, because you'll have those additional months to save for it (and for your own travel expenses, of course).

If you send out invitations to a postwedding get-together, make it clear that you don't expect your guests to give you gifts. A simple "No gifts, please" in the corner of the invitation will suffice. Chances are, if you invited them to your wedding, they already sent a gift. And those you didn't invite to the wedding may view your postnuptial invitation as a crass grab for more wedding loot.

Chapter 15

Honeymooning in Style — and in the Black

In This Chapter
- Factoring the honeymoon into your budget
- Finding honeymoon sites that won't break the bank
- Adjusting your plans to save money

The honeymoon industry, although puny by general wedding industry standards, takes in about $8 billion a year. According to The Wedding Report (www.theweddingreport.com), an industry analysis Web site, 99 percent of marrying couples take a honeymoon, and they spend an average of $3,800 — three times more than the average for any other vacation. Honeymoon expenses account for about 14 percent of the average $20,000 wedding budget.

Of course, you don't have to spend that much to have a super honeymoon. In fact, even if you choose an overseas location, you can still keep your honeymoon costs in check. The first step is establishing a budget for your getaway. After you know how much you want to spend, you can begin researching locations that fit your budget. Then you're ready for the fun part: tweaking your plans to get the most value for your dollar.

Thinking About the Kind of Honeymoon You Want

Just as you envision the kind of wedding you want, draw up a mental picture of how you want to spend your postnuptial getaway. Do you want to be pampered on a cruise or at a full-service tropical resort? Or would you and your new spouse prefer to hop in the car and go on your ultimate road trip? Maybe you're more interested in mountain biking than in Mayan ruins, or maybe a week in Venice or Prague appeals to you more than sunbathing on a Caribbean beach.

The point is that there's no such thing as a "proper" honeymoon. The best honeymoon is the one that you and your sweetie will enjoy without overdrawing your bank accounts or overextending your credit limits. In the following sections, I explore some common honeymoon options, including the popular cruise or resort vacation and some lesser-known alternatives.

Saving money on cruises and resorts

All-inclusive packages are becoming more and more popular with honeymooners, because, in theory, you know upfront exactly how much lodging, food, beverages, and entertainment are going to cost. Having that all-inclusive figure at your fingertips can make budgeting easier.

But the term "all-inclusive" is, at best, elastic. At some resorts, the all-inclusive rate does indeed cover your room, all meals, your bar tab, snacks at the poolside bar, and the bands and other entertainers who perform around the resort. Many resorts even offer free use of nonmotorized land and water vehicles like bicycles and kayaks. Even at these resorts, though, you'll pay extra to rent a personal watercraft or motorized scooter, and some resorts charge extra if you want to have dinner at their specialty restaurants. Most resorts also charge you if you fail to return the "free" beach towel it provides. (And, of course, all-inclusive doesn't include purchases at the resort's convenience store or gift shop.)

At other resorts, the all-inclusive label doesn't cover your entire bar tab. It may only cover domestic beers, wines, and liquors. And remember that when you're in a foreign country, your native beer is imported beer.

Cruises don't typically use the all-inclusive label, but that doesn't stop many travelers from experiencing sticker shock when they board their ship. Most cruise lines charge for alcoholic beverages; only soft drinks, coffee, tea, juice, and milk are included in your cabin rate. On many ships, the charge for a drink includes an automatic tip for the bartender or server, too. You'll also be charged a daily room-cleaning fee, typically $10 per person — or $140 for a seven-day cruise for the two of you.

Whether you're at a land-based resort or on a cruise ship, you'll pay extra for *excursions* — tours or activities in the area you're visiting. Even if you decide to explore on your own, be sure to factor certain excursion expenses — such as cab or bus fare, car rental, off-site meals, and souvenirs — into your travel budget.

Even though cruise lines and many resorts can book excursions for you, you may save money by making reservations on your own. Check the excursions available on your cruise or at your resort, and then search the Internet to find the Web sites of the companies that provide the excursions. Check the companies' listed prices against the prices that the cruise line or resort offers; then you can go with the least expensive alternative.

Also look into packages that combine bus tours, for example, and museum passes. You may not always save money with these deals, but you can save a lot of time, especially at popular sites; tour bus companies often arrange with sites to get their passengers in ahead of "walk-ups."

Considering hotels, condos, and other alternatives

Weeklong cruises and resort stays may be stereotypical honeymoon vacations, but they are by no means the only way to travel. Here are some less costly options to think about:

- ✔ **Book a regular hotel instead of a room at a resort.** Some hotels offer complimentary breakfast, so you only have to budget for two meals a day instead of three; depending on where you go and what kinds of eateries you prefer, you can lunch and even dine inexpensively. However, you also have to budget for other expenses — such as bike rentals, use of the beach, and, naturally, drinks (even soda) — that are typically included in the room rate at all-inclusive resorts.

- ✔ **Rent an apartment or condo instead of staying at a hotel.** A week's rent at a beachfront condo may cost less than a standard room in a resort. Cost aside, with a condo you also get a sense of privacy and space that hotels lack. And because you'll likely have a kitchen, you can save money on meals, too, by cooking breakfast, lunch, and even romantic dinners yourself.

  Check out www.vacationrentals.com for apartments, condos, and even houses in popular vacation spots.

- ✔ **Stay at a campground.** Some campgrounds have cabins, so you don't even need your own tent or RV. Cabins also are more fun for those couples who don't like to rough it in a tent with the bugs and other critters.

- ✔ **Look for a getaway close to home.** Destinations within a six- to eight-hour drive can be a lot cheaper than a cross-country or international location simply because transportation is less expensive. Pull out the atlas and see what's in your region that you and your sweetie would like to see.

✔ **Check out bed-and-breakfast inns.** B-and-Bs tend to be more personal — and often more lavishly furnished — than hotels, and prices often are comparable to other local hotels. Many B-and-Bs are in historic buildings, which adds to their charm.

Budgeting for Your Postwedding Getaway

Unfortunately, honeymoons, like weddings, don't pay for themselves. And, like weddings, you can easily be blindsided by unanticipated expenses. In this section, I point out some common, but often overlooked, expenses that you need to budget for as well as tips on saving for your honeymoon — including the relatively new phenomenon of honeymoon registries.

Covering all your travel expenses

The typical honeymoon costs go beyond just the destination (and the transportation to get there). If you're like most soon-to-be-married couples, you probably intend to purchase new clothes, luggage, and incidentals like bathing suits, sunglasses, and sunscreen for your honeymoon. You may even buy a new camera or video camera.

How much do these purchases add to your honeymoon costs? If you and your spouse-to-be are true to the averages, you'll likely spend more than $1,600 before you even buy your airline tickets and hotel room or purchase that weeklong cruise.

One way to avoid some of these expenses is to add items such as luggage and cameras to your wedding registry — just be sure you make time to open your gifts before you leave on your trip. You also can register for gift cards at your favorite clothing stores. (However, if you leave for your honeymoon immediately after your wedding, you probably won't have time to use those gift cards to buy honeymoon attire.)

When you're figuring out how much you can or want to spend on your postnuptial trip, make sure you factor in *all* the expenses you're likely to have, including activities, airfare, entertainment, transportation, lodging, meals, passports, visas, vaccinations, and incidentals (souvenirs, toiletries, snacks, tips, clothes, and so on).

Use the "Budget Cruncher" worksheet at Honeymooner's Review Guide (`www.honeymoonersreviewguide.com/planning/Budget_Cruncherpdf.pdf`) to make sure you've covered all your expenses. You can print the blank form as often as you like to compare costs for different honeymoon destinations.

Saving for the trip

The best way to make sure you have enough money for your dream honeymoon is to open a honeymoon savings account as soon as you get engaged. The average engagement lasts 16 months, so if each of you contributes $100 a month to the honeymoon account, you'll have $3,200 saved (plus any interest) by the time you're ready to leave. If you're both confident that you can stick to your savings plan, you can start looking for destinations that fit your budget.

If you don't have enough room in your monthly budget to set aside a specific amount for your honeymoon, consider "giving up" certain nonessentials (brown-bag your lunch, for example, or skip that afternoon latte) for the months leading up to your honeymoon; reassessing your wedding priorities and budget to come up with honeymoon funds; or scaling back your honeymoon plans to something more affordable — perhaps a weekend at a nearby bed-and-breakfast instead of a week in Cancun. And, if you like, you can begin planning (and saving for) a more spectacular trip for your first anniversary.

Some couples pay for their honeymoon with credit cards. I'm not a big fan of this option, because you can easily end up paying thousands more in interest if you don't pay the cards off promptly. However, if you're expecting a bonus from your job or some other one-time payment, or if your household budget allows you to pay off your honeymoon charges within 3, 6, or 12 months, using a credit card may work for you. If possible, use a card that offers cash back on all purchases (the most useful kind of reward card) or one that has a low interest rate.

Even if you decide to save so you can pay for your honeymoon in cash, you'll probably end up putting at least some expenses — especially booking fees or reservation deposits — on a credit card. The trick is to make sure you include any credit card charges in your overall budget. In other words, charging your $1,000 resort bill to your credit card means you have to reserve $1,000 of your honeymoon money to pay off that charge — not that you have an extra $1,000 spending cash for the trip.

Registering for your honeymoon

A relatively new trend in the wedding industry is *honeymoon registries*. Instead of giving you traditional gifts from a traditional registry, guests can use a honeymoon registry to pay for part of your postnuptial trip. They may pay one night's stay in the hotel, for example, or provide money toward airfare. Most sites convert these gifts into points or credits that you can use toward your trip.

Some of these registries are available through hotel and resort chains. Several hotels cover their registry programs on their own Web sites. Others set up their honeymoon registries through Weddingchannel.com (`weddings.weddingchannel.com/default.aspx?MsdVisit=1`).

Here are a couple of catches to honeymoon registries that you need to be aware of:

- ✔ **Fees:** All honeymoon registry sites charge some sort of fee, either to the registering couple or to those who purchase gifts through the site. Some charge registering couples a percentage of the value of gifts others buy for them through the site. Others charge a flat rate to set up the registry (say, $150 or so), and then charge gift-givers an additional percentage fee.

- ✔ **Deposits:** Unless you're planning to hold off on your honeymoon until well after your wedding is over (see "Delaying your honeymoon" later in this chapter), you'll have to pay for deposits and any other charges yourselves and then wait to see whether your guests choose to ante up for honeymoon costs.

  Most couples get a lot less than they expect in both cash gifts and these relatively new honeymoon gifts. So be prepared to pay for the honeymoon yourselves; then, if you do receive gifts to offset those costs, you'll be ahead of the game.

- ✔ **Expiration dates:** On some sites, registry credits or points expire. For example, at this writing, one hotel's credits are only good for two years from the date of purchase.

To avoid any of these surprises, make sure you know how a registry works, including all costs, expiration dates, and limitations, before you sign up. Be sure to explain to your wedding guests how the registry works, too, including any extra fees they may incur. Even though it's tacky to include registry information in your wedding invitations, you can post links to your gift registries on your wedding Web site, along with a brief description of the registry and, if necessary, instructions on how to use it.

Researching Honeymoon Spots with Cost in Mind

Being on a budget doesn't mean you can't have a wonderful honeymoon. There are lots of romantic getaways that won't flatten your wallet. And the Internet has made deals easy to find — although you may want to consult a travel agent, too.

Turning your Internet know-how into travel savings

You can visit countless travel sites online, including popular ones like Expedia (www.expedia.com) and Travelocity (www.travelocity.com). Most travel sites have links to the airlines, hotels, resorts, and cruise lines they list. Be sure to use these links to complete your research. Why? An airline site may offer a better price than the travel site, or it may give you an idea of how much you'd save by going through a particular travel site.

Be sure to check out reviews of any vacation spot you're considering — either on the company's own site or on sites like Trip Advisor (www.tripadvisor.com) or Virtual Tourist (www.virtualtourist.com). Pay attention to the negative comments and weigh them against the positive ones. If a place gets only so-so reviews overall, you may be happier if you continue your search. No matter how inexpensive a vacation spot is, you aren't getting a good deal if your experience is miserable.

Enlisting a travel agent

The reports of the death of travel agents, to borrow from Mark Twain, have been greatly exaggerated. Certainly the Internet has made agents' jobs more challenging, but sometimes you just can't find a substitute for a live, breathing, and talking person who's experienced in all the aspects of travel.

Besides knowing what kind of documentation and vaccines you need when you're going overseas, a good travel agent may know of special deals that aren't available online. Plus, he may have been to the place you're planning to visit and can give you valuable info about what to really expect. And when you know what to expect, you can plan and budget better — and thus save some bucks.

Start your search for the perfect honeymoon spot online with the preceding section, and then make an appointment with a travel agent to see whether you can get a better deal — or get the inside scoop on places you're considering. If you know what you'll be charged online, you can better judge the prices an agent will quote. You don't have to pay for the appointment or the services that an agent provides; travel agents are paid by the airlines, hotels, and other travel-related companies they book (not by the people who make reservations through them).

Tweaking Your Plans for Value

You can stretch your honeymoon dollars without giving up the things you really want. Honest! The first, and most obvious, tactic is scheduling your honeymoon when fewer people will be at your destination. But you also can save money by traveling on slower days of the week, by booking early, or by waiting for last-minute deals. I explain all this and more in the following sections.

Don't be shy about telling agents or staff at your destination that you're on your honeymoon. You may bag some extras reserved just for newlyweds — things like complimentary champagne, breakfast in bed, or a fruit basket or flowers in your room.

Hitting hot spots in the off-season

Nearly every vacation spot has an *off-season* — usually a time when the weather isn't ideal and when many attractions in the area close down because there aren't enough visitors to justify staying open. You can save a ton of money by visiting during the off-season, but I don't recommend it unless both of you have intense hermitlike characteristics.

However, vacation destinations also have *shoulder seasons,* which are the few weeks leading up to the season and the few weeks after the season "officially" ends before the hot spot becomes a virtual ghost town. Prices typically are lower during shoulder seasons, and popular spots usually are less crowded, so you may find your honeymoon more enjoyable.

"High season" doesn't always refer just to the destination's best weather. Convention business can drive prices up just as much as terrific weather can, so be sure to contact your destination's tourism or convention bureau to find out whether you'll be competing with thousands of conventioneers for lodging and amenities.

Here are the shoulder seasons for some of the most popular honeymoon locations:

- ✔ **Alaska:** May and September are the best months to find deals on Alaskan cruises.

- ✔ **Australia and New Zealand:** In May and June, Australia's northern section has great weather, and airfares from the U.S. are usually at their lowest during these months. New Zealand is lovely in April (before winter begins there) and in November and December (early spring in that country).

- ✔ **The contiguous United States:** Get great deals at ski resorts in the Rockies in April. Nantucket still has summer-like weather, but virtually none of the crowds, in September and October. Golf courses in Arizona aren't nearly as full in November and December, but the weather is still warm and sunny.

- ✔ **Europe:** April, May, and September are good times to visit major European cities like London, Paris, and Rome. These months are on the shoulders of the high summer season, so popular attractions will be less crowded. You'll also be more likely to find good deals on airfare and lodging during these months. If you're interested in a European ski vacation, December is the time to go.

- ✔ **Hawaii:** You're likely to find the best Hawaiian deals in September as the summer crowds leave the islands.

- ✔ **Latin America and the Caribbean:** April and November are the shoulder months for the Caribbean islands — just before and just after the official hurricane season (of course, weather systems don't read calendars, so you can't completely rule out a hurricane). You can find deals for Mexico's Baja Peninsula (below California) in June and October. May and December are good times to visit Belize and Costa Rica.

- ✔ **The Mediterranean:** You're likely to find the best deals at Mediterranean resorts in April and October, before and after the summer crowds. The Greek Islands' shoulder months are September and October.

- ✔ **The Pacific Rim:** India is more temperate in March than later in the spring or summer. The beaches in Malaysia are less crowded in March and April; December is a good time to visit here, too. Visit Bali in September and October, before the rainy season begins. The South Pacific islands are best in May and November.

You won't find any significant shoulder seasons in January, February, July, or August. However, many destinations drop their prices right after New Year's Day and offer lower rates until their shoulder seasons begin in earnest. The exception often is mid-February, when demand for romantic getaway spots is spurred by Valentine's Day.

Choosing cheaper days of the week

Sometimes you can save money — or get more value for the same money — by adjusting your travel plans. For example, it's usually less expensive to fly on Tuesdays and Wednesdays, and you may get another price break for staying over until at least the following Sunday.

Lots of hotels, particularly in hot honeymoon or vacation spots like Las Vegas, offer significantly lower room rates Sunday through Thursday. So you could save money by trimming your stay to four days. Or you could use the savings from midweek flights to finance the higher room rates on Friday and Saturday and still spend a full week at your honeymoon destination.

On weekdays, early-morning and late-afternoon flights often are more expensive than mid-day or evening flights, because these are prime slots for business travelers. You may save $100 or more per ticket by leaving at 10 a.m. or 10 p.m. instead of 6 a.m. or 4 p.m.

Looking into other transportation options

Unless you live near your honeymoon destination — say, within a few hundred miles — the only practical way to get there may be to fly. If that's the case, your job is relatively simple: You just need to use your computer skills or your travel agent to compare the costs of different flight options.

However, if flying isn't the only way to get where you're going, you should check out options — train service, bus travel, or even driving — to see whether you can save money.

Driving or taking the train may be cheaper than flying, but often the trade-off is time. If you have to spend eight hours driving or riding on a train, you may decide that the extra expense of flying is worth the time you'll save. Also, remember that these modes of transport have their own hidden costs: meals, tolls, and (if you're taking a train) cab fare to your lodgings.

The early bride gets the deal: Booking early

If you want to honeymoon in a popular vacation spot at the height of the season, booking early — 9 to 12 months in advance — is the way to go. Prices for both flights and lodging typically go up as supply dwindles. Plus, the earlier you book, the more likely you are to get exactly what you want.

You face potential downsides to booking early, though. You may forfeit part or all of your deposit if you cancel your flight or reservation; this is especially true of cruises. You also may miss out on special deals or promotions if you book *too* early. However, many companies will arrange for you to take advantage of these deals, so be sure to call and ask.

Flights are typically cheapest when they're booked at least three weeks in advance. However, if you're heading to a popular destination at a popular time — Cancun during spring break, for example — book your flight as early as possible to make sure you get what you want.

Some online booking sites like Orbitz (www.orbitz.com) offer price guarantees on their airfares. If the price on a flight you book through Orbitz drops by more than $5 before your trip, Orbitz automatically refunds the difference, up to $250. You'll get a check about a month after your trip. See the earlier section "Turning your Internet know-how into travel savings" for more online tips.

If you don't live near a major airline hub and can't get a direct flight to your destination, try booking each leg of your flight separately; you may save money over the automatic routing of your itinerary. Just remember to take into account connection times and travel-through-the-terminal time if you book with different airlines. Missing your honeymoon flight would definitely ruin the moment.

When being late pays off: Booking your trip at the last minute

Sometimes you can get great deals by waiting until the last minute to book your trip. Of course, "last minute" is a fluid term. For airlines, you typically get the best deals if you book at least three weeks in advance. For cruises, resorts, and hotels, you may be able to score great deals as little as a week in advance. Generally, though, "last minute" is anywhere between 30 and 90 days before your planned departure date.

The leading online travel sites all have sections devoted to special deals for last-minute travelers, and some companies actually target those travelers. Vacations To Go (www.vacationstogo.com), for example, sends out regular (and free!) e-mail newsletters with last-minute deals on cruises, safaris, and resort vacations. Cruise lines are especially prone to offering deep discounts in the 90 days before a ship sails; they want their cabins filled even if they have to slash their regular prices to do it.

Even though waiting until the last minute to book your trip can save you a lot of money, you do risk not being able to go to your top-choice hotel or destination. If your heart is set on a week in the Bahamas, you're better off booking as early as possible to make sure you get the dates and accommodations you want.

Delaying your honeymoon

For numerous reasons, many couples decide to delay their honeymoons. Maybe it isn't convenient for one or both of you to take the time off from work right after your wedding. Maybe you'd rather wait so you can save up for the really lavish honeymoon you want. Or maybe you want to get married in January but would rather wait until April for your Caribbean honeymoon so you can take advantage of lower prices and less crowded beaches.

Whatever the reason, there's nothing wrong with putting your honeymoon on hold for a while. In fact, if trying to cram your honeymoon in right after your wedding would strain your finances, the smart thing to do is to delay it until you can afford it.

Part IV
The Part of Tens

The 5th Wave   By Rich Tennant

"They saved a bundle on the tent. Just watch your step around the trapeze rigging."

In this part...

Here you can find ten ways to stretch your wedding dollar. I also suggest ten inexpensive wedding favors and ten things you can cut from your wedding if your budget gets even tighter. Enjoy these nuggets of useful information, which are presented in a quick-read format.

Chapter 16

Ten Ways to Get the Most for Your Wedding Dollar

*I*n your quest for the perfect budget wedding, you may have realized that the word "wedding" pumps up the price of just about everything. But when you're trying to stick to a budget, you want to make every dollar you spend go as far as it can. So in this chapter, I give you my top ten suggestions for stretching your money so you can have a fabulous wedding that you won't regret paying for.

Shop Around and Get Several Different Quotes

Legwork costs you some time, but it can save you a bundle of cash. When you're looking for wedding vendors — caterers, photographers, florists, bakers, and so on — get price quotes from at least three of each. Then compare the values — what you're getting in return for your money. A florist may seem inexpensive at first glance, for example, until you add delivery and setup fees into the quote. Similarly, another florist's higher price may actually be quite reasonable if it includes those fees.

Getting several quotes helps you judge whether a vendor's prices are close to the average for your area or way out of line. You also avoid making impulse decisions that you may regret later.

Get Referrals from Trusted Sources

A bargain is no bargain at all if you don't get what you expect. So ask family and friends to recommend trustworthy vendors. And ask the vendors whether you can speak to a couple of their clients or at least see some thank-you letters from satisfied customers. You want to get a sense of whether others have had good experiences with this vendor. If they haven't, or if the same issues come up with several clients, you may want to look elsewhere.

When talking with a vendor's former clients, get answers to these questions:

- Did the vendor provide the appropriate level of service?
- Were items delivered correctly and on time?
- Did you have any problems with this vendor? If so, how were they resolved?
- Did you discover any unexpected charges on your bill?
- Did you feel the price you paid was fair for what you received?

Hit the Suburbs

Vendors in suburbs and small towns often charge significantly less than their big-city counterparts, so it's worth checking them out. If you're searching for vendors online, many sites let you set a range for your search — within 10, 20, or 50 miles, for example. Many metropolitan telephone books include suburbs and outlying areas. So you shouldn't have trouble finding some vendors in these less expensive areas.

Some vendors may charge mileage or an extra delivery fee for going out of their primary service area. Depending on how much extra they charge, you still may save 5 percent to 15 percent on your total bill for that vendor. You then can put those savings toward another wedding day priority or keep them in the bank for a rainy day.

Search the Internet for Deals and Advice

The Internet is an astounding tool for finding products at rock-bottom prices. It's an especially good option for bulk purchases, such as fresh or artificial flowers (see Chapter 8 for do-it-yourself floral ideas); materials for making centerpieces, decorations, and favors; and candy and nuts.

If you aren't careful, shipping charges can erase a good portion of the savings you can gain by ordering online. Delivery times also can be problematic, especially if you're on tight deadlines. Be familiar with the prices in your local bricks-and-mortar stores so you can judge whether ordering from a Web site makes sense.

Of course, you also can get tons of free information, including step-by-step instructions and even demonstration videos for do-it-yourself wedding projects, on the Internet.

Ask Vendors for Extras

You won't be able to negotiate a 50 percent discount on the cake or photos, but you may be able to convince the vendor to waive the delivery fee or give you an extra 30 minutes of service at little or no charge.

You're more likely to get extras thrown in if you aren't getting married at the height of wedding season. A vendor who can book her goods or services at full price during June or October probably won't be in a mood to negotiate much. But if you're getting married on a Saturday morning in August or a Friday evening in January, you have the advantage of offering the vendor business at a slow time, making negotiation much more attractive to her. (See Chapter 3 for information on how to save money by tweaking the timing of your wedding.)

Wedding vendors are trying to make a living like everyone else, so don't expect them to give away their service or product for nothing. Make sure the extras you ask for are reasonable. In general, the most you should ask for — or expect — is the equivalent of a 5 percent to 10 percent discount.

Negotiate Discounts with Vendors

Knowing what the competition offers is your best weapon when negotiating discounts, giving you another reason to shop around (see the earlier section "Shop Around and Get Several Different Quotes" for details). Say, for example, that the reception site you really like charges a banquet hall rental fee in addition to the catering, cake-cutting, and other charges. If another reception site in the area waives the rental fee for a minimum guaranteed number of guests, point that out to the manager of the first site and ask for a similar deal.

The trick to successful negotiating is offering something in return for something else. In the preceding reception example, the trade is a guaranteed head count in exchange for waiving the rental fee; you're offering to pay for a minimum of, say, 100 guests, so the vendor is still making money.

Use this approach with all your vendors. For example, ask the photographer if he'll give you all the proof sets for free if you order a certain number of albums. Or ask him to throw in a few free enlargements if you agree to purchase the negatives.

Again, timing is everything when asking for discounts. You'll be more successful getting vendors to shave prices if you aren't competing with other marrying couples for the same resources. In other words, although it never hurts to ask, don't expect to score deep discounts in the height of wedding season.

Use Your Social Network to Your Advantage

You know the theory that everyone is connected to everyone else by no more than six other people? Well, that theory, broadly speaking, is what using your network is all about. You may not know any singers personally, but your family or friends may have direct or indirect contacts with singers. More important, such personal contacts often lead to discounts you wouldn't get — and couldn't expect — in a strictly vendor-client relationship. So don't be shy about putting out a call for help among your family and friends. It could net you great talent at a low cost.

Opt for Services Instead of Gifts

Do you have a friend who's a whiz at cake baking and decorating? Ask her whether she'd be willing to make your wedding cake as a gift. Similarly, your artistic niece may be thrilled to do the calligraphy for your invitations as a special gift to you and your betrothed. And your computer geek buddy from college may be willing to put together digital photo albums or design your wedding Web site in lieu of buying you towels or a crystal bowl.

Having friends and relatives lend their talents to your celebration saves you money, makes those friends and relatives feel good about being an important part of your day, and lends a uniquely intimate and personal touch to your wedding.

Become a DIY Expert

Unless you're having a super-formal wedding, you can do many of the things that go into a nuptial celebration yourself — and save a lot of money. You can buy bulk flowers and create your own arrangements for bouquets and centerpieces, for example. If you have a computer and a good printer, you can create your own invitations, programs, and place cards.

You can even save money by making, instead of purchasing, gifts for your intended, your wedding party, and other important people. You can make scrapbooks of your history together for your maid of honor and earrings or bracelets for your bridesmaids. For the best man and groomsmen, decorate canning jars with photos of them with the groom, and then fill the jars with homemade trail mix. Check with your local crafts store for kits and other ideas.

Pay with a Rewards Credit Card

If you don't have the cash saved when deposits are due, consider putting those deposits on a credit card that gives you rewards like cash back or frequent flyer miles. Then use the reward to help pay for other aspects of your wedding or honeymoon.

It's easy to go over your budget when you don't actually see the cash you're handing over or have to deduct a huge amount from your checking account register.

To avoid unintended splurging, follow these steps:

- ✔ Earmark one credit card for wedding expenses, and don't use it for anything else.

- ✔ Keep a running tally of charges, so you don't get any unpleasant surprises when the statement arrives.

- ✔ Commit to paying off that credit card as soon as possible. Finance charges alone can throw your wedding budget way off and put you into much more debt than you anticipate.

Chapter 17

Ten Inexpensive Wedding Favors

In This Chapter

▶ Saying thanks to your guests without going over budget

▶ Exploring inexpensive favor options

*T*he cost of wedding favors can get out of control quickly. Something that looks like a bargain at $3 per unit translates into a $300 bill if you have 100 guests. And don't forget sales taxes and shipping costs. Go for a $10 favor, and suddenly you've added at least $1,000 to your 100-guest wedding budget. Yikes!

Fortunately, if you want to give favors (but remember that you don't have to; see Chapter 18), you have lots of inexpensive options to choose from. The ten listed here can be found (as of this writing) for less than $2 a piece, but they still provide a nice thank-you to your guests. Many of the ideas here have even cheaper do-it-yourself alternatives, too.

For most favors, and particularly those you order online, the per-unit cost goes down as your total quantity goes up. So, for example, if you decide to order 50 personalized shot glasses, each one may cost $1.10. But if you order 150, the per-unit price may drop to $0.60. I'm not suggesting you order twice as many favors as you need. However, if your order is close to a price-reduction threshold — say you need 130 units, and the price drops significantly if you order 144, it may be more cost-effective to place a slightly larger order. (By the way, an order of 144 is called a *gross,* and many vendors offer discounts if you purchase a gross.)

The Internet makes shopping and price comparisons easier than ever. Here are a few general Internet tips before you start browsing the thousands of favor options out there:

✔ **Crash the online clearance bins.** Many favor Web sites have "clearance" tabs, where you can find great deals on more expensive favors. Here's the catch: If an item is being cleared out, the e-tailer may not have enough in stock to meet your needs. However, don't fret; you can always mix and match favors, collecting great bargains from the virtual clearance bins.

✔ **Set aside money to order samples.** If you're leery about ordering favors online — or if you just prefer to see and touch what you buy, no matter what it is — set aside $50 to order samples. Most Web sites allow you to order one item as a sample. You won't get the discount for quantity, obviously, but it's better to spend $5 or $10 to be sure a favor is what you want rather than be disappointed in what you get (and be out $100 or $150). Remember, many personalized items can't be returned.

Bookmarks

Bookmarks are useful and inexpensive. Wedding-themed metal bookmarks can be had for less than $1 each at the many wedding favor Web sites I mention in this chapter. Or you can order custom-printed bookmarks from online sites like www.printingfor less.com, where the base price for 500 2- by 6-inch bookmarks with full color and scuff-resistant coating on the front is less than $125 — or $0.25 a piece.

If you have a home computer, printer, and laminating machine (or access to one), you can create and print your own bookmarks for even less money.

Candles and Candle Holders

You can get candles and candle holders in any number of styles, so you can fit virtually any theme or hobby. Want to go really romantic? Lay a long-stemmed rose candle across each place setting at your reception. Wedding Favors Unlimited (www.weddingfavors unlimited.com) has white and red rose candles for less than $2 each when you buy 96 or more.

Dollar stores are good places to shop for candles and candle holders, too, especially if you want to mix and match styles, colors, and
scents.

Candy

Sites like the Candy Wrapper Store (www.candywrapperstore.
com) offer full- and fun-size candy bars in personalized wrappers;
most have a variety of designs to choose from. You also can order
Jordan almonds, Hershey Kisses, and other confections with personalized stickers or packaging. Prices vary widely, depending on
the size and quantity you order. Personalized fun-size or miniature
candies typically start at less than $1 a piece.

Many sites allow you to buy either the candy with the custom
wrapper, or just sets of wrappers or stickers. For example, at
Custom Candy Bar Wrapper (www.customcandybarwrapper.
com), you can buy a set of 120 personalized stickers for the bot-
toms of Hershey Kisses for less than $20, or you can get 120 Kisses
with the stickers affixed for a few dollars more. If you can get a
good deal on candy locally — and you have the time to do the
wrapping yourself — you can save at least a few bucks.

Another option is to purchase favor tins and fill them with candy
that you buy in bulk or on sale. The Web site www.wrapwithus.
com has tins and other favor containers for less than $1 each.

Buy glass serving bowls at your local dollar store, fill them with
bulk candy and use them as centerpieces at your reception.
Provide a scoop and small plastic bags or favor tins so your guests
can take the candy home.

Coasters

Coasters come in all kinds of materials and themes; you can even
find photo coasters. A set of four cork coasters, including packaging, such as a clear plastic box or tulle bag, runs about $1 to $1.20.
You can find glass coasters for less than $2 a piece. Stoneware
coasters usually cost more, but you may be able to find bargains
online. Check out the wedding-themed coasters at American Bridal
(www.americanbridal.com), for example, or look at discount
stores for deals.

Drink Mix Packets

Coffee, tea, lemonade, hot cocoa, and other drink mixes are popular favors, and you can get them personalized for your wedding at reasonable prices. Wedding Favors Unlimited (www.wedding favorsunlimited.com) offers personalized cosmopolitan and margarita drink mix packets for $1.25 a packet (minimum order is 30 pieces). This site offers other drink mix packets as well.

 Buy your favorite coffee, tea, hot cocoa, or lemonade mix in bulk, and fill snack-sized plastic bags with four to eight scoops of the mix. Then put the bagged portions in mini gift bags from your local dollar store (you usually can get three or four bags for $1). Don't forget to tag the favors with directions for use. This do-it-yourself project takes more time, but you may be able to save a few bucks.

Magnets

Nearly everyone has a magnet or two on the refrigerator, so this is a useful and universal favor idea. Price depends in large part on what kind of magnet you choose, but you can find them for less than $1.50 a piece. Remember that personalized magnets usually are sold in lots of 50 or 100, so you may see a total price for the lot, rather than a per-unit price.

Check out Web sites like Zazzle (www.zazzle.com) — which offers discounts on larger orders but doesn't require a minimum purchase — and Memory Magnets (www.memorymagnets.com).

 "Save the date" magnets are a cool substitute for traditional wedding announcements, and, as long as they aren't oversized, postage is the same as for paper announcements. Plus, if you use magnets as your announcement, you may decide not to buy separate favors: Everybody you invited already has your wedding souvenir on their fridge!

Photo Frames and Keychains

Miniature photo frames are popular wedding favors, and you can get nice ones for around $1 a piece. Use your home computer to print your names and the date — and any message you care to include, such as "Thank you for coming" or "We're glad you're here" — on paper that complements your color scheme, and slip it into the frame.

Photo keychains are another inexpensive option (also less than $1 each). Again, you can put your own message in the photo slot — or you can even use your engagement picture or another photo of you and your new spouse. E-Favors (www.efavors.com) has a variety of inexpensive favors, including photo frames and keychains.

 Buy wood or metal coffee mug trees at your local dollar store or discount retailer, and decorate them with the keychains and ribbons as centerpieces for your reception tables.

Plantable Favors

Miniature pots of herbs, cacti, or lucky bamboo are quite expensive — typically $4 or more a piece. But you can give your guests seed packets or plantable paper for a much more reasonable price.

Milkweed Café (www.milkweedcafe.com) offers "Confetti to Grow" — special paper laced with wildflower seeds that your guests can plant after your wedding. You can choose from eight shapes (which are about 1-inch square) and a rainbow of colors. Six hundred pieces of confetti costs $50. Place a few pieces (along with planting instructions) in an inexpensive "Thank you for attending" note at each place setting.

Milkweed Café also has larger plantable paper favors at reasonable prices. Their Celebration Grows and Share & Blossom favors cost between $1 and $2 per unit.

Botanical Paperworks (www.botanicalpaperworks.com) also has inexpensive plantable favors, including a wedding cake–shaped plantable card (available in six colors and customizable with five ink colors) for less than $2, including matching envelopes.

Soaps

Many favor Web sites offer good prices on wedding-themed soaps packaged in pretty gift boxes. Wedding Favors Unlimited (www.weddingfavorsunlimited.com), for example, has a broad variety of soaps starting at less than $1 a piece.

 You often can find miniature soaps at dollar stores and discount retailers; you can then personalize them with paper tags or self-stick labels that you create on your home computer.

Swizzle Sticks

Swizzle sticks are inexpensive and unusual favors. You can buy different styles in bulk at your local party supply store, or you can order personalized swizzle sticks from countless online favor sites. At Only Wedding Favors (www.onlyweddingfavors.com), for example, you can get 50 personalized swizzle sticks for about $25. If you're planning for 100 guests, you could order 200 swizzle sticks for about $100 and give two — tied together with a ribbon — to each guest.

Chapter 18

Ten Traditions to Reconsider When You're on a Budget

. . . .

In This Chapter

▶ Opting out of wedding industry propaganda

▶ Choosing to forgo the usual wedding traditions

. . . .

*T*he wedding industry is built on the premise that every bride and groom *must* do certain things to have the wedding of their dreams — and the businesses in this industry do their best to convince you that your day just won't be complete if you don't conform to their ideas of what's appropriate.

The truth is that you can make your wedding whatever you want it to be. If you don't have much money and don't want to start your newly married life with a lot of wedding debt, you can find lots of ways to save. Regardless of what wedding professionals would like you to believe, here are ten things you can do without or find inexpensive alternatives for. For details on deciding what's most important to you and your intended — and what you can do without — see Chapter 1.

A Traditional Location

More and more couples are forgoing the church-and-reception-hall wedding in favor of less traditional sites. Sometimes it's simply a matter of personal preference, but it also can be a way to significantly trim your costs. After all, renting a pavilion in a public park is a lot cheaper than renting a ballroom at a fancy hotel.

These days, you can go pretty much as far afield as you like in choosing a location for your ceremony and reception. Couples have been married in bowling alleys and fast-food restaurants, on beaches and golf courses, and even in carwashes and in midair while skydiving. If you and your betrothed share a hobby or met in unusual circumstances, you may be able to save a lot of money by choosing a site that reflects your interests and your history together. (See Chapter 4 for more on selecting ceremony sites.)

The reception typically eats up at least half of a wedding budget, because you're paying for food, entertainment, and decorations (and alcohol, if you decide to have it). If your budget is particularly tight, you can ease the strain substantially by looking for fun alternatives to a conventional reception hall, such as a clambake on the beach or a backyard barbeque. (Chapter 11 tells you what you need to know to choose the best reception site for you.)

Traditional Wedding Clothes

Brides get married wearing everything from prom-style dresses to business suits, and plenty of grooms bypass the traditional tuxedo for a suit or even less formal wear. All these options are much cheaper than traditional wedding garb, and most of them can be worn again.

In fact, until the end of the 19th century, most marrying couples wore outfits that later became their "Sunday best" clothes. Even Queen Victoria reused part of her wedding dress; she wore the lace overskirt many times, including as part of the outfits she wore for her Diamond Jubilee celebrations nearly 50 years after her nuptials.

Your wedding outfit should reflect your style and personality — not the wedding industry's conventions. Why spend $800 or more on a traditional wedding dress if you can look stunning in a $150 evening gown — especially if you can wear that same gown again? (Refer to Chapter 6 for more on inexpensive wedding gown and tuxedo options.)

A Romantic Limo Ride

No rule says that you have to be whisked away from your ceremony to your reception in a spotless white (or black, or pink, or baby blue) limousine. Instead of paying $75 an hour or more (plus the tip for the chauffeur) for a traditional fancy ride, look into renting a cool convertible or a luxury sedan and having the best man act as your driver. In many areas, you can get a 24-hour rental for around $100, compared with an average of $500 to hire a limo for a measly four hours. (Chapter 11 provides more information on transportation options.)

Check out free-standing car rental agencies — ones that aren't located at airports, train stations, or other transportation hubs, where rental fees are often higher. If you live in a metro area, look to the suburbs for a car rental; you could save a lot by going out of town.

Does a friend or relative have a car you just love? If so, ask about borrowing it for the day. Or you can eliminate this expense entirely if you have your ceremony and reception at the same place.

Professional Photography or Videography

If you're reluctant to pay $1,000 or more for professional photography or video services, you're in luck; you have lots of reasonable alternatives to choose from. If all you really want is a collection of candid shots, for example, you can supply your guests with single-use cameras and encourage them to take pictures at will. Or you can ask your guests to take pictures with their digital cameras and then drop off their memory cards with a designated person at the reception.

If you have your heart set on group shots of your wedding party and families, but want to be kind to your budget, you can ask a friend to take those pictures for you. Friends or family members also may be willing to take video of the ceremony and reception; if no one has a decent video camera, you can rent one for a fraction of what hiring a professional costs.

These are all valid alternatives you may want to try, but do remember that the quality will likely decrease if you decide to use them. Chapter 9 goes in depth into your options and provides pros and cons of using a professional versus going the friends and family route.

The Tossing of the Bouquet (Or the Garter)

Not only do you not have to throw a bouquet or garter, you don't even have to include these two traditional items in your wedding. In fact, a great way to trim your budget is to cut down on the number of fresh flowers you use.

For example, instead of carrying a bridal bouquet down the aisle, consider carrying something that holds sentimental or symbolic value for you, such as a family member's Bible. This item also can count as your "something old" or "something borrowed" from the traditional bridal adage. Or you can carry a simple bouquet of three of your favorite flowers. You can discover some more money-saving tips on picking flowers in Chapter 8.

A Traditional Reception

The wedding reception is really just a party — a way for your guests to help you celebrate your marriage. But you don't have to confine yourself to traditional ideas about what your wedding reception should look like. Instead, focus on what you, your new spouse, and your family and friends enjoy.

For instance, maybe all of you are more comfortable at a backyard barbeque than in a vast ballroom. Or maybe you'd rather play board games than dance. I heard of one couple that took their guests to a college basketball game after the ceremony. Another exchanged vows at a park, and then changed clothes and captained softball teams with their guests. Yet another couple held a potluck dinner in a barn they decorated for the occasion.

You also can elect not to have a reception at all; instead throw a party at home on your first anniversary. Such a party is a lot cheaper, simply because it doesn't have the word "wedding" in front of it: Your guests won't expect a wedding cake, for example, or floral centerpieces, or even formal invitations, for that matter. Even if you decide to have a more wedding-like reception at a hotel ballroom or other facility, you can save as much as 30 percent by calling it a reunion instead of a wedding celebration.

A Traditional Tiered Cake

According to The Bridal Association of America, the average wedding cake costs $543. But, of course, no rule says you have to have a cake for your wedding. You can serve whatever dessert you like; you can even opt for a dessert buffet. Some popular (and often less expensive) options include the following:

- ✔ A chocolate fountain with fruit and other foods for dipping
- ✔ Doughnuts or cupcakes (which can be arranged in tiers to resemble a cake)
- ✔ Ice cream novelties

    ✔ Italian cookies

    ✔ Pie (even a variety of flavors)

    ✔ Truffles

If you choose a dessert from the caterer's menu, you probably won't even pay extra for it. The per-person price usually includes dessert.

Anytime you put the word "wedding" in front of a product, the price goes up — often by 25 to 50 percent or more. If you want to have a cake, ask to see party cakes instead; you may find one you really like for much less money. (For more ways to trim cake costs, see Chapter 12.)

Professional Musicians

You don't have to pay an organist, harpist, or another musician to serenade you up and down the aisle or to provide dance music at the reception. Today's portable CD players have excellent sound quality, and virtually every store that sells CDs has wedding collections for $25 or less. (See Chapter 13 for other ways to trim music costs.)

At Wedding Music Central (`www.weddingmusiccentral.com`), you can download entire wedding programs — all the music you need for your ceremony and reception — for a fraction of what you'll pay professional musicians or DJs. This site even provides you with a guide to an iPod wedding (with packages starting at $18) and guidance on selecting the right music for every phase of your ceremony and reception.

Monogrammed Napkins

People who sell monogrammed napkins argue that they're an easy way to incorporate your wedding colors into your reception décor. Compared with other wedding paraphernalia, napkins emblazoned with your names and wedding date are relatively cheap; you can get 100 embossed cocktail or dinner napkins for about $50 to $100. But if your budget is tight, this is one item you can cut without anybody noticing. Plain cocktail napkins work just fine, and they're a lot cheaper; depending on where you shop, you can get 100 for $5 or less.

Most reception sites offer different colors of table linens, so you can select colors that match or complement your wedding colors. Best of all, the reception site's linens are nearly always included in the cost of using the facility.

Expensive Favors

Back in the day — that is, since ancient times — newly married couples gave out favors to their guests as a way of sharing their good fortune. In the 15th century, guests at weddings (and other celebrations) were sent home with trinket boxes made of crystal, porcelain, or precious metal. Inside these boxes were five sugared almonds or other sweets to represent health, wealth, fertility, happiness, and longevity.

These days, I'm sure few people know the meaning behind that little mesh bag of Jordan almonds at each place setting. And I doubt guests come home bragging about the good luck they expect to get from the miniature silver picture frame or heart-shaped measuring cup they were given at the reception. In fact, many wedding guests leave the favors behind, simply because it's something they won't use and don't want cluttering up their own homes.

If you really want to give your guests favors, check out Chapter 17 for inexpensive ideas. But, really, this is one area you can safely cut without worrying about offending anyone. Concentrate your efforts (and limited funds) on making the party as fun as it can be; that's the best way to favor your guests.

Part V
Appendixes

The 5th Wave   By Rich Tennant

"We're trying to save money for the wedding by buying in bulk. Caviar?"

In this part...

So many details are involved in planning a wedding that it's easy to lose track of what tasks you still have to complete and where you are in your spending plan. So in this part, I provide worksheets to help keep you organized.

With these worksheets, you can plan when things need to be completed, record prices from different vendors, and even make a to-do list for you and your betrothed (and anyone else who's taking charge of an element of your wedding). You also can stay on top of your budget with these worksheets by plugging in actual costs or vendor estimates, comparing them with your original budget, and adjusting your budget as needed.

Appendix A

Your Planning Calendar

• •

*T*he planning calendar in this appendix is based on a 12-month timeline leading up to a wedding. If you have less time to plan your wedding, you can still use this calendar; just do upfront tasks more quickly, and be a little more ruthless in what you decide to forgo. For example, if you have only three months to plan your wedding, tackle the tasks under "12 to 9 Months in Advance" first. However, in this circumstance, I suggest you skip the expense of an engagement photo, newspaper announcement, and party.

No matter how long your planning calendar is, I recommend giving yourself a starting date and completion deadline for each task to help counter any tendencies toward procrastination.

You don't have to do everything on this list. If you don't want to go through premarital counseling or send announcements to your local newspaper, just cross it off your list.

12 to 9 Months in Advance

To Do	Start By	Complete By
To mark your engagement		
Have your engagement photo taken.		
Send an engagement announcement to the newspaper.		
To create the wedding you really want		
Research wedding themes, colors, and attire.		
Discuss the kind of wedding you and your betrothed want (see Chapter 2 to jumpstart this discussion).		
Set your wedding date.		
Discuss prenuptial agreements or premarital counseling.		
To avoid financial stress		
Set your wedding budget (see Chapter 2 for tips).		
Create savings plans for your wedding and honeymoon.		
Start your preliminary guest list (with your budget in mind).		
To match what you want with what you can afford		
Research and visit ceremony and reception locations.		
Choose your ceremony and reception locations, sign contracts, and make deposits.		
Start looking for vendors (flip to Chapter 4).		
To get the vendors you want before they're booked up		
Book the caterer.		
Book the photographer.		
Book the videographer.		
Book the musicians or the DJ.		
Research florists.		
Research and book officiant.		

To Do	Start By	Complete By
To find what you want in wedding attire		
Research wedding dresses and accessories.		
Research tuxedos or suits for the groom.		
Research attire for the wedding party.		
To be surrounded by the people you love		
Send save-the-date notices (especially for destination or holiday weddings) to the people you definitely intend to invite.		
Choose your wedding party.		

8 to 6 Months in Advance

To Do	Start By	Complete By
To create your ideal atmosphere		
Select a florist.		
Place your floral order.		
Order decorations (or supplies, if you're making your own) for the ceremony and reception.		
Order miscellaneous ceremony items, such as a unity candle and send-off favors (birdseed, bubbles, or confetti).		
Research favors and gifts for the wedding party.		
Go over music selections for the ceremony and reception with the musicians or DJ, or begin collecting recordings to make your own CDs or iPod wedding library.		
Reserve any rental items (tables, chairs, tents, arches, or plants).		
To make travel go smoothly		
Reserve lodging for out-of-town guests.		
Reserve accommodations for your wedding night.		
Finalize honeymoon plans and make reservations.		
Get or renew your passports, if necessary.		
To get the wedding attire you want		
Order wedding dress and accessories.		
Select bridesmaid attire and accessories.		
Select attire for the groomsmen.		
Select attire for the ring bearer and flower girl.		
Begin researching wedding rings.		

To Do	Start By	Complete By
To get the word out		
Research invitation styles and prices.		
Decide on ceremony programs, printed napkins, place cards, thank-you notes, and other printed materials.		
Decide whether you need map or direction cards.		
Research and hire a calligrapher.		
Order printed materials.		

5 Months in Advance

To Do	Start By	Complete By
To make sure your vendors know what you want		
Meet with your caterer to discuss the menu and alcohol options.		
Find a baker and order the cake or other dessert.		
Confirm ceremony and reception decorations, or begin assembling them if you're creating your own.		
Book transportation for your wedding day.		
To stay on top of other wedding-related events		
Schedule the rehearsal dinner.		
Confirm your honeymoon plans.		
Plan any post-wedding events (gift-opening party, bridesmaids' luncheon, post-wedding brunch, and so on).		

4 Months in Advance

To Do	Start By	Complete By
To make you look your best		
Consult with your hair stylist and beautician for ideas on wedding hair and makeup.		
Schedule any beauty treatments for the weeks leading up to the wedding.		
Schedule hair and makeup sessions for your bridesmaids.		
To be sure you have everything you need		
Purchase wedding bands and order engraving.		
Purchase a gift for your spouse-to-be.		
Purchase wedding party gifts.		
Purchase any other needed gifts.		
Purchase reception extras, such as a cake knife, toasting flutes, and a guest book and pen.		
Register for gifts.		
Schedule a bridal portrait.		

3 to 2 Months in Advance

To Do	Start By	Complete By
To ensure that everyone is well-dressed		
Arrange for a final wedding dress fitting.		
Make sure the bridesmaids and flower girls have their dresses and accessories.		
Make sure groom, groomsmen, ushers, and ring bearer have been measured for tuxes or suits and have the needed accessories.		
To take care of your guests		
Address invitations and add postage.		
Mail invitations.		
Decide on and purchase wedding favors.		
Plan the rehearsal dinner details, including location, time, and menu.		
Invite people to the appropriate pre- and post-wedding events.		
To keep yourself on track		
Write thank-you notes for any gifts you've received.		
Go over your wedding checklist to make sure you haven't overlooked anything.		
Review the earlier tasks in your calendar to make sure they're completed.		

1 Month in Advance

To Do	Start By	Complete By
To get your paperwork in order		
Finalize prenuptial agreement, if necessary.		
Get your marriage license.		
Alert your local post office of any address changes.		
Take care of name changes, including driver's license, credit cards, passport, bank accounts, and utilities.		
Change beneficiaries on insurance policies and retirement accounts.		
Arrange for any necessary changes on health insurance plans.		
To make sure you and your vendors are on the same page		
Order wine, beer, and liquor (if not provided by your caterer).		
Finalize wedding day transportation plans.		
Review parking arrangements at ceremony and reception sites.		
Verify lodging reservations for out-of-town guests.		
Verify wedding night accommodations.		
Finalize ceremony and reception music selections with the musicians or DJ.		
Finish assembling do-it-yourself decorations and favors.		
To keep your guests in the loop		
Mail rehearsal dinner invitations.		
Mail wedding announcements to those who won't attend.		
Send a wedding announcement to your local newspaper.		
To prepare as bride and groom		
Pick up the wedding gown and accessories.		
Practice hair and makeup styles.		
Finalize your vows.		
Review toasts and speeches with those giving them.		

3 Weeks in Advance

To Do	Start By	Complete By
To make sure the ceremony and reception go as planned		
Discuss ceremony details with your officiant.		
Assign duties to your ushers.		
Go over the final music list with the musicians or DJ and discuss the timing of dances, toasts, and speeches. (If you're providing your own music, finish creating CDs or loading music into your iPod.)		
Create a schedule for your wedding day and give copies to your wedding party and vendors.		
Confirm orders and deliveries with all vendors and make sure they have locations and times correct.		
Confirm vendor accessibility with your ceremony and reception sites.		
To get a handle on your guests		
Contact anyone who hasn't responded to the wedding invitation.		
Finalize the head count for the rehearsal dinner and any other pre- or post-wedding events.		
To avoid overlooking any details		
Pick up the wedding bands.		
Wrap any gifts you bought for the wedding party or your spouse-to-be.		
Find old, new, borrowed, and blue items (if you're using them).		
Keep up on thank-you notes for gifts you receive before the wedding.		
Confirm hair and beauty treatment appointments.		
Confirm wedding night and honeymoon reservations.		

The Week before the Wedding

To Do	Start By	Complete By
To ensure your comfort		
Break in your wedding shoes.		
Pick up groom's rental tuxedo or suit and make sure it fits properly.		
Schedule some alone time together.		
To finalize the details		
Give a final head count and seating chart to the caterer and reception manager.		
Confirm all vendors, including times, locations, and final payment arrangements.		
Confirm vendor accessibility to the ceremony and reception sites.		
Gather honeymoon documentation, including tickets, passports, currency, and traveler's checks.		
Pack for your honeymoon.		
To prepare on the day before the wedding		
Gather all items you need for the wedding, including vendor payments and tip envelopes.		
Go to hair or beauty appointments.		
Attend the rehearsal ceremony and dinner.		

Appendix B

Price Comparison Worksheets

● ●

*A*lways get written estimates when you interview wedding vendors. Then you can use the information on those estimates to fill out this worksheet, which allows you to compare what is and isn't included with each vendor and see at a glance which packages and pricing best suit your needs.

Refer to the appropriate chapters to discover pointers on the questions to ask vendors and the information you need to make an informed decision.

Amend any of the following worksheets to suit your needs. If, for example, you want to serve something other than a traditional wedding cake at your reception, ask bakers for a cost-per-guest figure to make your comparisons as accurate as possible.

Bakers

Vendor Name and Phone Number	Tier Cake	Sheet Cake	Side Cakes	Icing and Decorations	Delivery / Setup	Deposit (Amount/ Terms)	Balance Due (Amount/ Terms)	Total Cost
ABC Cakes 555-1212	$2.50 per slice; 3-tier – 75 slices; 4-tier – 100 slices	$2 per slice	20 servings each; $2.25 per slice	Fondant: add $2 per slice	$50 flat fee	$100 deposit, refundable up to 2 weeks in advance	Cash or check on delivery; credit card if pay in store	$240-$450

Catering Services

Vendor Name and Phone Number	Meal Cost Per Guest	Appetizer Cost	Alcohol Cost Per Guest	Extra Charges*	Deposit (Amount/ Terms)	Balance Due (Amount/ Terms)	Total Cost
City's Best Party Hall 555-1217	Menu A: $14.95; Menu B: $19.95; Menu C: $26.95	Menu A/B: $3 per guest; Menu C: included	$15 per hour per guest	Cake-cutting: $1 per slice; 18% staff gratuity	$500 deposit, nonrefundable	72 hours in advance; credit card imprint required in case of overages	Menu A: $4,472 + tax; Menu B: $4,767 + tax; Menu C: $5,190 + tax

*Cake cutting, staff gratuities, corking fees, and so on

Ceremony Sites

Vendor Name and Phone Number	Available (Date/Time)	Other Events That Day? (Y/N)	Decorations	Music Restrictions	Deposit (Amount/Terms)	Balance Due (Amount/Terms)	Total Cost	Items Not Included
My church 555-1213	6/26 after 1 p.m.	Yes: Morning wedding	Need to provide	Sacred songs only; no recorded music	$50 reservation/clean-up fee	$250 suggested donation	$300	Aisle runner, musicians, candles

Florists

Vendor Name and Phone Number	Bouquets and Corsages	Ceremony Flowers	Reception Flowers	Locally Grown/Seasonal? (Y/N)	Delivery/ Setup	Deposit (Amount/ Terms)	Balance Due (Amount/ Terms)	Total Cost
Acme Floral SSS-1214	Bridal: $75 Maids: $50 each Corsages: $30 each	Altar spray: $50 Side plants: $20 each	Head table spray: $75 Centerpieces: $20 each	Yes	$30 for ceremony $5 per table at reception	50% due 30 days in advance	Pay on delivery Cash/check	$870

Musicians/DJs

Vendor Name and Phone Number	Ceremony Cost (Per Hour or Flat Fee)	Reception Cost (Per Hour or Flat Fee)	Availability/ Restrictions	Reception: Meal Required?	Extra Fees*	Deposit	Balance Due (Amount/ Terms)	Total Cost
Super DJ 555-1215	$150 flat fee (includes setup)	$125/hour	Can't start before 6 p.m.	Yes	50 cents per mile over 25 miles	25% to hold date; refundable more than 30 days in advance	Cash/check at end of reception	$775

*Setup fees, overtime charges, and so on

Photographers

Vendor Name and Phone Number	Items Included in Package	Hours/Number of Shots	Overtime Fees	Travel Fees	Extra Charges*	Online Viewing/ Ordering? (Y/N)	Deposit	Balance Due	Total Cost
Pica-a-plenty SSS-1216	5 hours; 200 prints + CD; 11 x 14 portrait; $100 in additional prints	5 hours; unlimited shots	$40/half hour; $75/hour	N/A	Shipping ($9-$15 USPS); $75 to shoot rehearsal	Yes	$350 to reserve date	Half remaining balance due 30 days in advance; final payment due on/before wedding day	$1,395 + tax for package (no extras)

*Special effects, additional prints or albums, and so on

Printers

Vendor Name and Phone Number	Invitations	Place Cards	Thank-You Notes	Additional Materials*	Extra Charges+	Deposit	Balance Due (Amount/Terms)	Total Cost
Retro-chic.com	$140/100 (includes invites, reply cards, info/map cards, thank-you notes, envelopes)	N/A	Included in package	N/A	$110 for color ink; 27 cents each for inner envelopes; shipping ($15)	Pay in full on ordering	N/A	$155 b/w; $265 w/color ink

*Save-the-date cards, announcements, napkins, and so on
+Foil lining, embossing, calligraphy, and so on

Reception Sites

Vendor Name and Phone Number	Available (Date/Time)	Other Events That Day? (Y/N)	Decorations	Additional Fees*	Deposit	Balance Due (Amount/Terms)	Total Cost	Items Not Included
City's Best Party Hall 555-1217	Afternoon only on 6/26; afternoon or evening available on 6/22	Evening wedding 6/26; no other events 6/22	Basic decorations, centerpieces included	Chair covers: $2 each + $2 pressing/placing fee; 18% service staff gratuity	$500 to reserve date	Rental fee waived if we use in-house caterer; deposit applied to final bill	$0 if we don't use chair covers	N/A

*Table and chair rental, audio/visual equipment, and so on

Videographers

Vendor Name and Phone Number	Items Included in Package	Hours	Overtime Fees	Travel Fees	Extra Charges*	Online Viewing/ Ordering? (Y/N)	Deposit	Balance Due (Amount/ Terms)	Total Cost
Let's Make a Movie 555-1218	8 hours; two DVDs; raw footage tapes	8	$150/hour	N/A	Raw footage DVD: $175; extra DVDs: $25 each; highlights video: $200	N/A	$500	On or before wedding day	$1,990 + tax

*Additional copies, purchase of raw footage, and so on

Appendix C

Your Wedding Checklist

● ●

*T*he checklist in this appendix is designed to help you keep track of the things you need and want for your wedding. Use the checkboxes to mark things off as you purchase or line them up.

 You probably don't need or want everything on this list, so I suggest you cross out the things that you don't want and highlight the ones that top your priority list. Doing so makes it easier to remind yourself — at a glance — what really matters for your wedding and what you can do without. Use the blank lines to fill in items that are important to you but aren't included here.

Apparel

For the bride:

❑ Alterations

❑ Garter

❑ Gloves

❑ Jewelry

❑ Shoes

❑ Undergarments (lingerie, slip, and hosiery)

❑ Veil/headpiece

❑ Wedding dress

❑ _____

❑ _____

❑ _____

For the groom:

❑ Accessories (pocket square, handkerchief, tie pin, and cuff links)

❑ Alterations

❏ Cummerbund

❏ Shirt

❏ Shoes

❏ Socks

❏ Tie

❏ Tuxedo/suit

❏ Vest

❏ _____

❏ _____

❏ _____

For the bridesmaids:

❏ Accessories (jewelry and hair decorations)

❏ Dresses

❏ Shoes

❏ _____

❏ _____

❏ _____

For the groomsmen/ushers:

❏ Accessories (pocket square, handkerchief, tie pin, and cuff links)

❏ Cummerbunds

❏ Shirts

❏ Shoes

❏ Socks

❏ Ties

❏ Tuxedos/suits

❏ Vests

❏ _____

❏ _____

❏ _____

Ceremony

- ❏ Aisle runner
- ❏ Altar decorations
- ❏ Candles
- ❏ Chair rental
- ❏ Chair/pew decorations
- ❏ Flower girl basket
- ❏ Guest book and pen
- ❏ Marriage license
- ❏ Music
- ❏ Musicians
- ❏ Officiant
- ❏ Other decorations
- ❏ Photographer
- ❏ Singers
- ❏ Sound system
- ❏ Readers
- ❏ Rings
- ❏ Ring pillow
- ❏ Transportation
- ❏ Unity candle
- ❏ Videographer
- ❏ _____
- ❏ _____
- ❏ _____

Flowers

- ❏ Altar/ceremony flowers
- ❏ Arch/bower flowers
- ❏ Bridal bouquet
- ❏ Bridesmaid bouquets

❏ Boutonnieres

❏ Corsages

❏ Flower girl flowers

❏ Maid or matron of honor bouquet

❏ Pew or chair flowers

❏ Reception centerpieces

❏ Reception cake table flowers

❏ Reception head table flowers

❏ "Throwing" bridal bouquet

❏ _____

❏ _____

❏ _____

Gifts/Favors

❏ Attendant gifts

❏ Bride and groom gifts

❏ Parent gifts

❏ Guest favors

❏ Reader/singer/musician gifts

❏ _____

❏ _____

❏ _____

Honeymoon

❏ Airline reservations

❏ Hotel reservations

❏ Passports

❏ Other travel documents (vouchers, etc.)

❏ Vaccinations

❏ _____

❏ _____

❏ _____

Miscellaneous

❐ Engagement ring

❐ Guest book and pen

❐ Hairdresser

❐ Makeup

❐ Manicure

❐ Marriage license

❐ Massage

❐ Name-change forms

❐ Pedicure

❐ Wedding consultant/coordinator

❐ Wedding rings

❐ Wedding ring engraving

❐ _____

❐ _____

❐ _____

Photography/Videography

❐ Bridal portraits

❐ Engagement photo

❐ Ceremony coverage

❐ Reception coverage

❐ Master tape/raw footage

❐ Negatives

❐ Photo albums

❐ Proof sets

❐ Video discs

❐ _____

❐ _____

❐ _____

Printing

- ❐ Address labels
- ❐ Announcements
- ❐ Bridesmaids' luncheon invitations
- ❐ Calligraphy
- ❐ Ceremony cards
- ❐ Embossing
- ❐ Engraving
- ❐ Envelopes
- ❐ Favor labels
- ❐ Foil lining
- ❐ Maps/direction cards
- ❐ Napkins
- ❐ Postage
- ❐ Programs
- ❐ Rehearsal dinner invitations
- ❐ Reply cards
- ❐ Save-the-date cards
- ❐ Thank-you notes
- ❐ Wedding invitations
- ❐ _____
- ❐ _____
- ❐ _____

Reception

- ❐ Alcohol
- ❐ Balloons
- ❐ Band
- ❐ Bartenders
- ❐ Cake
- ❐ Cake knife

❏ Cake table decorations

❏ Card basket

❏ Caterer

❏ Centerpieces (nonfloral)

❏ Champagne

❏ Chairs

❏ Coat check

❏ Decorations (nonfloral)

❏ DJ

❏ Disposable cameras

❏ Favors

❏ Gift table

❏ Glassware

❏ Groom's cake

❏ Microphone

❏ Napkins

❏ Parking

❏ Place cards

❏ Photographer

❏ Servers

❏ Silverware

❏ Sound system

❏ Tables

❏ Table linens

❏ Table settings

❏ Tents/canopies

❏ Toasting flutes

❏ Transportation

❏ Video camera (if a relative is taking video)

❏ Videographer

❏ _____

❏ _____

❏ _____

Rehearsal Dinner

❐ Bartender

❐ Caterer

❐ Centerpieces

❐ Chairs

❐ Coat check

❐ Decorations

❐ Glassware

❐ Microphone

❐ Music

❐ Napkins

❐ Parking

❐ Servers

❐ Silverware

❐ Sound system

❐ Tables

❐ Table linens

❐ Table settings

❐ _____

❐ _____

❐ _____

Appendix D

Your Wedding Budget

●●

*F*iguring out how much you can spend may be the most stressful aspect of planning a wedding, especially if you don't take the time to set a budget and identify your priorities. At the beginning of your planning process, write down ballpark estimates for the things that you want for your wedding in the "Estimated" column of the following table. As you get more reliable information, such as written quotes from vendors, plug those numbers into the "Actual" column. Don't forget to make any necessary adjustments to other budget lines when you make changes. Build a cushion (of between 10 percent and 15 percent) into your overall budget to account for unexpected expenses.

Fill out the columns in pencil so you can easily make changes if your priorities shift — if, for example, you decide you'd rather put money toward the cake than pay for the fancy aisle runner you initially envisioned.

If others are involved in financing your wedding, give them a copy of your budget so they know where you do and don't want to spend money.

Wedding Budget

	Estimated	Actual
Total Budget	$	$
Cushion	$	$

Apparel	Estimated	Actual
Alterations	$	$
Bride's shoes	$	$
Engagement ring	$	$
Garter	$	$
Groom's accessories	$	$
Groom's socks and shoes	$	$
Groom's suit/tuxedo	$	$
Hosiery and undergarments	$	$
Jewelry and gloves	$	$
Wedding dress	$	$
Wedding rings	$	$
Veil/headpiece	$	$
Other _____	$	$
Total apparel	$	$

Decorations	Estimated	Actual
Altar plants/other nonfloral decorations	$	$
Aisle runner	$	$
Arches/bowers	$	$
Balloons	$	$
Candles	$	$
Chair covers/bows	$	$
Lighting	$	$
Pew decorations	$	$
Photo collage/slideshow	$	$
Table centerpieces (nonfloral)	$	$
Table linens	$	$
Other _____	$	$
Total decorations	$	$

Flowers	Estimated	Actual
Altar/ceremony flowers	$	$
Arch/bower flowers	$	$
Bridal bouquet	$	$
Bridesmaid bouquets	$	$
Boutonnieres	$	$
Cake table flowers	$	$
Centerpieces	$	$
Corsages	$	$
Flower girl flowers	$	$
Head table flowers	$	$
Maid/matron of honor bouquet	$	$
Pew/chair posies	$	$
Other _____	$	$
Total flowers	$	$

Gifts	Estimated	Actual
Attendants	$	$
Bride and groom	$	$
Parents	$	$
Readers	$	$
Singers	$	$
Other _____	$	$
Total gifts	$	$

Miscellaneous Expenses	Estimated	Actual
Beauty treatments	$	$
Cake knife	$	$
Camera/camcorder rental/purchase	$	$
Card basket	$	$
Church/ceremony site rental fees	$	$
Disposable cameras	$	$
Guest book and pen	$	$
Hotel rooms (for wedding/honeymoon suite and/or guests)	$	$
Marriage license fee	$	$
Officiant fee	$	$
Rehearsal dinner	$	$
Ring pillow	$	$
Send-off favors (such as bubbles, birdseed, and so on)	$	$
Toasting flutes	$	$
Wedding coordinator/planner	$	$
Other _____	$	$
Other _____	$	$
Other _____	$	$
Total miscellaneous	$	$

Music	Estimated	Actual
Ceremony musicians	$	$
Ceremony singer(s)	$	$
Reception band/DJ	$	$
Total music	$	$

Photography/Videography	Estimated	Actual
Bridal portrait	$	$
Engagement photo	$	$
Enlargements	$	$
Extra prints/copies	$	$
Master tape/raw footage	$	$
Negatives	$	$
Package	$	$
Photo albums	$	$
Proof sets	$	$
Other _____	$	$
Total photography/videography	**$**	**$**

Printing/Stationery	Estimated	Actual
Announcements	$	$
Calligraphy	$	$
Invitations	$	$
Maps/direction cards	$	$
Napkins	$	$
Postage	$	$
Programs	$	$
Thank-you notes	$	$
Other _____	$	$
Total printing/stationery	**$**	**$**

Reception	Estimated	Actual
Alcohol	$	$
Cake-cutting fee	$	$
Catering	$	$
Coat check	$	$
Favors	$	$
Linens	$	$
Room/hall fees	$	$
Sound system	$	$
Staff	$	$
Tables and chairs	$	$
Taxes	$	$
Tent/pavilion rental	$	$
Wedding cake or other dessert	$	$
Other _____	$	$
Total reception	$	$

Related Events	Estimated	Actual
Bridal luncheon	$	$
Gift-opening party	$	$
Rehearsal dinner	$	$
Other _____	$	$
Total related events	$	$

Tips/Gratuities	Estimated	Actual
Altar boys/girls ($10 to $15 each)	$	$
Baker* ($10 to $20)	$	$
Bartenders (10% of liquor bill)	$	$
Catering/reception manager* ($50 to $100)	$	$
Ceremony/reception musicians* ($5 to $10 per hour for each musician)	$	$
Chauffeurs (10% to 15% of bill)	$	$
Coat check/restroom attendants (50 cents to $1 per guest)	$	$
DJ ($50 to $100)	$	$
Florist* ($10 to $20 per staff member)	$	$
Hair stylist/makeup artist (10% to 15% of bill)	$	$
Officiant* ($75 to $150)	$	$
Photographer/videographer* ($50 each)	$	$
Valet parking attendants (50 cents to $1 per car)	$	$
Wait staff (15% of catering bill)	$	$
On-site wedding coordinator* ($50)	$	$
Wedding planner* (10% of total bill)	$	$
Other _____	$	$
Total tips/gratuities	**$**	**$**

* These tips are optional (see Chapter 2 for more on doling out gratuities).

Transportation	Estimated	Actual
Car rental	$	$
Horse-drawn carriage	$	$
Limousine	$	$
Parking/valet service	$	$
Taxis	$	$
Other _____	$	$
Total transportation	**$**	**$**

Index

BUSINESS, CAREERS & PERSONAL FINANCE

Accounting For Dummies,
4th Edition*
978-0-470-24600-9

Bookkeeping Workbook
For Dummies†
978-0-470-16983-4

Commodities For Dummies
978-0-470-04928-0

Doing Business in China For Dummies
978-0-470-04929-7

E-Mail Marketing For Dummies
978-0-470-19087-6

Job Interviews For Dummies,
3rd Edition*†
978-0-470-17748-8

Personal Finance Workbook
For Dummies*†
978-0-470-09933-9

Real Estate License Exams For Dummies
978-0-7645-7623-2

Six Sigma For Dummies
978-0-7645-6798-8

Small Business Kit For Dummies,
2nd Edition*†
978-0-7645-5984-6

Telephone Sales For Dummies
978-0-470-16836-3

BUSINESS PRODUCTIVITY & MICROSOFT OFFICE

Access 2007 For Dummies
978-0-470-03649-5

Excel 2007 For Dummies
978-0-470-03737-9

Office 2007 For Dummies
978-0-470-00923-9

Outlook 2007 For Dummies
978-0-470-03830-7

PowerPoint 2007 For Dummies
978-0-470-04059-1

Project 2007 For Dummies
978-0-470-03651-8

QuickBooks 2008 For Dummies
978-0-470-18470-7

Quicken 2008 For Dummies
978-0-470-17473-9

Salesforce.com For Dummies,
2nd Edition
978-0-470-04893-1

Word 2007 For Dummies
978-0-470-03658-7

EDUCATION, HISTORY, REFERENCE & TEST PREPARATION

African American History For Dummies
978-0-7645-5469-8

Algebra For Dummies
978-0-7645-5325-7

Algebra Workbook For Dummies
978-0-7645-8467-1

Art History For Dummies
978-0-470-09910-0

ASVAB For Dummies, 2nd Edition
978-0-470-10671-6

British Military History For Dummies
978-0-470-03213-8

Calculus For Dummies
978-0-7645-2498-1

Canadian History For Dummies, 2nd
Edition
978-0-470-83656-9

Geometry Workbook For Dummies
978-0-471-79940-5

The SAT I For Dummies, 6th Edition
978-0-7645-7193-0

Series 7 Exam For Dummies
978-0-470-09932-2

World History For Dummies
978-0-7645-5242-7

FOOD, HOME, GARDEN, HOBBIES & HOME

Bridge For Dummies, 2nd Edition
978-0-471-92426-5

Coin Collecting For Dummies,
2nd Edition
978-0-470-22275-1

Cooking Basics For Dummies,
3rd Edition
978-0-7645-7206-7

Drawing For Dummies
978-0-7645-5476-6

Etiquette For Dummies,
2nd Edition
978-0-470-10672-3

Gardening Basics For Dummies*†
978-0-470-03749-2

Knitting Patterns For Dummies
978-0-470-04556-5

Living Gluten-Free For Dummies†
978-0-471-77383-2

Painting Do-It-Yourself
For Dummies
978-0-470-17533-0

HEALTH, SELF HELP, PARENTING & PETS

Anger Management For Dummies
978-0-470-03715-7

Anxiety & Depression Workbook
For Dummies
978-0-7645-9793-0

Dieting For Dummies, 2nd Edition
978-0-7645-4149-0

Dog Training For Dummies,
2nd Edition
978-0-7645-8418-3

Horseback Riding For Dummies
978-0-470-09719-9

Infertility For Dummies†
978-0-470-11518-3

Meditation For Dummies with CD-ROM,
2nd Edition
978-0-471-77774-8

Post-Traumatic Stress Disorder
For Dummies
978-0-470-04922-8

Puppies For Dummies,
2nd Edition
978-0-470-03717-1

Thyroid For Dummies,
2nd Edition†
978-0-471-78755-6

Type 1 Diabetes For Dummies*†
978-0-470-17811-9

* Separate Canadian edition also available
† Separate U.K. edition also available

Available wherever books are sold. For more information or to order direct: U.S. customers visit www.dummies.com or call 1-877-762-2974.
U.K. customers visit www.wileyeurope.com or call (0) 1243 843291. Canadian customers visit www.wiley.ca or call 1-800-567-4797.

INTERNET & DIGITAL MEDIA

AdWords For Dummies
978-0-470-15252-2

Blogging For Dummies, 2nd Edition
978-0-470-23017-6

**Digital Photography All-in-One
Desk Reference For Dummies,
3rd Edition**
978-0-470-03743-0

**Digital Photography For Dummies,
5th Edition**
978-0-7645-9802-9

**Digital SLR Cameras & Photography
For Dummies, 2nd Edition**
978-0-470-14927-0

**eBay Business All-in-One Desk
Reference For Dummies**
978-0-7645-8438-1

eBay For Dummies, 5th Edition*
978-0-470-04529-9

eBay Listings That Sell For Dummies
978-0-471-78912-3

Facebook For Dummies
978-0-470-26273-3

**The Internet For Dummies,
11th Edition**
978-0-470-12174-0

**Investing Online For Dummies,
5th Edition**
978-0-7645-8456-5

**iPod & iTunes For Dummies,
5th Edition**
978-0-470-17474-6

MySpace For Dummies
978-0-470-09529-4

Podcasting For Dummies
978-0-471-74898-4

**Search Engine Optimization
For Dummies, 2nd Edition**
978-0-471-97998-2

Second Life For Dummies
978-0-470-18025-9

**Starting an eBay Business
For Dummies, 3rd Edition†**
978-0-470-14924-9

GRAPHICS, DESIGN & WEB DEVELOPMENT

**Adobe Creative Suite 3 Design
Premium All-in-One Desk Reference
For Dummies**
978-0-470-11724-8

**Adobe Web Suite CS3 All-in-One
Desk Reference For Dummies**
978-0-470-12099-6

AutoCAD 2008 For Dummies
978-0-470-11650-0

**Building a Web Site For Dummies,
3rd Edition**
978-0-470-14928-7

**Creating Web Pages All-in-One Desk
Reference For Dummies, 3rd Edition**
978-0-470-09629-1

**Creating Web Pages For Dummies,
8th Edition**
978-0-470-08030-6

Dreamweaver CS3 For Dummies
978-0-470-11490-2

Flash CS3 For Dummies
978-0-470-12100-9

Google SketchUp For Dummies
978-0-470-13744-4

InDesign CS3 For Dummies
978-0-470-11865-8

**Photoshop CS3 All-in-One
Desk Reference For Dummies**
978-0-470-11195-6

Photoshop CS3 For Dummies
978-0-470-11193-2

**Photoshop Elements 5
For Dummies**
978-0-470-09810-3

SolidWorks For Dummies
978-0-7645-9555-4

Visio 2007 For Dummies
978-0-470-08983-5

**Web Design For Dummies,
2nd Edition**
978-0-471-78117-2

**Web Sites Do-It-Yourself
For Dummies**
978-0-470-16903-2

**Web Stores Do-It-Yourself
For Dummies**
978-0-470-17443-2

LANGUAGES, RELIGION & SPIRITUALITY

Arabic For Dummies
978-0-471-77270-5

Chinese For Dummies, Audio Set
978-0-470-12766-7

French For Dummies
978-0-7645-5193-2

German For Dummies
978-0-7645-5195-6

Hebrew For Dummies
978-0-7645-5489-6

Ingles Para Dummies
978-0-7645-5427-8

Italian For Dummies, Audio Set
978-0-470-09586-7

Italian Verbs For Dummies
978-0-471-77389-4

Japanese For Dummies
978-0-7645-5429-2

Latin For Dummies
978-0-7645-5431-5

Portuguese For Dummies
978-0-471-78738-9

Russian For Dummies
978-0-471-78001-4

Spanish Phrases For Dummies
978-0-7645-7204-3

Spanish For Dummies
978-0-7645-5194-9

Spanish For Dummies, Audio Set
978-0-470-09585-0

The Bible For Dummies
978-0-7645-5296-0

Catholicism For Dummies
978-0-7645-5391-2

The Historical Jesus For Dummies
978-0-470-16785-4

Islam For Dummies
978-0-7645-5503-9

**Spirituality For Dummies,
2nd Edition**
978-0-470-19142-2

NETWORKING AND PROGRAMMING

ASP.NET 3.5 For Dummies
978-0-470-19592-5

C# 2008 For Dummies
978-0-470-19109-5

Hacking For Dummies, 2nd Edition
978-0-470-05235-8

**Home Networking
For Dummies, 4th Edition**
978-0-470-11806-1

Java For Dummies, 4th Edition
978-0-470-08716-9

**Microsoft® SQL Server™ 2008
All-in-One Desk Reference For Dummies**
978-0-470-17954-3

**Networking All-in-One Desk Reference
For Dummies, 2nd Edition**
978-0-7645-9939-2

**Networking For Dummies,
8th Edition**
978-0-470-05620-2

SharePoint 2007 For Dummies
978-0-470-09941-4

**Wireless Home Networking
For Dummies, 2nd Edition**
978-0-471-74940-0